Asia Bible Commentary Series

PHILIPPIANS

Asia Bible Commentary Series

PHILIPPIANS

Roji Thomas George

General Editor
Federico G. Villanueva

Old Testament Consulting Editors
Yohanna Katanacho, Tim Meadowcroft, Joseph Shao

New Testament Consulting Editors
Steve Chang, Andrew B. Spurgeon, Brian Wintle

© 2019 Roji Thomas George

Published 2019 by Langham Global Library
An imprint of Langham Publishing
www.langhampublishing.org

Langham Publishing and its imprints are a ministry of Langham Partnership

Langham Partnership
PO Box 296, Carlisle, Cumbria CA3 9WZ, UK
www.langham.org

Published in partnership with Asia Theological Association

ATA
QCC PO Box 1454 – 1154, Manila, Philippines
www.ataasia.com

ISBNs:
978-1-78368-585-1 Print
978-1-78368-586-8 ePub
978-1-78368-588-2 PDF

Roji Thomas George has asserted his right under the Copyright, Designs, and Patents Act, 1988 to be identified as the Author of this work.

All rights reserved. No part of this publication may be reproduced, stored in a retrieval system, or transmitted in any form or by any means, electronic, mechanical, photocopying, recording, or otherwise, without the prior written permission of the publisher or the Copyright Licensing Agency.

Requests to reuse content from Langham Publishing are processed through PLSclear. Please visit www.plsclear.com to complete your request.

Scriptures taken from the Holy Bible, New International Version®, NIV®. Copyright © 1973, 1978, 1984, 2011 by Biblica, Inc.™ Used by permission of Zondervan.

British Library Cataloguing in Publication Data
A catalogue record for this book is available from the British Library.

ISBN: 978-1-78368-585-1

Cover & Book Design: projectluz.com

Langham Partnership actively supports theological dialogue and an author's right to publish but does not necessarily endorse the views and opinions set forth and works referenced within this publication or guarantee its technical and grammatical correctness. Langham Partnership does not accept any responsibility or liability to persons or property as a consequence of the reading, use, or interpretation of its published content.

Roji Thomas George's commentary faithfully bridges two worlds of the text: Paul's own and that of Asian believers today, especially in India. The step-by-step exposition of Paul's thought with an eye toward the experience of the Asian church will also help readers in other contexts uncover the significance of Paul's message in new ways. George's work is therefore highly recommended!

Scott J. Hafemann, DTh
Honorary Reader in New Testament,
School of Divinity, St Mary's College,
University of St Andrews, UK

Thoroughly engaging both the biblical text's ancient background and his modern South Asian setting, Roji George connects these horizons skilfully. With well-reasoned and sound conclusions, George articulates the significance of Philippians for Asian contexts today.

Craig S. Keener, PhD
F. M. and Ada Thompson Professor of Biblical Studies,
Asbury Theological Seminary, Wilmore, Kentucky, USA

George's careful and nuanced reading of Philippians is enriched with suggestive similarities to the multi-religious contexts of the modern Asian readers. For him, Paul's critical adaptation to cultural-political discourses with difference, in other words, embracing the "scandalous" pattern of the "self-emptying Messiah," is the crux of negotiating modern mission praxis even when facing persecution. Here is an excellent tool for pastors, missionaries and serious students of the Bible who care to be shaped as authentic *Yesu bhaktas* in a religiously pluralistic and volatile contexts.

Idicheria Ninan, PhD
Professor of New Testament,
South Asia Institute of Advanced Christian Studies, Bangalore, India

To my beloved wife, Anjana Roji

CONTENTS

Commentary

Series Preface	xi
Author's Preface	xiii
Acknowledgments	xv
List of Abbreviations	xvii
Introduction	1
Commentary on Philippians	19
Selected Bibliography	165

Topics

A Comparison of Perspectives on Suffering in Paul and Other Religions	42
Christian Discipleship by Imitation in the Context of the *Gurukula Pathashala* System in India	131
"Dual Citizenship" of Christians in a Hostile and Pluralistic Religious Context	136
Partnership in Mission: Defining the Donor-Recipient Relationship	159

SERIES PREFACE

In recent years, we have witnessed one of the greatest shifts in the history of world Christianity. It used to be that the majority of Christians lived in the West, but Christians are now evenly distributed around the globe. This shift has implications for the task of interpreting the Bible from within our respective contexts, which is in line with the growing realization that every theology is contextual. Thus, the questions that we bring into our reading of the Bible will be shaped by our present realities as well as our historical and social locations. There is a need therefore to interpret the Bible for our own contexts.

The Asia Bible Commentary Series addresses this need. In line with the mission of the Asia Theological Association Publications, we have gathered evangelical Bible scholars working among Asians to write commentaries on each book of the Bible. The mission is to "produce resources that are biblical, pastoral, contextual, missional, and prophetic for pastors, Christian leaders, cross-cultural workers, and students in Asia." Although the Bible can be studied for different reasons, we believe that it is given primarily for the edification of the Body of Christ (2 Tim 3:16–17). The ABCS is designed to help pastors in their sermon preparation, cell group or lay leaders in their Bible study groups, and those training in seminaries or Bible schools.

Each commentary begins with an introduction that provides general information about the book's author and original context, summarizes the main message or theme of the book, and outlines its potential relevance to a particular Asian context. The introduction is followed by an exposition that combines exegesis and application. Here, we seek to speak to and empower Christians in Asia by using our own stories, parables, poems, and other cultural resources as we expound the Bible.

The Bible is actually Asian in that it comes from ancient West Asia, and there are many similarities between the world of the Bible and traditional Asian cultures. But there are also many differences that we need to explore in some depth. That is why the commentaries also include articles or topics in which we bring specific issues in Asian church, social, and religious contexts into dialogue with relevant issues in the Bible. We do not seek to resolve every tension that emerges but rather to allow the text to illumine the context and vice versa, acknowledging that we do not have all the answers to every mystery.

Philippians

    May the Holy Spirit, who inspired the writers of the Bible, bring light to the hearts and minds of all who use these materials, to the glory of God and to the building up of the churches!

Federico G. Villanueva
General Editor

AUTHOR'S PREFACE

The apostle Paul wrote his letters in response to particular issues that his Christian communities in different Greco-Roman cities faced. This is also true of his *Letter to the Philippians*. In writing a commentary on Paul's letters, we must first hear and understand the apostle's words, tone, and rhetorical intent within the particular context of his original addressees. Only then can we apply those to the present context of readers today.

As an Indian living in a sociocultural and political pluralistic context, I share a similar situation with Paul's audiences in Philippi. Many of my Asian or South Asian readers may also share a similar experience. I feel Paul's heart when I face the multidimensional challenges of my pluralistic context, such as violent opposition to Christians and their mission from non-Christians, the dependence of many Christians upon their religious pedigrees, the complacent attitude of Christians towards caste system within the churches in India, and the desire to look righteous before others through human efforts. Reading Philippians with an understanding of my present Indian context not only helps me identify the core of Paul's rhetorical thrust, but it also brings the text alive in the here and now. Hence, rather than becoming entangled with the nitty-gritty details of doctrinal and textual debates in the historical study of Philippians, my interest has been to capture the significance of Paul's words for the original audience and for present readers who are, like me, living in South Asia.

Since the Asia Bible Commentary Series seeks to cater to missionaries and pastors so that they can hear the text speak into their ministerial context, I pay careful attention to Paul's missional and pastoral contexts in Philippi. I also explain the missional and pastoral insights from the text with religious-cultural materials from the Indian context. I believe this exercise will help my readers find parallels in their own specific contexts so that they can hear Paul speaking directly to them.

I pray that this commentary will enrich the church at large to be inspired by the profound (and perhaps last) words of the apostle to serve our Lord faithfully in the days to come.

Roji T. George
Professor and Head of the Department of New Testament Studies
South Asia Institute of Advanced Christian Studies (SAIACS),
Bangalore, India

ACKNOWLEDGMENTS

I am grateful to God through whom all opportunities come to participate in his continuing mission in the world. It is his grace alone that enabled me to persist in completing this project. I am full of gratitude to Dr. Federico G. Villanueva, who not only introduced me to the ABCS, but also extended the opportunity to write a commentary on Philippians as part of the series. His critical comments have been helpful throughout the project. A special thanks to Ms. Bubbles Lactaoen for all the hard work she put in to bring out this work in time. I am thankful to the Langham Publishing House and the dedicated staff there who have spent immense time and energy to publish the book. My special thanks to Dr. Eric Clouston, my dear friend, whose sacrificial efforts in proofreading and language editing have relieved me of a lot of hard work. Finally, I would not have finished writing this commentary without the sacrificial support of my wife, Anjana Roji, and my two beautiful daughters, Joanne and Janet. Their sacrifices I cannot pay back, but can only say, "Thank you for your unconditional love and support."

LIST OF ABBREVIATIONS

BOOKS OF THE BIBLE

Old Testament
Gen, Exod, Lev, Num, Deut, Josh, Judg, Ruth, 1–2 Sam, 1–2 Kgs, 1–2 Chr, Ezra, Neh, Esth, Job, Ps/Pss, Prov, Eccl, Song, Isa, Jer, Lam, Ezek, Dan, Hos, Joel, Amos, Obad, Jonah, Mic, Nah, Hab, Zeph, Hag, Zech, Mal

New Testament
Matt, Mark, Luke, John, Acts, Rom, 1–2 Cor, Gal, Eph, Phil, Col, 1–2 Thess, 1–2 Tim, Titus, Phlm, Heb, Jas, 1–2 Pet, 1–2–3 John, Jude, Rev

BIBLE TEXTS AND VERSIONS

Divisions of the canon
NT	New Testament
OT	Old Testament

Ancient texts and versions
LXX	Septuagint
MT	Masoretic Text

Modern versions
NIV	New International Version

Journals, reference works, and series
AB	Anchor Bible
ABD	*Anchor Bible Dictionary*
AJPS	*Asian Journal of Pentecostal Studies*
BDAG	*A Greek-English Lexicon of the New Testament and other Early Christian Literature*
BECNT	Baker Exegetical Commentary on the New Testament
BNTC	Black's New Testament Commentaries
BTF	*Bangalore Theological Forum*

BZNW	*BeiheftezurZeitschrift fur die neutestamentliche Wissenschaft und die Kunde der*
CBQ	*Catholic Biblical Quarterly*
CTR	*Criswell Theological Review*
DJG	*Dictionary of Jesus and the Gospels*
DPL	*Dictionary of Paul and His Letters*
DTJ	*Doon Theological Journal*
ECS	Epworth Commentary Series
GNBC	Good News Bible Commentary
HBT	*Horizons in Biblical Theology*
HTR	*Harvard Theological Review*
IBC	Interpretation: A Bible Commentary for Teaching and Preaching
ICC	The International Critical Commentary
IVPNTC	IVP New Testament Commentary
JBL	*Journal of Biblical Literature*
JETS	*Journal of the Evangelical Theological Society*
JSNT	*Journal for the Study of the New Testament*
LCBI	Literary Currents in Biblical Interpretation
LTQ	*Lexington Theological Quarterly*
NAC	New American Commentary
NCBC	New Century Bible Commentary
NICNT	New International Commentary on the New Testament
NIDNTT	New International Dictionary of New Testament
NIGTC	The New International Greek Testament Commentary
NovT	*Novum Testamentum*
NovTSup	Supplements to Novum Testamentum
NTC	New Testament Commentary
NTS	*New Testament Studies*
PCNT	Paideia Commentaries on the New Testament
PNTC	Pillar New Testament Commentary
PRSt	*Perspectives in Religious Studies*
ResQ	*Restoration Quarterly*
SBL	Society of Biblical Literature
SNTSMS	Society for New Testament Studies Monograph Series

List of Abbreviations

TC	Thornapple Commentaries
TDNT	*Theological Dictionary of the New Testament*
THNTC	Two Horizons New Testament Commentary
TNTC	Tyndale New Testament Commentary
TynBul	*Tyndale Bulletin*
WBC	Word Biblical Commentary
WEC	Wycliff Exegetical Commentary

INTRODUCTION

Letters from prisoners, especially those who are awaiting execution for political reasons, are interesting to read for people from across the world because they open a window into prisoners' spiritual, emotional and psychological state during their last days. These letters also help to reconstruct the silenced historical realities and voices through the eyes of the oppressed subjects, the prisoners. Prison letters are often heart-touching emotional conversations with loved ones, encouraging them not to grieve over the prisoner's imminent death. At other times, these letters contain important advice to children and spouses for the future, such as Nehru's letters to his daughter, Indira.[1] They also often reflect joy, contentment, and hope for dying as martyrs for a legitimate cause.

Paul's letter to the Philippians is a short but significant letter in the New Testament (NT). As a prison letter, it offers readers a window into the apostle's experience and thoughts while he was in jail. The letter reflects Paul's strong conviction and joyful disposition towards his own uncertain future along with his love and care for friends in Philippi. In other words, Philippians is not written by a discouraged or repentant author who is regretting what he has done that has led him to prison. Rather, Paul continues to be zealous about preaching as new opportunities open up before him in jail. Paul repeatedly commands the church in Philippi to rejoice (Phil 3:1; 4:4). Amidst the realities that could cause Paul to despair, Paul explores his source of joy, which is based on his eschatological vision (Phil 2:16; 3:20–21). This vision causes him, though in confinement, to send a positive report to the church (Phil 1:12–18). He opens up his mind regarding the struggles taking place within himself concerning the future, and he also expresses his concern for the well-being of his beloved friends. He is a cordial, loving, and courageous person who encourages, invites, and directs others to follow his path in imitating Christ.

SIGNIFICANCE OF THE LETTER TO PHILIPPIANS FOR TODAY

The words and message of Paul's letter to Philippians are relevant for Asian readers today. The original first-century readers of Paul's letter in Philippi

---

1. Pt. Jawaharlal Nehru was the first Prime Minister and one of the frontline leaders of Indian freedom struggle against the British Empire. The letter to his beloved daughter, Indira Gandhi, who became the fourth and the second longest serving Prime Minister of India, was written during Nehru's imprisonment during British rule. Later, these letters were collected and published.

shared a historical context that was not very different from the context of modern Asian readers. Like present-day Asia, first-century Philippi was multi-cultural, multi-ethnic, and multi-religious in its social composition. This not only facilitated a cross-pollination of multiple cultural-religious ideas, but it also resulted in ideological clashes and an unleashing of violence against the new religious minority called the Christians. Paul's letter to the Philippians reflects its context and, in turn, implies significance for us today.

At least five vital areas can be identified to highlight the significance of Philippians for present-day Asian readers.

First, Philippians encourages its readers to see new opportunities amidst violent resistance and the victimization of the gospel and Christians. Today, Christians in Asian countries such as India, Pakistan, Nepal, China, and elsewhere face violent resistance for the sake of their faith in Christ. The Philippian believers also suffered from the non-Christian population in Philippi (1:28–29) because of their faith and witness. It is not rare among Asian Christians to hear testimonies about martyrdom, threat, imprisonment, and the destruction of life and property by non-Christian opponents for preaching the gospel and making disciples of Christ. However, Paul's ability to see positive results amidst the dark moments of his forced confinement in jail (1:12–14) provides us with a new set of lenses to see opportunities for advancing the gospel in quarters that lie beyond our easy reach. Paul's repeated exhortation to rejoice amidst suffering for Christ's sake makes his letter to the Philippians uniquely valuable as a precious gift to a persecuted community that instils patience, courage, and vitality in Christians.

Second, Philippians identifies the significance of a cruciform Christian lifestyle both inside and outside the church. Philippians neither approves of passive and aimless suffering, nor romanticizes suffering and martyrdom for its own sake. Instead, it teaches that Christian suffering is an active fulfilment of God's will for us (1:29), while it also helps Christians complete their spiritual sacrifices (2:17). Such a community-oriented Christian existence coheres with traditional Asian cultural values, where an individual's interest is meant to be in balance with communal well-being and fulfilment. Interestingly, Paul and his companions leave behind no other form of Christian conduct for the Philippian believers to replicate (2:8, 19–30; 4:9) than demonstrating a self-sacrificial lifestyle for the sake of others.

Third, Philippians identifies the supremacy of the Christian gospel above every cultural and political discourse. Paul's refusal to blur single-minded devotion to Christ with reliance upon earthly pedigrees (3:2–14) deters those of us

Introduction

(particularly Indians) who are uniquely prone to seek righteousness and a higher spiritual standing in society based on clan, caste, family lineage, and so on. Philippians warns us from seeking true righteousness in anything except faith in Christ alone.

Fourth, Philippians identifies patriotism amidst religious nationalistic movements. In India, Christians are often called anti-nationals, and their patriotism is viewed with suspicion. The primary reasons for this suspicion are simple: (a) Christians seem to follow a Western religion that entered the country as an ally of the Western colonizers. Hence, current Christian missionary activities must remain under close surveillance as they not only maintain close relations with the church in the West but are also a potential threat to the national interest; (b) Christians (missionaries) not only pollute but destroy traditional Indian social and cultural values with their propagation of Christianity, which alienates them from the broad native cultural landscape. Thus, Indian Christians do not completely integrate into the Indian society. However, Paul's appeal to live out our dual citizenship (1:27; 3:20) – both heavenly and earthly – suggests that Indian Christians can be both patriotic Indians and faithful Christians at the same time. The two are not mutually exclusive. Thus, Paul's words to the Philippian believers help us to configure our absolute loyalty to God as well as genuine patriotism towards the nation.

Fifth, Philippians identifies the church's role in partnering with frontier missionaries in the unhindered advancement of the gospel. In seeking to spread the gospel throughout the world, the active partnering of the Philippian church through the mission of Paul – in addition to the regular support they extended to him in need – is a model for every church in Asia. Reaching the unreached with the love of God is not just the task of select (native or foreign) missionaries, but rather is the consequence of a church's sacrificial support to missionaries and evangelists in the name of God. The churches in India ought to realize this with greater conviction in order to encourage self-reliant, self-sufficient, and self-governed indigenous Christian missions to grow.

FLASHBACK

At the beginning of a movie, the audience is often flashed back into certain crucial instances in the past so that they can understand the unfolding sequence of events, plot of the story, and setting of the narrative. This flashback helps the audience tie together the logical coherence of the entire narrative. Similarly, we need a flashback into the actual context of Paul's letter to the Philippians.

This context will help us to understand the mind of Paul as the author and will help us to hear both the breadth and depth of his written communication, along with its rhetorical significance. We can perform a flashback into the background of the letter to the Philippians at two levels: (1) the story of the city of Philippi, and (2) the story of the origin, growth, and challenges faced by the first-century Christian community in the city.

Story of the City of Philippi

The origins of the city can be traced back to the lesser known pre-Hellenistic times as a Thracian settlement.[2] Later, the city was brought under Macedonian rule after Philip II, the father of Alexander the Great, captured and named it after himself in 356 BC. During the Roman times, in order to sustain an interest in the city, the Thracians cooperated with the Roman military in the region. Rome reciprocated to the Thracian military support by duly bestowing civic honors upon the Thracian elites, who acted on their behalf as client-rulers in Philippi.[3]

In second century BC, Rome included Philippi within the province of Macedonia.[4] In the later centuries, Philippi became significant to Rome for two reasons: (1) Philippi served as a Roman outpost on the *Via Egnatia*, which connected the Roman Empire with the East by facilitating imperial commerce and serving as a "frequent passage of [Roman] troops";[5] (2) Philippi was situated near the depleted gold mines, and the vast cover of fertile land that surrounded the city was "unusual in Greece where only 18 percent of the land was arable."[6] The strategic geographical location of Philippi caused the double colonization of the city, first in 42 BC and again in 30 BC. The city continued to flourish in the later Roman centuries with new building constructions.[7]

At 42 BC, Philippi became part of the Roman Empire when Octavian and Antony defeated the murderers of Julius Caesar, and Antony founded a colony for Roman veterans. Then in 30 BC, Augustus re-founded a Roman

---

2. Joseph H. Hellerman, *Reconstructing Honor in Roman Philippi: Carmen Christi as Crusus Pudorum*, SNTSMS 132 (Cambridge: Cambridge University Press, 2005), 64.
3. Holland L. Hendrix, "Philippi," *ABD* 5:314.
4. Hendrix, *ABD* 5:314.
5. James S. Jeffers, *The Greco-Roman World of the New Testament Era: Exploring the Background of Early Christianity* (Downers Grove: InterVarsity Press, 1999), 282.
6. Robert L. Brawley, "An Alternative Community and an Oral Encomium: Traces of the People of Philippi," in *The People beside Paul: The Philippian Assembly and History from Below*, ed. Joseph A. Marchal, Early Christianity and Its Literature 17 (Atlanta: SBL Press, 2015), 225.
7. Hendrix, "Philippi," 314.

colony in the city after defeating Antony in the Battle of Actium.⁸ This laid the foundation for "one of the most Roman cities in the East,"⁹ a Romanized Philippi. On both occasions, the Roman veterans were resettled in Philippi after they had lost their claim to land in Italy. In the first century, Philippi was known as "the place commemorating the victory of Octavian (later called Caesar Augustus) over the murderers of Julius Caesar."¹⁰ The city continued to flourish in the later Roman centuries with new building constructions.¹¹ James S. Jeffers states that Philippi was honored with *ius Italicum* by Augustus because it was already "in many respects a miniature Rome. The plan of the city was distinctively Roman. . . . Latin, not Greek, was the language of the city."¹² As a result, Philippi had a "dominant minority – initially veterans and displaced Italians" who "possessed the right of self-government structured and operated according to Roman law, freedom from tribute and taxation."¹³ This required the Philippian population to behave like a "loyal imperial outpost."¹⁴

During Paul's missionary visit, he encountered the descendants of these Roman colonists in Philippi (Acts 16). Moreover, all the inhabitants – Roman citizens or not – must have felt a powerful Roman presence in their everyday life in the city. Owing to the resettlement of the Roman veterans and the continued Roman domination, the city officials were mostly the "descendants of the original Roman colonists" along with some native elites and the Roman loyalists who obtained personal benefits, such as Roman citizenship and a role in the political structure.¹⁵ While the settler minority community continued their domination, the native beneficiaries of power remained closely attached to the colonists with their pro-Roman attitudes.

In contrast to the Roman colonies in Asia Minor, there was minimal assimilation of Hellenistic values and culture into the day-to-day social life in

---

8. David W. J. Gill, "Macedonia," in *Greco-Roman Setting*, vol. 3 in The Book of Acts in Its First Century Setting, ed. David W. J. Gill and Conrad Gempf (Grand Rapids: Eerdmans/Carlisle: Paternoster, 1994), 411.
9. Jeffers, *Greco-Roman World*, 282.
10. Clinton E. Arnold, *Acts*, Zondervan Illustrated Bible Backgrounds Commentary, ed. Idem. (Grand Rapids: Zondervan, 2002), 154.
11. Hendrix, "Philippi," 314.
12. Jeffers, *Greco-Roman World*, 282.
13. Brian Rapske, *The Book of Acts and Paul in Roman Custody*, vol. 3 in The Book of Acts in Its First Century Setting, ed. David W. J. Gill and Conrad Gempf (Grand Rapids: Eerdmans/Carlisle: Paternoster, 1994), 116.
14. Michael J. Gorman, *Apostle of the Crucified Lord: A Theological Introduction to Paul and His Letters* (Grand Rapids/Cambridge: Eerdmans, 2004), 413.
15. Jeffers, *Greco-Roman World*, 282.

Philippi.[16] Instead, the normal pattern that regulated every social interaction was "the principle of social replication," whereby "cultural values and social codes tend to 'trickle down' from elite to lower status groups who, in turn, mimic the practices of their social betters."[17] Historical evidence proves that when the Roman occupants colonized the city, Philippi had 60 percent of the prosperous agrarian population who had been dispossessed of their ancestral lands living in urban areas.[18] However, the loss of land by the native population not only impacted the economy of the city, but because of its significance to culture and religion, it also paved the way for the destruction of "ethnic heritage" and the "relationship of patron gods to the land."[19] Thus the natives were not only reduced to a non-citizen status, but were also forced to become unskilled, low paid daily waged laborers.[20]

During the time of Paul, the Philippian population was a mixture of several cultures and ethnic groups. Peter Oakes observes that "the catch-all term 'Greeks'" in Philippi included indigenous tribes,[21] who had already been Hellenized before the Roman colonizers arrived.[22] The mixed population was colored with Thracian religious habits and also included Jews (perhaps negligible in size), a later generation of Greek colonists from the fourth century BC, migrant workers, and Greek speaking slaves from the east. These various groups "were almost all economically dependent on Romans."[23] Unlike the rest of the empire, the Roman colonial system greatly impacted the social hierarchy of the Greeks. The colonists rigorously enforced a social hierarchy that determined the daily interpersonal socio-economic transactions.[24] For example, the non-Roman population knew beyond doubt that the rich Romans were of higher status within the social system. However, even a poor Roman received better treatment by the local magistrates and was above the wealthy Greeks in the social hierarchy. In the same way, while *Pax Romana* provided a conducive environment for better trade relations with the native business class,

---

16. Hellerman, *Reconstructing Honor in Roman Philippi*, 66.
17. Hellerman, 71–72.
18. Peter Oakes, *Philippians: From People to the Letter*, SNTSMS 110 (Cambridge: Cambridge University Press, 2001), 19–20, 29–30, 50.
19. Robert L. Brawley, "An Alternative Community and an Oral Encomium," 226.
20. Hellerman, *Reconstructing Honor in Roman Philippi*, 66; Brawley, "An Alternative Community and an Oral Encomium," 226.
21. Oakes, *Philippians*, 75.
22. Gill, "Macedonia," 407.
23. Oakes, *Philippians*, 75. Arnold, *Acts*, 154; G. F. Hawthorne, "Philippians, Letter to the," *DPL* 707.
24. Oakes, 73–75.

Introduction

the Romans had absolute control over everything in Philippi.[25] In short, the Roman hierarchy prevailed over every level of social, political, and religious interactions in Philippi, and the non-Roman population completely depended upon the Roman colonists, who were a minority, for their existence.

The religious context of Philippi was quite pluralistic, as it is today in India. Hendrix mentions the archaeological remains of a temple for Apollo and Artemis that date back to late-fourth century BC, an Egyptian cult that appears to have been quite influential among the wealthy citizens during the early period of Roman colonization in the first century AD. There is a sanctuary built of imported marbles dedicated to the Egyptian gods, and five inscriptions were found in a Roman bath complex – one each dedicated to Liber, Libera, and Hercules, and two dedicated to Liber pater.[26] Although there is no evidence of a major Jewish worship place in the city during the first century, it is beyond doubt that along with the emperor cult, there were several other local deities worshiped in Philippi, including Silvanus (the Roman god of lower class male members), Bacchus/Dionysus, Diana/Artemis, Apollo, Jupiter/Zeus, and Isis.[27] In short, Philippi had an important role in the Roman Empire due to its strategic geographical location. It was culturally Romanized, and the native Hellenistic inhabitants lived subordinate to the Roman colonizers in day-to-day life in the city. This led to a cultural, ethnic, and social intermingling during the Roman colonial era. Religiously, the society was pluralistic, and many different gods and goddesses managed to survive. In this context, Paul arrived in Philippi with the gospel of Christ and, through his evangelism, made new followers of Christ in the city.

Story of Christian Community in Philippi

Luke's historical writing, the Acts of the Apostles, provides the primary source for our knowledge about Paul's arrival in Philippi, his mission, and the founding of the Christian community there. Paul first came to the city during his second missionary journey and stayed for some days, preaching and teaching the gospel of Christ (Acts 16:6–40). According to Luke, Paul arrived in Philippi after passing through the region of Phyrgia and Galatia after being forbidden by the Holy Spirit to preach in Asia. Again, having been restricted by the Spirit from going into Bithynia, Paul received the Macedonian call in a dream during his short stay in Troas of Mysia. In that dream, he saw a man

---

25. Oakes, 75–76.
26. Hendrix, "Philippi," 314–315.
27. Gorman, *Apostle of the Crucified Lord*, 413–414.

saying, "Come over to Macedonia and help us" (Acts 6:9). Paul recognized this as God's call to continue his transcontinental missionary journey[28] and set out to cross the sea.

Philippi was "a Roman colony and the leading city of the district of Macedonia" (Acts 16:12), where Paul's transcontinental mission in Europe began with powerful encounters, both with spiritual powers and the inhabitants. Timothy (Acts 16:1), Silas (Acts 16:25), and Luke (identified by "we" in Acts 16:11–17) were Paul's companions during his ministry in Philippi. The initial audience to whom Paul witnessed about Christ was a group of women at the city gate. Paul found his first converts in Lydia and her household. Lydia was from the city of Thyatira, a city that was involved in the business of selling purple fabric. She was "a worshipper of God," which means that she was familiar with the salvation story of God that Paul preached from Jewish Scriptures. Lydia, along with her household, took baptism. Upon her insistence, Paul and his companions stayed on with her household and began their evangelistic activities in the city.

Very quickly, Paul landed in conflict with the natives, whose business was negatively affected after Paul exorcised a slave girl who had brought profit to her owners through her prophesies. The primary accusation levelled against them was that "[t]hese men are Jews, and are throwing our city into an uproar by advocating customs unlawful for us Romans to accept or practice" (Acts 16:20–21). Following a huge commotion in the city, Paul and Silas were stripped, flogged, and imprisoned. However, they were later released by the city magistrate (Acts 16:11–40). Interestingly, their release came after an earthquake that crashed the gates of the prison, which led to the dramatic conversion of the jailer, who in his panic attempted to kill himself. Later, the magistrate ordered to release Paul and Silas quietly after learning that they were Roman citizens (Acts 16:25–39). Paul and Silas departed from the city soon after their release from jail, per the request of the magistrate (Acts 16:40). Nevertheless, Paul visited the believers in Philippi again (Acts 20:6). If the references to "Macedonia" in 2 Corinthians 2:13 and Acts 20:1 refer to Philippi, then it seems that Paul continued to have contact with his converts in Philippi.

The initial opposition that Paul faced during his mission in the city (Acts 16:19–24) appears to have continued even later against the Christian believers (Phil 1:29–30; 1 Thess 2:1–2). Internal evidence from the letter proves that

---

28. Keener argues that it is most possible that Luke recognized the expansion of the gospel from Asia to Europe as transcontinental with postcolonial significance. Craig S. Keener, "Between Asia and Europe: Postcolonial Mission in Acts 16:8–10," *AJPS* 11 (2008): 3–14.

Introduction

Paul shared an intimate relationship with the believers there. In return, they stood with him in the advancement of the gospel, whether he was free or in a Roman prison, and continued to supply resources in his need (Phil 1:4–5; 4:14–19). The concrete evidence of their sacrificial support is proved when they sent Epaphroditus on their behalf to serve Paul (Phil 2:25–30; 4:18). In addition, Epaphroditus carried gifts with him for Paul (4:10–20). Most probably, despite their affliction and poverty, the Philippian church played a generous role in the collection project of Paul for the saints in Jerusalem (2 Cor 8:1–6). Hence, as Paul writes in the letter, he is overwhelmed with joy when he thinks about them in prayer (Phil 1:3, 7).

While Paul was writing his letter from prison, the Philippian church was struggling with internal strife, the arrival of troublemakers with a distorted gospel, and persecution from outsiders. These struggles worried Paul, for he felt torn between his willingness to be martyred for Christ and his desire to visit Philippi to ensure their continuity in faith by being present among them (Phil 1:21–26). Paul used his apostolic authority as their servant-leader to keep them together as a flock of God. He encouraged them to imitate him in order to preserve the suffering community. Hence, many have identified his letter to the Philippians as a "friendship letter,"[29] where Paul emphasizes his partnership with the church in Philippi in spreading the gospel.

BACKGROUND TO THE LETTER TO PHILIPPIANS

In modern times, a letter is typically sent with a clear identification of the intended recipient, the date, and greetings from the sender at the beginning, along with the name and signature of the sender at the end.[30] However, in Paul's time, the letter writing practices were different. The letter to the Philippians contains a clear mention of the recipient, an initial salutation, and the sender, but the date is omitted.[31] This omission creates hurdles for modern readers in

---

29. L. Michael White, "Morality Between Two Worlds: A Paradigm of Friendship in Philippians," in *Greeks, Romans and Christians: Essays in Honor of Abraham J. Malherbe*, eds. David L. Balch, Everett Ferguson and Wayne A. Meeks (Minneapolis: Fortress Press, 1990), 201–215; John T. Fitzgerald, "Philippians in the Light of Some Ancient Discussions of Friendship," in *Friendship, Flattery and Frankness of Speech: Studies on Friendship in the New Testament World*, ed. John T. Fitzgerald, NovTSup 82 (Leiden: Brill, 1996), 141–160.
30. It is not uncommon to see Christians begin a letter with, "Praise the Lord," "Greetings in Jesus name," or a drawing of a cross. Even Hindus do that by either drawing the symbol of "Om" or greeting in the name of their gods (Ram, et al).
31. Calvin J. Roetzel, *The Letters of Paul: Conversations in Context*, 2nd ed. (Atlanta: John Knox Press, 1982), 29–39.

understanding several details in the ancient letter due to our lack of knowledge about the immediate occasion that prompted Paul to send the letter. This omission requires us to consider several vital questions related to the general background of the letter.

Who Wrote the Letter?

There is no doubt that the letter is sent by a prisoner (of Christ) who is waiting with uncertainty to hear the final verdict from the emperor in Rome. He claims to have been imprisoned "for Christ" (1:12–13). The effect of this uncertainty is evident within the letter. Although the sender desires to depart and be with Christ, he understands the significance of his speedy release from the jail for the benefit of his followers. For multiple reasons, the details found within the letter point towards Paul, the apostle, as the author of the letter.

The internal evidence tells us that Paul, along with Timothy, has sent the letter to his dear friends in the city (1:1–2). He uses the term "servants" with a genitive expression "of Christ Jesus" to introduce himself and Timothy to his readers (Rom 1:1; Titus 1:1). Such self-identification by the apostle is, generally, done only where his relationship with the recipient church is cordial. In other situations, Paul affirms his authoritative position as the apostle of Christ Jesus (Gal 1:1; 1 Cor 1:1; 2 Cor 1:1; 1 Thess 1:1; 2 Thess 1:1). Among the four prison letters traditionally ascribed to Paul, Philippians is the only undisputed prison letter. Seldom has anyone questioned Paul as the author of the letter to the Philippians.

Where Was It Written?

The possible provenance of the letter includes Rome, Ephesus, Corinth, and Caesarea.[32] The fundamental reasons for these different proposals are: (1) needing to reconcile quick travels with gifts and the letter between the city of imprisonment and Philippi, (2) the mention of a "palace guard" (*praitōrion*) in 1:13, (3) Paul's plan to re-visit the city (in the east) after his anticipated release, and (4) uncertainty about his safe release from the jail.

Traditionally, the letter is considered to be sent from the Roman jail after Paul was arrested in Jerusalem and then deported to Rome, following his

---

32. James W. Thompson, *Philippians*, PCNT (Grand Rapids: Baker Academic, 2016), 11–12 (he is inconclusive about a particular city); Gerald F. Hawthorne, *Philippians*, WBC 43 (Waco, TX: Word Books, 1983), xliii–xliv (Caesarea); Gorman, *Apostle of the Crucified Lord*, 417–418 (Rome); J. Peter Bercovits, "Paul at Ephesus and the Composition of Philippians," *Proceedings* 8 (Grand Rapids, 1988): 61–76. Online: http://web.a.ebscohost.com/ehost/pdfviewer/pdfviewer?vid=4&sid=45634aac-71d7-4a8a-8d1f-5fe9b9beef3a%40sessionmgr4008.

Introduction

appeal to appear before the emperor for a fair judicial hearing (Acts 21:27–36; 28:11–31). Such an appeal is an example of Paul's use of his right as a Roman citizen (Acts 25:10–12). The evidence supplied in favor of Roman provenance is as follows. First, Luke's statement that he lived in house arrest in Rome guarded by a soldier but with freedom to preach and meet the Jewish leaders (Acts 28:17–31) assures us of Paul's imprisonment in Rome as it coheres well with his words in Philippians 1:7, 13, 17. Second, Rome is the most probable place for Paul to be guarded by the *praetorium* ("palace guards") mentioned in Philippians 1:13 and Acts 28:16. Third, the mention of "those who belong to Caesar's household" (Phil 4:22) suggests that Paul is writing from Rome. Fourth, the church in Rome was well established, and Paul would have known both sympathetic members and rival missionaries there (Phil 1:13, 15–17). In fact, his letter to the Romans as rhetoric against the Jewish preachers, who were teaching a gospel that was contrary to what he preached, may be implied in Philippians 1:15–17.

A major objection raised against Roman provenance is its geographical distance from Philippi, making frequent travels between Paul in a Roman jail and Philippi difficult. Although this is a valid objection, no other proposed place for Paul's imprisonment seems defensible, either on account of geographical distance or on account of our knowledge of his imprisonment for a longer period of time. While Corinth and Ephesus can help explain the possibility of multiple quick trips (sending a gift, the return of Epaphroditus to Philippi, sending Timothy to Philippi, Paul's plan for a quick visit after his release, etc.) due to their shorter distance from Philippi, one cannot be certain that Paul was imprisoned in these cities. The arguments in favor of Paul's imprisonment in Corinth or Ephesus are essentially conjectural in nature, and so they are not a viable choice.

Caesarea raises more likely challenges to Rome as the provenance for the letter, given our knowledge of Paul's imprisonment there. Paul was imprisoned in Caesarea for two years (Acts 24:27), but its distance from Philippi is just as much of a problem as Rome.[33] In this light, the traditional position of favoring Rome appears to be the best choice, despite the difficulties. Paul stayed in Rome for two years (28:30), facing uncertainty about the emperor's decision regarding the quantum of his punishment.

---

33. D. A. Carson, Douglas J. Moo, and Leon Morris, *An Introduction to the New Testament* (Grand Rapids: Zondervan, 1992), 320.

When Was It Written?

If the letter was written from Rome, it must have been sent between AD 60–62 (the first Roman imprisonment) during the reign of Nero[34] to the believers in Philippi, after which Paul was released unhurt from the prison. Paul must have made a quick trip to Philippi as he desired (2:24) before undertaking his planned missionary journey to Spain (Rom 15:24). He must have been arrested again after the Neronian persecution broke out in AD 63/64 in the imperial capital, when he was brought back to Rome. He must have been, finally, martyred in AD 66/67.

What Was the Occasion?

To reconstruct the possible immediate occasion for dispatching this letter to Philippi, we must ask, who are the troublemakers that are intruding into the church? The letter itself identifies the following reasons for writing: Paul's imprisonment in Rome (Phil 1:12–14, 17) and his desire to express his gratitude for the Philippian church's participation and the Philippian believers' support in his mission (Phil 1:4–5; 4:10–20). Moreover, the immediate occasion for dispatching the letter is the complex situation that has arisen in Philippi due to: (1) the persecution of the believers by some outsiders (1:28), (2) the internal situation marred by disunity among believers (Phil 1:27–2:5; 2:12–14; 4:2–3), and (3) the entry of some who are preaching a distorted version of the gospel in the church (Phil 3:1–4, 18–19). Paul, the founding apostle of the church in Philippi, sends the letter through Epaphroditus, writing with joy that is mingled with concern for the well-being of the church. Paul's letter represents him in absentia[35] before the believers, encouraging and interpreting their suffering as their participation with him in mission (Phil 1:30; 4:14). In other words, as the letter from Paul is read out in front of the believers in Philippi, it is as if Paul is speaking to them directly.

Concerning the identity of Paul's opponents, the internal evidence points towards Jewish Christian Judaizers, who taught reliance upon the fleshly credentials. Paul paints their portrait as Jews quite clearly by the selection of sharp polemic terms. Paul identifies them as "mutilators of the flesh" (Phil 3:2) – in other words, circumcision – and highlights their reliance upon the flesh. They

---

34. Donald A. Hagner, *The New Testament: A Historical and Theological Interpretation* (Grand Rapids: Baker Academic, 2012), 557.
35. Robert W. Funk, "The Apostolic Parousia: Form and Significance," in *Christian History and Interpretation*, eds. W. R. Farmer, C. F. D. Moule, and R. R. Niebuhr (Cambridge: Cambridge University Press, 1966), 249–268.

are pitched as opposed to a Christian identity apart from Jewish laws: "we are the circumcision" who put "no confidence in the flesh" (Phil 3:3). The sharp contrast between the two is further emphasized by Paul's presentation of himself as a model for imitation without submitting to the Jewish religious pedigrees (Phil 3:4–6). Similarly, Paul's exhortation for his companions to imitate him (Phil 3:17; 4:9) is a tool to dissuade the Philippian believers from aligning with the troublemakers (3:18–19; compare 1:15, 17). By calling the troublemakers "dogs" and "evildoers" (Phil 3:2), Paul may be re-employing the Jewish vocabulary, taking the word "dogs" – which they used for gentiles (Mark 7:27) because of their defilement – and then throwing it back at them.[36] Unlike Paul, these troublemakers are seeking perfection apart from Christ, which is evil because it leads to confidence in the flesh.

These Jewish Christian Judaizers disturbed Galatian Christians by their rival mission to coerce them to be circumcised (Gal 6:12). The troublemakers' easy acceptance among the believers in Philippi, even though Paul says they were living "as enemies of the cross of Christ" (Phil 3:18), confirms their Christian identity. The Philippians clearly saw them as fellow Christians, and perhaps the church thought they had more interesting or more beneficial teaching than Paul about how to attain perfection through the law. If the troublemakers in Rome who are mentioned in Philippians 1:15–17 are related to the group that was active in Philippi, then they are preachers of the gospel of Christ. Though they are preaching the gospel with the wrong motives, they are Christians.[37]

Why Was It Written?

If Philippians is a single literary unit (as I will argue later in the discussion of Phil 3:1–4:1), then Paul seems to have had multiple purposes for sending the letter.

First, as discussed above, Paul is writing to express his gratitude to the Philippian church for their financial and personal assistance as his missional partners (Phil 4:10–20). Paul repeatedly acknowledges his receipt of gifts from them as well as Epaphroditus's sacrificial service for him in the Roman jail (Phil 2:25–30; 4:10–20). However, he also wants to defend his decision to send Epaphroditus back to Philippi, and so he heaps praises on Epaphroditus, using cruciform language in order to ensure that Epaphroditus will receive a

---

36. Scott C. Ryan, "The Reversal of Rhetoric in Philippians 3:1–11," *PRS* 39 (2012): 70.
37. Hawthorne, *Philippians*, xliv.

favorable reception in Philippi. Paul does not want his decision to disturb his intimate relationship with the church.

Second, Paul is writing to update his mission partners about his whereabouts (Phil 1:7), and he also wants the Philippians to know that his imprisonment has not hindered his ministry of preaching the gospel. In contrast, his imprisonment has opened the unexpected door of advancing the gospel to the "palace guards" in Rome, which otherwise may not have been possible (Phil 1:12–13). Moreover, he wants to inform the Philippians that his imprisonment has had a positive effect upon those who are with him in Rome, as they have been emboldened to preach Christ fearlessly (Phil 1:14).

Third, even though God has been working among the Philippian church (Phil 1:6; 2:13), they have been struggling with disunity (Phil 2:1–4; 4:2–3). Thus Paul expresses his pastoral concern by dedicating a major chunk of the letter to encourage them to be united by having the same mind of Christ. He asks them to practice a cruciform lifestyle by seeking to serve others' interests above their own, just as Christ did (Phil 2:5–11). He also exhorts them to shine as stars amidst the perverted generation (Phil 2:12–15). In order to do this, they need to set their eyes upon all those who have put the teaching of Christ into practice (Phil 3:17; 4:9). In short, they ought to join with Paul and others in learning to imitate Christ.

Fourth, suffering is an important component of Paul's theology and his exhortations to the Philippians, and so he encourages the persecuted community of believers to stand firm in their faith and to be strong in their corporate living (Phil 1:27; 4:1). He himself is a good model for standing firm in Christ amidst suffering (Phil 1:19–26), relinquishing religious pedigrees in order to know Christ through the power of his resurrection and the fellowship of his suffering (Phil 3:5–14), and becoming like Christ by practicing a cruciform lifestyle (Phil 2:17–18).

Finally, Paul is greatly concerned about false teachers entering the church in Philippi. He earnestly desires for the church to recognize this grave danger to their faith, and so he reiterates his earlier warning to be cautious (Phil 3:2). The troublemakers are described with strong negative words – "dogs," "evildoers," and "mutilators of the flesh" (Phil 3:2) – who live as "enemies of the cross of Christ" (Phil 3:18) and whose end is "destruction" because "their god is their stomach" (Phil 3:19). Paul wants the Philippian believers to take careful notice of such people coming among them.

Introduction

What Type of Letter Is It?

The practice of letter writing existed very early in antiquity, and its broad purpose was to communicate about a particular situation. The form and structure of ancient letters depended upon several factors. According to White, "there are identifiable Greek letters with fixed formal patterns and stereotyped phrases which constitute specific epistolary types."[38] He enumerates four major types: "Letters of Introduction and Recommendation," "Letters of Petition," "Family Letters," and "Royal Correspondence."[39] However, the classification is neither exhaustive nor fully satisfactory. One must remember that "Family Letters" were never considered as a distinct type of letters in the Greco-Roman antiquity. Hence, Stowers maintains that it can be treated as a type similar to the generally recognized category of friendship letters.[40] Letters of friendship helped maintain friendship between physically separated friends who shared deep affection for each other. Such letters treated long-lasting relationships and the reciprocity of benefits received in the past as the basis for a fresh request.[41] Many recent scholars consider Philippians as a "Letter of Friendship" within the broad tradition of letter writing in antiquity.[42] These scholars note that the terms and phrases related to ancient friendship language, such as "partnership" and "thinking the same thing," are repeatedly used by Paul.[43] Hansen enlists ten expressions parallel to the friendship motifs in Hellenistic letters, which provide a framework for critically looking at Philippians: (1) "affection" (1:8), (2) "partnership" (*koinōnia* 1:5, 7; 2:1; 3:10; 4:15), (3) "unity of soul

---

38. John L. White, "Ancient Greek Letters," in *Greco-Roman Literature and the New Testament*, ed. David E. Aune (Atlanta: Scholars Press, 1988), 88.
39. White, "Ancient Greek Letters," 88–95.
40. Stanley K. Stowers, *Letter Writing in Greco-Roman Antiquity* (Philadelphia: Westminster Press, 1986), 71.
41. Stowers, *Letter Writing in Greco-Roman Antiquity*, 58–60.
42. Stanley K. Stowers, "Friends and Enemies in the Politics of Heaven: Reading Theology in Philippians," in *Pauline Theology: Thessalonians, Philippians, Galatians, Philemon*, ed. Jouette M. Bassler, vol. 1 (Minneapolis: Fortress Press, 1991), 107–114. Stowers classifies Philippians specifically as "a hortatory or psychagogic letter of friendship" (108).
43. This treatment of Philippians in the past decades of Pauline studies has become a general trend, though there are some exceptional voices who speak otherwise. Philippians as a letter of friendship is maintained by Gordon D. Fee, *Paul's Letter to the Philippians*, NICNT (Grand Rapids: Eerdmans, 1995), 12; Fitzgerald, "Philippians in the Light of Some Ancient Discussions of Friendship," 141–160. Ken L. Berry argues specifically that 4:10–20 is loaded with friendship terms, "The Function of Friendship Language in Philippians 4:10–20," in *Friendship, Flattery and Frankness of Speech*, 107–124. However, John Reumann judges this classification of Philippians as "something of a jump from the mood created by certain words and phrases to a proposed letter form" (105), "Philippians, Especially Chapter 4, as a 'Letter of Friendship': Observations on a Checkered History of Scholarship," in *Friendship, Flattery and Frankness of Speech*, 83–106.

and spirit" (1:27; 2:2, 20), (4) "like-mindedness" (2:2; 4:2), (5) "yokefellow" (4:3), (6) "giving and receiving" (4:15), (7) "common struggles and joys" (1:30; 3:18), (8) "absence/presence" (1:27; 2:12, 24), (9) "virtue friendship" (4:8, 11), and (10) "moral paradigm" (3:3–14, 17; 4:9).[44]

Malherbe argues that the language of friendship is not unique to 4:10–20, but "is in fact the culmination of a letter that employs such language from its very beginning."[45] Drawing from Aristotle, he maintains that the defining features of friendship are that "friends are people of one soul (1:27; compare 2:2), and they think the same thing (2:2; 4:2); . . . that friends have all things in common, is reflected in Paul's repeated concern with sharing in the letter (1:5, 7; 2:1)." Along with this, friends rejoice together (1:4, 18, 25; 2:2, 28, 29), share confidence based on mutual loyalty (1:25; 2:24), and engage in activities together (Paul employs the cognate of *syn* in 2:25, 27, 30; 4:2–3).[46]

Johnson takes a more nuanced position even though he identifies Philippians as a letter of friendship, saying, "I do not suggest that it precisely follows the letter form for the 'friendly letter' (*epistolēphilikē*) as attested in the rhetorical handbooks (compare Pseudo-Demetrius)."[47] Rather, its rhetorical function is to evoke a desired response of "equality and unity" that "counters the impulse of self-assertion."[48]

Fitzgerald acknowledges that the mixed and complex nature of Paul's letters defies any straightjacket classification. He says that it is "an oversimplification" to identify Philippians as a letter of friendship, but he argues that "this designation is quite useful in calling attention to the presence in the letter of a remarkable number of terms that were associated in antiquity with the topics of friendship."[49] Often, the absence of traditional friendship terms, such as *philia* and *philos*, has been used as evidence that Philippians cannot be identified as a letter of friendship.[50] However Paul does make frequent use of kinship terms, such as "brother" (1:12; 3:1, 13, 17; 4:1, 8). In Greek philosophical writings, kinship terms were used to describe friendship, but that

---

44. G. Walter Hansen, *The Letter to the Philippians*, PNTC (Grand Rapids/Cambridge: Eerdmans/Nottingham: Apollos, 2009), 8–11.
45. Abraham J. Malherbe, "Paul's Self-Sufficiency (Philippians 4:11)," in *Friendship, Flattery and Frankness of Speech*, 128.
46. Malherbe, "Paul's Self-Sufficiency," 127–128, cited from 127. See Luke Timothy Johnson, *The Writings of the New Testament: An Interpretation*, rev. ed. (Minneapolis: Fortress Press, 1999), 372.
47. Johnson, *Writings of the New Testament*, 372.
48. Johnson, 373.
49. Fitzgerald, "Philippians in the Light of Some Ancient Discussions of Friendship," 143.
50. Reumann, "Philippians as a 'Letter of Friendship'," 100–105.

Introduction

connection is absent in Paul's letters. Todd Still observes that "[i]t is possible that the apostle regarded kinship and friendship metaphors to be incompatible. In any event, he does not use these metaphors interchangeably in his letters."[51] However, even though there is an absence of friendship language in Philippians, proponents explain that as an intentional omission by the apostle because of the specific social context in Philippi.

For example, Melherbe argues that traditional friendship language is strategically avoided by Paul for two reasons. First, he wanted to avoid anthropomorphic connotations that were contrary to the Christian view that "relationships were determined by God."[52] In this way, Paul preserves his independence in partnering with the Philippians by identifying God as his provider. Second, Paul avoids the terms *philia* and *philios* because of the social obligations associated with them.[53] Moreover, Paul subtly claims authority over the Philippians by defying their Greek understanding of equal friendship when he exhorts them to "watch out" for "the dogs" (3:2) while addressing himself as a "slave" (1:1), whose "Lord" has become the sovereign Lord by taking the nature of a slave (2:7, 11). For Still, this servile term is "a manipulative tool, whereby Paul attempts to pull a verbal bait and switch, feigning to serve while seeking to rule and ride roughshod."[54]

In summary, we can reasonably recognize the importance of friendship between Paul and the Philippian community in his letter, but we cannot reduce the complex nature of the letter to one narrow literary category (i.e., a "letter of friendship"). While Paul does appeal to his strong friendship with the Philippian believers, he is doing so in order to influence an appropriate response from them, whether in their relations with him or in their relations with one another, by imitating the Christlike model that is visible in him and other faithful Christ followers.

---

51. Todd D. Still, "More Than Friends? The Literary Classification of Philippians Revisited," *PRS* 39 (2012): 61.
52. Malherbe, "Paul's Self-Sufficiency," 139.
53. Malherbe, 139.
54. Still, "More than Friends," 64.

PHILIPPIANS 1:1–2
OPENING GREETINGS

Cross-cultural missionaries and pastors in India, Sri Lanka, Nepal, and other places in southern Asia would recognize the significance of bearing a native name when establishing the initial contact with an audience. A name that sounds culturally familiar gives you an added advantage in gaining quick acceptance among your audience.[1] Perhaps Paul recognized this in his mission to the gentiles, for he introduces himself to his readers by his Hellenistic name, Paul, rather than his Hebrew name, Saul. This creates cultural affinity with his non-Jewish audience. He also addresses his readers as "all God's holy people" in Philippi (1:1). Unlike the modern letter writing practice in India, which is to begin with the greeting, "*Mere priyamitra (name) ko namaskar*" (Greetings to my dear friend [name]), the apostle begins his letter according to the Greco-Roman custom by first identifying himself along with Timothy (1:1), his spiritual son (1 Tim 1:18; 1 Tim 1:2; 1 Cor 4:17) and close associate, as the senders of the letter. Most probably, Timothy is mentioned not only because he was known to the church in Philippi (Acts 16:1–2, 12),[2] but also because Paul was planning to send him very soon to gather news about the Philippians' well-being (2:19). Because of Timothy's real concern for the welfare of the Philippians (2:20–24), he is mentioned as Paul's co-worker and close confidant, but throughout the letter, Paul alone is the speaker.

1:1 "SERVANTS OF CHRIST JESUS"

Paul, the senior pastor, demonstrates his great appreciation for Timothy by including him among the "servants of Christ Jesus" (using the plural of *doulos*, which literally means "slave," in 1:1). On this sole occasion, Paul shares the title "servant" with someone else in his salutation. Apart from Philippians 1:1,

---
1. I have experienced this issue personally as a village evangelist who has a south Indian Christian name, Roji T. George. Although my proficiency in Hindi, our national language mostly spoken in northern India, is relatively good and often appreciated by the native Hindi speaking folks, my south Indian Christian name often raises suspicion and questions about my intent to do mission in a cross-cultural context. It always takes time to be accepted among the natives, despite my upbringing in a north Indian context.
2. Hansen, *Philippians*, 37. Hansen maintains that Paul mentioned Timothy because he served Paul as an amanuensis. He may be right in this speculation, but the same rationale would require us to consider Silas and Timothy as co-authors with Paul for 1 and 2 Thessalonians.

the title "servant" is used twice in his epistolary salutations (Rom 1:1; Titus 1:1), but it is always reserved for Paul alone. The use of "servants" instead of "apostle" (compare 1 Cor 1:1; 2 Cor 1:1; Gal 1:1; Eph 1:1; Col 1:1; 1 Tim 1:1; 2 Tim 1:1) proves that Paul did not have to assert his authority before the Philippian believers.³

In the first-century Greco-Roman context, the term "*doulos*" signified a low social status for an individual, while in Greek culture, it meant submission to someone else's will and the loss of self-autonomy. So "the Greek felt only revulsion and contempt for the position of a slave."⁴ However, not all slaves were of the lowest position in the social hierarchy, as many held high administrative responsibilities within the Roman imperial hierarchy. Hence, a slave could be socially humble yet hold an honorable position in the Greco-Roman society, such as Felix, the governor of Syria (Acts 23:24; 23:26). On the other hand, in the OT (LXX), the title "servant" is used to describe Moses, Joshua, and David as ones who served the Lord (Josh 1:1, 13; 14:7; 24:29; 2 Chr 1:3; Ps 89:3; 2 Kgs 8:19; 2 Chr 6:42). Thus from the time of Moses, "servant" was a title of special honor, for "it stood for one who was commissioned by God for a special task."⁵

In this context, the title "servants of Christ Jesus" refers to two important things. First, Paul and Timothy are surrendered to the will of Christ Jesus, for whom and on whose behalf they work. Second, the title reflects their humble yet honorable position within the body of Christ. The honor implied in the title is not related to their own authority, but is derived from Christ Jesus, whose authority, position, and identity Paul invokes repeatedly. In this salutation, Paul honors Timothy.

The importance of the "servant" status of Paul and Timothy is magnified by the triple use of "Christ Jesus" in 1:1–2 (twice "Christ Jesus" and once "Jesus Christ"). Should the expression "Christ Jesus" be understood as "[t]he double name," treating Jesus as though Messiah were part of his name,⁶ or should it be seen as a name with a title, as Paul's proclamation of King Jesus?⁷ If understood merely as a "double name," then it simply means that the salvific role of Jesus is assumed to formulate his theology. However, if the titular

---

3. Richard R. Melick Jr., *An Exegetical and Theological Exposition of Holy Scripture: Philippians, Colossians, Philemon*, NAC 32 (Nashville: Broadman, 1991), 48.
4. R. Tuente, "δουλος," *NIDNTT* 3:593.
5. Melick, *Philippians*, 48.
6. Hansen, *Philippians*, 39.
7. N. T. Wright, *What Saint Paul Really Said: Was Paul of Tarsus the Real Founder of Christianity?* (Grand Rapids: Eerdmans/Cincinnati, Ohio: Forward Movement Publications, 1997), 52.

meaning of "Christ" is invoked, then, as Hendricksen observes, "[h]e focuses the light upon the heavenly Master rather than upon Rome which considered itself to be the master of the earth."[8] Further, Hendricksen maintains that Paul, who observes the servile attitude of the soldiers in the prison and the Roman subjects in the Roman colony of Philippi, "was comforted by the fact that the Anointed One, the Savior, and not the emperor, was his real Master."[9] This also defines Paul and Timothy's humble but honorable position as "servants." Like the slaves who conduct their administrative role on behalf of the Roman emperor within a Roman province, Paul and Timothy appear as representatives of "King Jesus" within the church and act according to the will of Christ Jesus.

1:1 "GOD'S HOLY PEOPLE IN CHRIST JESUS"

The letter is addressed to the whole community of God at Philippi, describing them as "God's holy people," which includes "the overseers and deacons" (1:1). The community is not a "holy people" in the sense that their holiness is innate in them, but the description signifies their separate status "in Christ Jesus." The phrase "in Christ Jesus" reminds us of the mystical space of union, where all believers are redeemed by grace to be holy, which is the sanctified state of a sinner, who is separated for God by faith in Christ Jesus, and continues to experience the sanctifying grace of God by the death of Christ upon the cross. More importantly, "all" implies no preference for the special functionaries within the church, "the overseers and deacons." "All" in the church are called the "holy people," and they all equally belong to God by being found "in Christ."

In a caste-ridden society such as India, only the highest caste (*varnas*),[10] the Brahmins (the priestly caste), have claimed to be religiously holy people. They have maintained their purity by strict ritualism and social separation from the so-called defiled, lowest caste people, such as the *Shudras* and *avarnas* (those who fell outside the four castes and were treated as less than human). Purity associated their caste identity by birth and was maintained through strict

---

8. William Hendricksen, *Philippians*, NTC (Edinburgh: Banner of Truth Trust, 1962), 45.
9. Hendricksen, *Philippians*, 45.
10. The term *Varna*, meaning caste, refers to the Hindu socio-religious system traditionally prevalent in India. Under the Hindu Vedic system, human beings are socially divided into four hierarchical levels (top to bottom): Brahmin (Priests), Kshatriya (Rulers/Warriors), Vaishya (Business class), and Shudra (untouchables), respectively. While this social system privileges those standing at the top of the social pyramid and relies upon the exploitation of the social class, which is placed lower at every level, the explanation that justifies the oppressive division is religious. However, there is a large population that is not included in the hierarchical structure, the *avarna*, who are not even considered fully human.

ritualistic practices, which qualified them to perform important religious roles within the Hindu *sanctum sacrum*. They claimed to be holy because they were believed to have originated from the head of Brahma, while others were made out of other parts of the body in descending order. Sadly, such divisive and, by biblical standards, evil practices have retained a foothold among Christians, too, who may get picky about caste differences in marital alliances. By addressing "all" at Philippi as "God's holy people in Christ Jesus," Paul contradicts the evil social practice in India. If the church is the body of Christ, in which "all" are brought in to share life in him, then "all" are "God's holy people" regardless of social differences. No one is holy except in Christ alone, and no one is holy in any sense that is intrinsic to themselves, such as by performing a special function within the church.

Further, Paul's mention of "overseers" in 1:1 must signify certain special functions fulfilled by some within the church. Because the plural form of "overseers" is used, it seems improbable that more than one functioned as an ecclesiastical office bearer within the church in Philippi. It also seems unlikely that one man was appointed as an "overseer" over many churches within a geographical region, because there was only one church in Philippi at that time. Hence, the term likely describes those who were appointed to fulfill a special function within the church by the Holy Spirit (Acts 20:28). The case with "deacons" (1:1) is similar. Although the function of deacons can be traced to Acts 6:1–6, they are not mentioned by this title there. In addition, Philippians makes no reference to the exact function that the "deacons" may have fulfilled.[11] Probably, they are specifically mentioned here for two reasons: (1) their important role in collecting support for Paul and sending him gifts through Epaphroditus (4:18); (2) they may have been instrumental in trying to prevent the emerging fissure within the community (see 2:3–4).[12]

1:2 GRACE AND PEACE TO THE READERS

In 1:2, Paul greets his audience at the outset following the Greek convention for letter writing. However, his use of two important terms, "grace" and "peace," from both Greek and Jewish conventional letter practices suggests his interest in speaking contextually.[13] Hansen observes that "[i]n fact, it expresses

---

11. Melick, *Philippians*, 49–50.
12. Hansen, *Philippians*, 42.
13. Elsewhere, I have argued that Paul's identity is formed at the interstitial space of multiple cultures, where it is natural for him to speak in the context of this interstitial space.

in condensed form the essence of his theology."¹⁴ The term "peace" (*shalom* in Hebrew) draws its meaning from the OT. Paul refers to God's "peace" again in 4:7, 9. This peace is accomplished by "the Lord Jesus Christ" (1:2), whose death upon the cross reconciled fallen humanity with God (Rom 5:1, 10; Eph 2:11–19) and put an end to God's enmity (Rom 1:18–32).

However, Paul slightly modifies the conventional Greek practice of using *chairein*, which means "greeting," by saying *charis*, which means "grace," thereby preserving the Christian message. Within the Greco-Roman context, Paul's modified greeting appeals to the reality of the divine grace that is available through Christ Jesus by his sacrificial death upon the cross (2:8). Christ's grace stands in contrast to Caesar's grace, which is only available to those who slavishly submit to Roman domination. In this greeting, Paul identifies Christ as "the Lord" (*Kyrios* 1:2) of God's "holy people."

Within the Roman world, "grace" and "peace" were believed to be brought in by Caesar Augustus, whose rule established an unprecedented universal peace within the empire (*Pax Romana*) and demonstrated the emperor's extravagant grace for his subjects. The emperor alone was the "Lord" in the Roman empire. However, Paul's appeal to the superior form of "grace" and "peace" available in "the Lord Jesus Christ" resists the false, inferior forms of "grace" and "peace" that originated from the Roman emperor, who was not the "Lord." For Paul, Jesus alone was worthy to be called "Lord" (2:11), and before him every knee, regardless of ethnicity, position, and power, would bow in absolute submission.

Paul identifies the sole source of "grace" and "peace" for "God's holy people" as "God our Father and the Lord Jesus Christ" (1:2). Mentioning Jesus Christ along with God the Father as the source of grace and peace reveals Paul's understanding about the supremacy of Christ (2:6), for he places Jesus Christ alongside and equal with God the Father. Indeed, Jesus himself bears the title "Lord" (1:2; 2:11). Hence, the blessings of grace and peace for the church are reminders of the incomparable gifts available to all believers.

He liberally adopts and adapts terms from different cultures in order to communicate his Christian thought aptly. Roji T. George, *Paul's Identity in Galatians: A Postcolonial Appraisal* (New Delhi: CWI, 2016).
14. Hansen, *Philippians*, 43.

PHILIPPIANS 1:3–11
THE APOSTLE'S THANKSGIVING
AND PRAYER

In India, as in Asia, religious teachers (*gurus*) and priests are revered for their presumably higher spirituality and devotion to God. However, this does not deny the possibility that a common believer might directly approach God in prayer. Often, *gurus* and priests are thought to commune more closely with God than others, and so their prayers are coveted. In an Indian context, Paul's assurance about his constant prayers on their behalf (1:3–11) would boost new converts, suggesting that they might receive special divine assistance. Moreover, Paul's confidence in God's continued activity among the Philippian church (1:6) would be viewed as an assurance of their well-being.

After the formal salutation in 1:1–2, Paul expresses his sincere gratitude to his readers for their partnership in advancing the gospel (1:3–11). Though Paul is a Jew, he has been influenced by the customary Hellenistic letter writing style, which he Christianizes and carefully adapts for his unique purpose.[1] In India, Christians use the culturally adapted expression, "*Jai Masih ki*" ("Hail Messiah!"), instead of the traditional Hindu greeting, "*Jai Ramji ki*" ("Hail Ram!"). This greeting is often incorporated into private letters. Paul's words in 1:3–11 suggest that Paul feels emotionally attached to his believers (vv. 3–8), for he offers a sincere pastoral prayer for their spiritual maturity and growth, so that they may praise and glorify God (vv. 9–11).

Based on the ancient Greek rhetorical practice, we know that Paul's primary intention is to secure the readers' "acceptance, receptivity and goodwill."[2] Hence, he iterates his gratitude to God for their sacrificial partnership with him in spreading the gospel, expresses his overflowing joy, affection, and love for them, and offers fervent prayers for their social and moral well-being.

---

1. Hawthorne, *Philippians*, 15. He states that "Paul takes a colorless, customary convention, reworks it and makes it express the intensity of his devotion to God and of his feelings for his friends." See Fee, *Philippians*, NICNT, 72.
2. Duane F. Watson, "A Rhetorical Analysis of Philippians and Its Implications for the Unity Question," *NovT* 30 (1988): 61–65. Watson contends that in Philippians we find a larger exordium that continues until 1:26.

1:3–8 HEARTFELT EXPRESSION OF GRATITUDE

1:3–6 Paul's Thanksgiving

In line with the ancient practice of letter writing, Paul mentions his gratitude to God, adding a rare personal touch by saying, "I thank my God" (1:3; Rom 1:8; 1 Cor 1:4; Phlm 4). There are at least three reasons for him to thank God: (1) the Philippians are partnering with him in furthering the gospel (1:5); (2) the Philippians sent Epaphroditus to serve him in jail (2:25); (3) the Philippians are sending financial support for his mission (4:15–18).

Reflecting about these acts of benevolence from the believers in Philippi, the apostle makes a personal offering of thanksgiving to God on their behalf. This offering gives us insight into Paul as a pastor and a team leader. Though the financial support received from the church in Philippi would have served the needs of the whole missionary team (both Paul and Timothy), Paul is the leader of the missionary team, and so he accepts the support as a personal favor. Paul's sense of obligation is implied by his use of "I" which seems to overlook Timothy's presence with him (compare 1:1).

From a sociological perspective, Paul's thanksgiving has further significance. His words of gratitude to God are an indirect compliment to his readers, aiming to encourage their continued partnership with him in the future.[3] Within the Greco-Roman system of *clientalia* in the first century AD, Paul's explicit verbal gratitude has a social function. Every social relationship under the system of *clientalia* was tied to the principle of reciprocity, where the client or beneficiary of a benefaction was obliged to reciprocate in an appropriate measure (in kind or words) to the patron.[4] Such reciprocity is not unusual in an Asian context either, as when Christian leaders acknowledge their supporters by openly expressing their gratitude in public. Such acknowledgments are often reciprocated with loud applause, and the intent of the speaker is to encourage the audience to continue such acts of benevolence in the future.

---

3. G. W. Peterman, *Paul's Gift from Philippi: Conventions of Gift-Exchange and Christian Giving* (Cambridge: CUP, 1997), 93. Peterson argues that the function of the thanksgiving sections in Paul's letters is to compliment the readers indirectly in order to encourage certain behavior among them.
4. See John E. Sambaugh and David L. Balch, *The New Testament in its Social Environment* (Philadelphia: Westminster Press, 1986), 63–64; Frederick W. Danker, "Benefaction," *ABD* 1: 669–671; Halvor Moxnes, "Patron-Client Relations and the New Community in Luke-Acts," in *The Social World of Luke-Acts: Models for Interpretation*, ed. Jerome H. Neyrey (Peabody, MA: Hendrickson, 1999), 245–249.

In 1:3b–4, Paul continues to express the intensity and consistency of his indebtedness to his readers by saying that he thanks God "every time" (*pantote* 1:4) he remembers them.[5] In fact, Paul reveals his intention to display his very positive disposition towards Philippians by repeating *pas* four times in 1:4. Paul means to say that he thanks God every time he remembers their benevolence (1:3–4). The term *deēsis* (which is repeated twice in different forms in 1:4) is translated as "prayer," but it is different than the term *proseuchē*, which means "prayer."[6] Instead, *deēsis* is "used for specific prayer (in case of 1:4, it refers to a prayer of petition) in concrete situations."[7] This term suggests that Paul's prayers were intercessory prayers, which he offered on their behalf amidst the problems they were facing (2:1–4; 3:2–3; 4:2). However, Paul's petitionary prayers were based on fond memories of their kind deeds, which is evidenced by the use of the term *meta charas* (1:4), which means "with joy" and is used repeatedly in the letter (see also 1:25; 2:2, 29; 4:1; its verb form *chairō* is also used in 1:18; 2:17, 18, 28; 3:1; 4:4, 10). By using the term *meta charas* in front of the phrase *tēn deēsin poioumenos* (literally "making the petition") in 1:4, Paul emphasizes his positive disposition towards the Philippians.[8] He wants his readers to realize that his constant prayer for them all (1:4), even in imprisonment, is full of thanksgiving and joy.

Moving further, 1:5 states the specific reasons for Paul's joy: "because of your partnership in the gospel from the first day until now." The term *koinōnia*, meaning "participation" or "fellowship," is a "two-sided relation"[9] that means either to share *in* something (participation) or to share *with* someone in something (fellowship).[10] In the given context, the former option appears to be more relevant, because it means the participation of the Philippians *in*

---

5. Scholars have repeatedly debated whether the term "remember" refers to Paul or the believers in Philippi. Syntactically, it is unclear. However, the context must suggest Paul as a better choice, which must then be understood in a temporal sense. See Hawthorne, *Philippians*, 15–17; Fee, *Philippians*, NICNT, 78; Melick, *Philippians*, 54; Jac J. Müller, *The Epistles of Paul to the Philippians and to Philemon*, NICNT (Grand Rapids: Eerdmans, 1955), 39; Hendricksen, *Philippians*, 50. Others have argued for the Philippian believers' remembrance in a causal sense. See Peterman, *Paul's Gift from Philippi*, 98 (Peterman states that here it is the remembrance of Philippians which "produces" thanksgiving in Paul); Paul Schubert, *Form and Function of the Pauline Thanksgiving*, ZNT 20 (Berlin: Topelmann, 1939), 73–74; Peter T. O'Brien, *Introductory Thanksgiving in the Letters of Paul*, NovTSup 49 (Leiden: Brill, 1977), 41–46.
6. Hawthorne, *Philippians*, 17.
7. Heinrich Greeven, "δεομαι, κτλ," *TDNT* 2:41, parenthesis added.
8. Gordon D. Fee, *Philippians*, IVPNTC (Downers Grove/Leicester: InterVarsity Press, 1999), 46.
9. Friedrich Hauck, "κοινονος, κτλ," *TDNT* 3:798.
10. Hauck, *TDNT* 3:797.

Paul's ministry of spreading the gospel through material support based on their friendship. The participation, which includes their readiness to share in Paul's preaching activities, makes Paul joyous in prayer for them.

What does the expression participation "in the gospel" mean? "Gospel" is an important term that appears repeatedly in Philippians (1:5, 7, 12, 16, 27; 2:22; 4:3, 15) and includes both the content of his proclamation (invariably the absolute use of "gospel" without a modifier, e.g., 1:5, 16, except in 1:27, "the gospel of Christ") and the further advancement of the gospel by preaching (1:7, 12; 2:22; 4:3). While the former meaning is possible, suggesting that Paul is rejoicing about the whole-hearted fellowshipping of the Philippians in the gospel, the latter meaning appears to be more appropriate in the present clause, where the expression "in the gospel" means their participation in his missionary activity. In this sense, he uses the term "gospel" in 2:22 and 4:3 to acknowledge the vital partnership of Timothy and the quarreling women, Euodia and Syntyche, in his ministry. However, we must not limit the scope of the participation of the Philippian believers "in the gospel" simply to their sharing of material resources with Paul. Instead, their sharing "in the gospel" also includes their life in Philippi, which is lived in the light of the gospel (1:27–30). In other words, it includes their witnessing in Philippi and sharing in the sufferings of Christ, just as Paul suffered for the gospel in the past and now in the Roman jail.

Further, Paul states that the Philippians have continuously participated from the beginning in the gospel, saying, "from the first day until now" (1:5). The "first day" refers to the day of their conversion, when they first believed in Christ Jesus while listening to the gospel that Paul preached at Philippi. Since that time, Paul has experienced a steady journey of mutual affection and participation in God's mission with the church at Philippi, and this has had a deep impact on his own missionary activity. Interestingly, despite Paul's general missionary policy of not accepting support from the newfound churches, lest he be robbed of his right to boast in sharing the gospel free of charge (1 Cor 9:15–18; 2 Cor 11:7–9), the Philippian believers appear to have convinced him to make an exception and accept their material/financial support regularly (e.g., 2 Cor 11:9; Phil 4:10, 16, 18).[11] This suggests that Paul did not refuse to accept support in ministry if it was given out of affection and sincere friendship.

Thus in 1:6, the apostle states that his joy on their behalf is also founded upon the confidence he has about their future. The participle form *pepoithōs*,

---

11. Hawthorne, *Philippians*, 20.

which means "having been persuaded," implies Paul's assurance that the partnership of the Philippians in the past will continue in future "until the day of Christ Jesus." Paul's words of confidence assure them of their being the field of God's activity. Interestingly, the focus here shifts from the Philippians to God himself, who has been active in the "good works" of the Philippian believers and will continue to be so in future. In other words, the visible partnership of the Philippians, which is the reason for Paul's "joy" and "thanksgiving" to God in 1:3–5, is in fact the visible expression of God's invisible activity in them (2:13). By this the believers in Philippi are instruments in God's hand to further God's mission in the world. Here, we find a double attestation about (1) the standing of Paul in God's mission as a missionary who sees both divine and human support in his moments of need, and (2) the special place that the Philippians have in the divine activity as shareholders with Paul in accomplishing God's salvific plan.

However, scholars disagree about the expression "good works" (*ergon agathon*) in 1:6. Some argue that it refers to Paul's partnership with the Philippians in the gospel by sharing "their resources with him to make the proclamation of the gospel possible."[12] Others argue that "More likely, however, it refers to God's good work of salvation itself, of creating a people for his name in Philippi," which "anticipates 2:12–13, where Paul urges them to keep working out their common salvation in the way they live together as God's people in Philippi, since God is at work in them both to will and to do for the sake of his own good pleasure."[13] While the latter view offers a broader space to understand the activity of God in the lives of the Philippians as the "good works," the former view appears more likely in the present context, rendering better meaning within the literary context because it appears to tie the "good works" closely with *koinōnia* in 1:5. In fact, Paul encourages them by reminding that their *koinōnia* is not merely their own human initiative but the result of God's activity. Despite the threat to *koinōnia* from outside (1:28) as well as within (4:2) the church, Paul raises "it above mere human relationships,"[14] identifying God as the initiator and consummator of that participation. God will lead this divinely secured relationship of partnership, "the good works," into completion on the eschatological day of Christ Jesus.[15]

---

12. Hawthorne, *Philippians*, 21; Hansen, *Philippians*, 50.
13. Fee, *Philippians*, IVPNTC, 48. See Moisés Silva, *Philippians*, BECNT, 2nd ed. (Grand Rapids: Baker Academic, 2005), 45–46.
14. Hansen, *Philippians*, 50.
15. Hansen, 50.

In the NT, the expression "the day of Christ Jesus" (1:6) refers to the final day of the Messiah's second coming, when the Messiah will be exalted and glorified and all who belong to him will share in it. This is the living hope of every true believer in Christ. However, in the incarnation of Christ, this process has already begun. Every believer in Christ experiences it here and now but also anxiously awaits its consummation on the eschatological day. During this intermediate period between faith in Jesus as Lord and the eschatological day, believers in Christ are to live out their otherworldly lifestyle as the citizens of heaven in this world (1:27). However, in light of 3:15–17, where Paul exhorts believers to engage in the pursuit of winning the prize of knowing Christ fully in the end, the expression "in the day of Christ Jesus" (1:6) must be understood as indicative of a problem in Philippi, when "some of them have apparently begun to lose the basic future orientation that marks all truly Christian life."[16] Paul manifests confidence to them about the certainty of the consummation of their "good works" in the end. Here, one may also hear the idea of judgment resonating due to its close semantic relationship with the OT concept of the Day of Yahweh (Joel 2:2; Amos 5:20), when everyone's deeds, including the Philippian believers', will be tested in fire (compare 1 Cor 3:13). Nevertheless, Paul is confident that on that day, their "good works" will be completed and his hard work among them will not be in vain (2:16).[17] The apostle anticipates God's continuing work in the lives of the believers until the final goal is attained.

1:7–8 Paul's Justification

In 1:7–8, Paul continues to justify his confidence in their continued partnership with him in the future. Paul's use of *kathōs* ("just as") without its correlative (*outōs*), which means something like "because," helps us to see the connection between 1:7 and 1:3–6.[18] Here Paul wants to impress upon the Philippian believers the love that he has for them in his heart (1:7). The sense of Paul's intimate feeling towards the Philippians implies his "certain 'mindset,' including attitudes and dispositions."[19] According to Hawthorne, the term "feel" in 1:7 "embraces both feeling and thought, emotions and mind."[20] Thus Paul not only cherishes the good relationship he shares with them in his heart

---

16. Fee, *Philippians*, IVPNTC, 48; Fee, *Philippians*, NICNT, 88.
17. Hawthorne, *Philippians*, 21–22.
18. Hawthorne, 22.
19. Fee, *Philippians*, IVPNTC, 49; Fee, *Philippians*, NICNT, 89.
20. Hawthorne, *Philippians*, 22.

(1:7), but he also anticipates a blessed ending on the last day (1:6). For Paul, feeling this way is "right" because it is based on his experience of their warm partnership in his ministry (1:3–6) and their sharing of God's grace with him (1:7). It would be unfair for Paul not to feel this way towards them because the term "right" in the neuter form denotes "that which is obligatory in view of certain requirements of justice, right, faith . . ."[21]

Does the phrase, "you share in God's grace with me," (v. 7) refer to the believers' co-suffering with him in ministry, their sending gifts to him, or the saving grace of God for all? One cannot be sure about its exact meaning, but their sharing in "grace" should not be narrowly understood as merely their sending of gifts to him,[22] or as God's offer of salvation to Paul and the Philippians. Within the present context, their sharing in "grace" must refer to their partnership in Paul's ministry[23] by giving gifts to Paul, whether he was in chain or defending the gospel (1:5, 7), by sending Epaphroditus to serve him in jail (2:25), as well as enduring the same suffering for Christ's sake in Philippi (1:29–30).

In 1:8, following the OT practice of invoking God as a witness (e.g., Josh 22:27; 1 Sam 12:5; 20:23), Paul calls God as his witness to insist on his deep affection for his readers. Paul uses a similar invocation of divine testimony for his missionary practice in other letters (1 Thess 2:5, 10; 2 Cor 1:23; Rom 1:9). Hence, in response to the love he has received from the Philippian believers, Paul assures them, invoking God as his witness, that he longs (*epipothō*) for all of them. In this way, Paul intensifies his claim of a deep emotional bond with the readers, which he already made in 1:7. He begins with "for" as a further explanation to 1:7. Paul's longing for his believers is characteristic of other letters (1 Thess 3:6; Rom 1:11).

Furthermore, Paul qualifies his affection (*ta splagchna*) with "of Christ Jesus" in the genitive form, which elevates his mere human emotional response to a higher form of love exhibited in Christ Jesus. This affection, which is modeled after Christ, is willing to sacrifice for his readers. In fact, having been put in jail and staring at possible death (although he hoped for his speedy release), Paul claims that if he lives, it is "for your progress and joy in the faith"

---

21. Walter Bauer, Frederick William Danker, W. F. Arndt, and F. W. Gingrich, *A Greek-English Lexicon of the New Testament and Other Early Christian Literature*, 3rd ed. (Chicago and London: University of Chicago Press, 2000), 247. Hereafter abbreviated as BDAG.
22. Silva, *Philippians*, BECNT, 47.
23. Brian Wintle, "Philippians," in *South Asia Biblical Commentary: A One-Volume Commentary on the Whole Bible*, ed. Brian Wintle (Udaipur: Open Door Publications, 2015), 1649.

(1:25). Similarly, in 2:17, Paul expresses his willingness to be sacrificed for their spiritual benefit (2:17) because of the love of Christ Jesus exhibited on the cross (2:8). Interestingly, Paul experiences such a strong emotion for them from his very inner being – his heart, liver, and lungs – which in later Jewish writings is the source of deep emotions, or the "seat of feelings."[24] In a sense, Paul claims to say: "God is my witness that I feel deep within me like dying for you if it is for your good." However, Paul's deep sense of affection is not oblivious to the actual reality in Philippi, about which he has some concern. Hence, in 1:9–11 he bursts out in prayer for the Philippians.

1:9–11 PAUL'S PASTORAL PRAYER

Philippians 1:9–11 states the content, reason, and goal of the apostle's prayer. In 1:9, Paul, who bursts out with joy and thanksgiving (1:3–6) to God for his partnership with the Philippian believers, informs his readers about the content of his prayer, saying, "And this is my prayer." The term "this," which is explained by the following reason clause (*hina*), introduces the content of his prayer. Interestingly, love does not have an object in 1:9. However, Paul's unique use of the term "love" (*agapē*) in the letter helps identify its actual sense in 1:9. Paul uses the term *agapē* twice in the section on ethical exhortation (2:1–2) as well as here in 1:9 and again in 1:15–16, where "love" characterizes the preachers who out of their good will for others act in love. The missional praxis of these preachers is contrary to those who act out of malice, "envy and rivalry" in order to "stir up trouble for" Paul (1:15, 17). Such a negative motive in mission contradicts the "attitude" of Christ Jesus. Paul wants the attitude of Christ, including "love," to characterize his believers (compare 2:1–2, 5). In this "other-oriented" lifestyle, self-sacrifice defines love, as in Christ's death on the cross (2:8). For Paul, the "love" in them must be the same that Paul has ("of Christ Jesus" in 1:8), which Jesus demonstrated by self-emptying, self-giving, and self-dying in order to bring them the benefit of salvation (2:6–8).

Thus, the love (*agapē*) which he describes in 1:9 is not a static feeling within, rather a dynamic process of constant growth in relation to others. By praying that their "love may abound more and more" (1:9), he recognizes the actual situation in the Philippian church, where strife and discord were taking root (4:2–3). Paul, as the pastor, knows that if this attitude of love is not among them, the life and testimony of the church will be in jeopardy.

---

24. Helmut Köster, "σπλαγχνον, κτλ," *TDNT* 7:548–550, cited from 550.

But how can they grow "more and more" in love? Their progress in love ought to be "*in* knowledge (*epignōsis*) and depth of insight (*aesthēsis*)" (1:9), which explains the context in which love must be practiced.[25] Love that is informed by *epignōsis* is not a higher, abstract form of philosophical knowledge, rather an experiential knowledge informed by the will of God (Col 1:9). This knowledge enables the Philippians "to conduct" themselves in a manner that is "worthy of and pleasing to the Lord."[26] Such knowledge enables love to serve others effectively.

Similarly, the term "insight" (*aesthēsis*) appears only here in the NT. In secular Greek, *aesthēsis* means moral understanding or insight.[27] In this sense, the term is also used in LXX (e.g., Prov 1:4, 7, 22; 2:10; 5:2; 11:9). Paul appears to be exhorting them to abound in a love that is informed by an experiential knowledge of God's will and a moral insight that will enable them to differentiate good from bad while seeking the interest of others. In short, the content of Paul's prayer for the believers in Philippi is guided by the actual need of the community, which is embroiled in strife and conflict. The purpose of the prayer in 1:9 is identified in the purpose clauses in 1:10: (1) "that you may be able to discern what is best" and (2) that you "may be pure and blameless." These two purposes need to be fulfilled in the life of the church continuously "until the day of Christ."

The term *dokimazein* ("discern") means "to make a critical examination of something to determine genuineness, put to the test, examine"[28] and suggests a conscious effort on the part of a Philippian believer to make choices for oneself or in relation to others. Like a goldsmith examining the genuineness of gold by rubbing it on a touchstone, discernment is a critical process that ensures the purity of the gold. In Romans 2:18, the same term is used to explain that which is known through the law. Here, the knowledge of God's will comes by testing every action against the standards of the law. However, in 1:10, discerning "what is best" is the goal of love, which is informed by the knowledge and moral insights mentioned in 1:9.

The term *diapherein* ("best") means that which is different from someone or something to one's advantage or "superior."[29] Again, Paul's prayer here has contextual relevance to the situation in the church in Philippi. In order to

---

25. Hansen, *Philippians*, 58.
26. Wintle, "Philippians," 1649.
27. BDAG, 29.
28. BDAG, 255.
29. BDAG, 239.

have a love that fosters unity in "spirit and purpose," "humility," and service to benefit others (2:2–4), it is important to be able to discern "what is best" (superior) amidst multiple options. Seeking one's own interest is not bad in itself, but it is better to seek to benefit others because it is beneficial to the larger life of the Philippian community.

The second purpose, that the community "may be pure and blameless," includes two vital terms that reflect Paul's heart for his believers. The first term, "pure" (*elikrinēs*), means "'tested by the light of the sun,' 'completely pure,' 'spotless'" implying moral purity (2 Pet 3:1; 1 Cor 5:8; 2:17).[30] The second term, *aproskopos* ("blameless"), means "to be without fault because of not giving offence" (1 Cor 10:32).[31] For the Philippians, they are to be pure in their personal life, their standing before God, and their co-existence with fellow believers. Paul most likely finds some behaving otherwise, and so he prays that they may live in harmony with others without causing offense and in moral purity "until the day of Christ" (1:10). This phrase appears twice within this short section (see 1:6), which points to Paul's mental orientation at the time of writing. He is concerned about those who have lost this futuristic dimension of Christian living (compare 1:6). The believers ought to live in moral purity, without blemish, to escape the rod of God's punishment.

Finally, in 1:11, Paul identifies the goal of his prayer, using the metaphor a "fruit of righteousness" from the field of agriculture. In the OT, this metaphorical expression refers to conducting oneself in a way that is pleasing to God (Prov 11:30; Amos 6:12).[32] This connotation is a logical extension of Paul's prayer in 1:10. But is "righteousness" a source or a nature of the fruit? If a source, then it identifies the legal standing of a believer before God by being justified. While such an interpretation of the expression is not impossible, the latter meaning of "nature" appears more appropriate within the context. Thus the present metaphorical expression must be understood as the sum total of the church's ethical living, which is modeled after the sacrificial life of Jesus (2:1–8). The Philippian believers are not merely sanctified subjects of God's grace but living trees of righteousness that can only bear fruit "through Jesus Christ," *dia Iēsou Christou* (3:9; compare John 15). Such a fruit-bearing righteous life will yield "glory and praise of God" (1:11).

---

30. Friedrich Büchsel, "εἰλικρινής, κτλ," *TDNT* 2:397.
31. BDAG, 125.
32. Hawthorne, *Philippians*, 29.

PHILIPPIANS 1:12–26
PAUL'S IMPRISONMENT

In Malayalam, which is a language spoken in Kerala, the southernmost state of India, there is this saying: "If you chase away a spider into another room, you will find new cobwebs created there." Although the saying implies that one must eliminate the spider to stop the formation of cobwebs, making cobwebs is obviously in the nature of a spider, and it will make them continuously wherever it may be. In Philippians 1:12–26, Paul, as a missionary, appears to be rather like a spider that cannot stop doing what is integral to his being, even when his accusers devise schemes to put him to death. He is an uncompromising missionary with no other purpose in life than to make Christ known to all. Hence, personal witness and mission are deeply rooted in Paul's self-consciousness, and he can scarcely see himself apart from his mission.

In 1:12–26, Paul reports his situation to his audience in Philippi because they are not only anxious to learn about his current situation in imprisonment, but they are also partnering with him in mission, both financially and by sending Epaphroditus to serve him in jail. Obviously, they would have heard recently about Paul from Epaphroditus, but he wants to explain how he views his present condition. From the perspective of nurturing and strengthening a church in eternal hope amidst persecution and suffering, Paul's encouraging report is vital for the spiritual life of the mission-minded believers in Philippi. It is always heart-warming for believers to hear that adverse circumstances faced by their minister (in this case, Paul) are unexpectedly helping to accomplish the goal of their partnership in Christ, which is the miraculous advancement of the gospel into unexpected quarters.

We can trace the structure of Paul's report in 1:12–26 as follows. First, in 1:12–14, Paul reports about how his imprisonment has enabled him to bear witness for Christ to the elite Roman guards in the prison. Next, in 1:15–18a, Paul rejoices that the advancement of the gospel among all is unhindered, irrespective of the good or bad intentions of the people involved in preaching. Finally, in 1:18b–26, Paul exhibits his single-minded devotion to the cause of Christ, whether through his life or in his death.

1:12–14 PAUL'S ENCOURAGING REPORT

Opposition to Christianity in India is not new, but the sudden increase of many unfortunate events in the past few years has sent alarm bells ringing loudly across the Christian community throughout the country. Christian pastors have been brutally attacked or murdered. Many churches have been either desecrated or destroyed. Christian worship services and spiritual meetings have been abruptly disrupted by agitated mobs accusing them of carrying out religious conversions and promoting blind faith among the masses. At times, democratically elected leaders, who have subscribed to certain ideological positions, have gone overboard in public, hurling abuses upon Christians and other minority communities, particularly those who adhere to Semitic religions. The new converts are harassed and reconverted into the dominant religion under the systematic program known as *Ghar Wapsi* ("Home Return") by some fringe elements of the dominant community. Court cases have also been lodged against Christian missionaries and pastors, entangling them in ongoing litigations that accrue huge financial burdens.

Amidst such a discouraging and fear-instilling environment, Paul's words in 1:12–14 are a model for how we can view our imprisonments and sufferings as new opportunities to reach inaccessible social quarters with the gospel of Christ rather than as setbacks or obstacles in mission. As a leader who wants to keep up the morale of his people, Paul focuses on how the purpose of their partnership – the advancement of the gospel – is being fulfilled even through his imprisonment. In 1:12–14, Paul adopts a positive approach as he reports on the unhindered advancement of the gospel. This subtly jibes the Roman exhibition of power because it scuttles the desire of Rome to control the activities of her subjects through imprisonment.

Paul's subtle jibe at Rome is deliberate, for he says, "I want you to know" (1:12). This is similar to other disclosure expressions, such as "I want you to realize" (1 Cor 11:3), or "I do not want you to be unaware" (Rom 1:13; compare 1 Cor 10:1; 12:1; 2 Cor 10:1). In Hellenistic letter writing practices, such formulaic expressions have four vital components: (1) naming the addresser's wish (i.e., "I want"), (2) identifying the addressee (i.e., "you," "brothers and sisters"), (3) using a "a *neotic verb* in the infinitive" (i.e., "to know"), and (4) imparting information (i.e., the sentence followed by "that").[1] Such expressions intend "to call attention to the fact that something of considerable interest

---

1. T. Y. Mullins, "Disclosure as a Literary Form in the New Testament," *NovT* 7 (1964): 44–50; T. Y. Mullins, "Formulas in New Testament Epistles," *JBL* 91 (1972): 382; J. T. Sanders, "The

or importance is going to follow."[2] Paul addresses the believers in Philippi as "brothers and sisters," implying their unique relationship as people redeemed by grace through Christ Jesus and brought into a family in Christ beyond ethnic, racial, and cultural differences (1:1–2).

Thus Paul continues to state his view on his current status in jail, claiming "that what has happened to me has actually served to advance the gospel" (1:12). The Greek expression *ta kateme*, which is translated as "what has happened" in the NIV, literally means "the things about me." The same expression appears in Ephesians 6:21 and Colossians 4:7, referring not only to his situation within the jail, but also to the entire series of episodes: from his arrest in Jerusalem, to his imprisonment in Jerusalem and Rome, to his standing before the Roman emperor (1:13–14; Acts 21:27–28:31).[3] However, Paul sees a dramatic turn to the whole course of events because of the prayers of the Philippian believers and "the Spirit of Jesus Christ" (1:19). While the former implies the broad scope of his audience's partnership with Paul in his service to the Lord Jesus Christ, the latter points to the constant divine presence, assistance, and protection in his missional involvement.

The term *mallon*, translated as "actually," implies an unexpected twist in this case. Although the term refers to a positive outcome, meaning "to a greater or higher degree,"[4] it must be understood here as "'rather' in the sense of 'instead'."[5] The believers in Philippi must have been anxious to hear about the actual proceedings and final outcome of Paul's case before the Roman emperor (Acts 28:14–16, 23, 30–31). As a corrective, Paul wants to direct them toward the alternative outcome, which is more positive. As Hansen observes, the apostle emphatically states that what might have hindered the advancement of the gospel has surprisingly advanced the gospel, using a slight wordplay between *prokopē*, which means "advance," and *proskopē*, which means

---

Transition from Opening Epistolary Thanksgiving to Body in Letters of the Pauline Corpus," *JBL* 81 (1962): 349.
2. Hendricksen, *Philippians*, 68.
3. Fee adopts a much narrower position on its meaning as referring to his imprisonment because the expression "in chains" appears three times in quick succession here (1:13, 14, 17). However, the expression can broadly imply the entire episode of his arrest and imprisonment together. Fee, *Philippians*, NICNT, 110.
4. BDAG, 613.
5. Peter T. O'Brien, *The Epistle to the Philippians*, NIGTC (Grand Rapids: Eerdmans/Carlisle: Paternoster Press, 1991), 90. See J. B. Lightfoot, *St. Paul's Epistle to the Philippians: A Revised Text with Introduction, Notes, and Dissertations* (Peabody, MA: Hendrickson, 1987), 87; Marvin R. Vincent, *A Critical and Exegetical Commentary on the Epistle to the Philippians and Philemon*, ICC (Edinburgh: T & T Clark, 1985), 16; Müller, *Philippians*, 48.

"hindrance."[6] Paul intentionally gives this twist to the whole process of his arrest and imprisonment, because it will not only assure his audience about the value of their financial and personal support, but it will also encourage and strengthen them in their struggle to stand firm in faith at Philippi.

The concrete evidence of the advancement of the gospel (1:12) through Paul's imprisonment consists of: (1) others knowing the reason for his imprisonment (1:13) and, thereby, knowing Christ himself and (2) the emboldening of the fellow believers in Rome to proclaim the gospel fearlessly (1:14). Grammatically, these two clauses (1:13–14) are tied to 1:12, which they explain.

First, in 1:13, Paul mentions how his imprisonment has given him easy access to a certain quarter of the Roman population that otherwise may not have been easy to reach. If Paul was imprisoned in Rome, the term "palace guard" (*praitōrion*) refers to the elite group of Caesar's Roman bodyguards and not merely to a place.[7] In the Roman imperial context, they held immense power on repeated occasions of major political crisis in Rome. These elite guards were first formed by Caesar Augustus, who chose efficient men "originally of Italian birth." From the time of Tiberius, they were permanently stationed in Rome in a "strongly fortified camp."[8] Without Paul's arrest and imprisonment in Rome, he would have found it difficult to find an opportunity to share the gospel with these elite soldiers.

Apparently, this is not the only group who heard about the reason for Paul's arrest. There were others (i.e., "everyone else" 1:13) to whom the news had spread about the unique prisoner who was in chains "for Christ" (1:13 literally, "in Christ"). It seems that the news of this prisoner for Christ must have spread from mouth to mouth among the "palace guards" and other fellow prisoners and from them, it must have gone to "everyone else." Though we are unsure whether "everyone else" refers literally to everyone in the whole city of Rome or just to the elite guards and prisoners in the jail, it is clear that when Paul wrote the letter to the Philippian believers, he had with him some who were from "Caesar's household" (4:22). Without implying that the news had reached every individual in Rome, it must certainly refer not only to the people who were with him in jail, but also to people beyond the jail.

The first important point here is that Paul, the prisoner, is unlike other prisoners in the Roman jail. In fact, the use of "in Christ" (1:13) suggests

---

6. Hansen, *Philippians*, 66–67.
7. Moisés Silva, *Philippians*, WEC (Chicago: Moody Press, 1988), 70; O'Brien, *Philippians*, 93.
8. Vincent, *Philippians*, 16–17.

that his very being is founded in Christ.⁹ Hence, his suffering in chains is "in Christ," for he is in jail due to his commitment to the gospel rather than any other reason, such as murder, treason, or robbery. He is a "true-blue" slave of Christ who is otherwise blameless before the Roman law. The message he is preaching and the suffering he is bearing are solely for the cause of Christ. Paul's gospel is about the universal Lord before whom every knee, including Caesar's, shall bow and every tongue confess that "Jesus Christ is Lord" (2:10–11). In this way he preaches Christ not only in his words (Acts 28:24), but also through his very being. To talk about his imprisonment is to talk about Christ. This is how Paul views the ongoing advancement of the gospel taking place at Rome, and so it is with every Christian who is fully committed to the cause of Christ.

The twentieth-century story of Prem Pradhan from Nepal offers a recent inspiring example. Like Paul, he was imprisoned for Christ by the Nepalese government, but he continued witnessing to Christ in the jail. They kept moving Prem Pradhan from prison to prison, but he remained undeterred by the opposition from the Nepal royalty and founded prayer groups in every single jail. Similar to the advancement of the gospel due to Paul's imprisonment, Nepal witnessed a steady growth of Christianity due to Prem Pradhan's total devotion to Christ even as he languished in jail.¹⁰

Second, the advancement of the gospel as a result of Paul's imprisonment emboldens "most of the brothers and sisters" to preach the gospel fearlessly (1:14). The ripple effect of Paul's bold witnessing to the palace guards in jail is revealed in the fearless witnessing of "most of the brothers and sisters." Now, they begin doing in Philippi the same work that Paul is doing within the jail. Paul's courage and devotion to the Lord Jesus Christ, even when confined in chains, is contagious. Paul says that "most" rather than *all* are "confident" and that their confidence is grounded "in the Lord" (1:14).¹¹ Naturally, some believers in Rome must have been afraid or hesitant to speak about their newfound faith amidst persecution (1:28). However, most had a change of attitude "in the Lord" after seeing how Paul conducted himself when "in chains." Hansen observes that the expression "in the Lord" refers to the one who initiates and works in a believer "to modify attitudes and actions that he

---

9. Fee, *Philippians*, NICNT, 113.
10. "'If I Ask My Lord, He Will Do It.' Prem Pradhan in Nepal." https://advancingnativemissions.com/ask-lord-jesus-will-prem-pradhan-nepal/ (accessed 27 September, 2017).
11. O'Brien, *Philippians*, 95; Vincent, *Philippians*, 17.

desires and commends."[12] Interestingly, Paul repeats the expression seven times in Philippians (2:19, 24, 29; 3:1; 4:1, 2, 4).[13] In other words, Paul witnesses God as an active agent – not only in his own life by the provision of "the Spirit of Jesus Christ" (1:19), but he also carefully acknowledges similar divine activity in the life of his brothers and sisters in Rome. For the fact that Paul is in chains does not instill confidence in them, rather they derive confidence from their rootedness "in the Lord."[14] In a nutshell, God is constantly at work in the lives of Paul and his fellow Christians in Rome, which encourages the believers in Philippi to stand firm in their faith and to continue to partner with Paul in the mission of God.

Interestingly, the "confidence in the Lord" of the brothers and sisters in Rome is evident in their boldness "all the more to proclaim the gospel without fear" (1:14). According to O'Brien, the word "confidence" assumes boldness amidst real danger. As an example, in an environment charged with hostility, Joseph of Arimathea dared to go and ask for the body of Jesus (Mark 15:43). Such confidence involves both moral and physical courage.[15] This courage is also evident in Paul's description of how the brothers and sisters are "daring" to preach the word fearlessly (1:14).

The Greek *ton logon* (literally "the word";[16] compare Gal 6:6; 1 Thess 1:6), which is translated as "the gospel" in the NIV, refers to the entire content of their teaching and preaching. For Paul, "the word" preached is nothing but Christ himself (compare 1:15–18, 27), who "being in very nature God . . . made himself nothing by taking the very nature of a servant, being made in human likeness, . . . [and became] obedient to death – even death on a cross!" Thus Christ is given a name "above every name" (2:6–11). One would certainly need courage and confidence, as modeled by Paul, to proclaim that "Jesus is Lord" in the Roman imperial context, where the title "Lord" was used by the Emperor Caesar himself. Caesar intentionally added this high title to

---

12. Hansen, *Philippians*, 69.
13. Hansen, 69.
14. Fee, *Philippians*, NICNT, 116.
15. O'Brien, *Philippians*, 95–96.
16. Some other ancient manuscripts have either *kupiou* or *tou Theou* following the word *logon*. However, textual critics have considered the shorter form *ton logon lalein* preferable because it explains the origin of other readings as scribal expansion, although *logon tou Theoulalein* has support of wider external evidences. See Bruce M. Metzger, *A Textual Commentary on the Greek New Testament: A Companion Volume to the United Bible Societies' Greek New Testament (Fourth Revised Edition)*, 2nd ed. (Stuttgart: Deutsche Biblgesellschaft/United Bible Societies, 1994), 544–545.

his name in order to claim the highest position within the empire.[17] Amidst this forceful political discourse in Rome, the imperial capital, and right under the nose of Caesar himself, Paul proclaimed the universal Lordship of Jesus, the crucified. Undoubtedly, this politically subversive message would have threatened the imperial system.

The single-minded devotion of Paul to Christ Jesus, even at the peril of tasting death, inspired his fellow believers in Rome. These fellow Christians were not encouraged so much by the expectation that Paul would be safely released from jail in the immediate future, but rather by his loyalty to Christ Jesus, his willingness to undergo suffering and pain for Christ's sake, and his dedication to make Christ known even in the jail. But the story of Paul's struggle is more complicated, because some are preaching Christ with the wrong intentions. Paul has a very different view of them.

---

17. H. Bietenhard, "κύριος," *NIDNTT* 2:511; Joseph D. Fantin, "Paul's Use of κύριοςas a Polemic against Caesar with Some Remarks towards the Contribution of the Study to the Exegesis of 1 Corinthians 8:5–6" (paper presented at the ECGRW Seminar, University of Sheffield, 29 April 2002), 1–18.

A COMPARISON OF PERSPECTIVES ON SUFFERING IN PAUL AND OTHER RELIGIONS

Various religions represent, understand, and explain suffering differently. In religions such as Hinduism, Buddhism, and Islam, suffering is perceived as a problem that humans face because of their deeds. In Paul's letter to the Philippians, the important theological theme of suffering is dealt very differently since the letter originated during Paul's imprisonment for the sake of his faith and mission (1:12–14) and also because the believers were facing threat and opposition in Philippi (1:28). A closer look at the letter reveals that Christians suffer for many reasons.

First, pain may be inflicted intentionally upon a Christian by those who are envious (1:17). Paul is clear that such ill-intended harmful acts do not threaten him, but those who act out of wrong motives are destined for eternal damnation (3:19). The Christians in Philippi also suffer due to opposition for their newfound faith. In Hindu mythology, the idea of a man (*Prahalad*) suffering under a wicked person (his father, king Hiranyakashyap) for his true devotion to his god (Narayana) exemplifies a similar idea. The story ends with Prahalad being delivered by the deity unharmed from fire, whereas Holika, his wicked sister, is burned to death in the same fire. The biblical story of Shadrach, Meshach, and Abednego being delivered unharmed after being cast into fire by the king (Dan 3:19–30) along with the story of Daniel in the lions' den (Dan 6:16–28) share close parallels with this Hindu mythology. The central truth is the victory of truth over untruth and righteousness over unrighteousness, with devotees of God being protected from wickedness. All these stories underline the truth that wicked plans devised against true devotees of God will be punished by eternal damnation.

Second, a Christian must be willing to suffer voluntarily – even unto death – if it helps to nurture a brother or sister's faith (2:17). This willingness reflects Paul's vision of a cruciform life that is inspired by the self-sacrificial death of Christ on the cross for the sake of fallen humanity.

Third, Christians must be willing to renunciate all earthly pedigrees to know Christ more and more (3:5–9). Paul counts all his cultural-religious credentials – both his acquired and earned privileges – as prideful "garbage" in order to know Jesus Christ more and more. Such tales of self-renunciation in search of god – the ultimate reality – are manifold in India. However, there is an underlying difference between Paul's self-renunciation to know Christ evermore and a Hindu *bhakta's* search to realize god. While a Hindu *bhakta* initiates the effort towards a mystical experience through penance and the renunciation of the world,

Paul's daily journey toward a greater knowledge of Jesus Christ is the consequence of Christ first taking hold of him (3:12).

There are several other similarities and dissimilarities between Paul's view of suffering in comparison with other Asian religions. In Hindu *advaitic* thought, *dukha* (suffering) is the consequence of *avidya* (ignorance). A soul under the sway of *maya* (illusion) experiences *dukha* because it fails to realize ultimate union in *Brahman* (the ultimate reality). Hence, humans begin to desire things that give room to the enemy residing within them (such as lust, anger, envy, greed, etc.) and produce bad deeds (*kukarma*). Thus in human existence, human deeds (*karma*) determine the experiences of joy and suffering.[1] In Buddhism, desire is the root of all suffering. In Islam, evil is inherent to humans, but it is necessary in order to be able to recognize its opposite: good. Even in Islam, human choices determine the extent of human suffering, for Allah allows the cycle of action and reaction to run its course in determining human lives.

However, it can also be divinely purposed, requiring a human to undergo the trials and sufferings patiently in order to attain ultimate peace. In short, suffering is not just the consequence of evil deeds in Islam, but it is also divinely ordained with purpose.[2]

But this is not the sort of suffering Paul speaks about in his letters. He does not suffer pain and hunger because of his evil *karma* or divine ordination. Instead, he suffers because of his divine vocation, which puts him under moral obligation to materialize his call fully. His loyalty, devotion, and unflinching love towards Jesus Christ yield him to offer himself sacrificially for the task of preaching the good news, so that he might work for the eternal benefit (salvation) of others. More importantly, Paul's positive response towards suffering as a Christian is inspired by two important ideals.

First, the selfless, voluntary experience of Christ's humiliation through his incarnation (2:6–8) inspires Paul because it enables him to identify with Christ in his suffering (3:10).

Second, Paul states: "it has been granted to you on behalf of Christ not only to believe in him, but also to suffer for him" (1:29). In other words, suffering for Jesus Christ is very much part and parcel of a Christian's call.

Hence, as a servant of Christ who is absolutely devoted to a heavenly call, Paul desires to be used for the benefit of the Philippian believers until the end (1:25). He finds encouragement to suffer despite his confinement, because the gospel is constantly advanced within the jail among the palace guards due to his imprisonment and also emboldens his fellow believers in the Lord to preach Christ fearlessly in Rome (1:13–14).

---

1. V. C. Pandey, "Problems of Death and Individual Suffering in Hindu Religion," in *The Problem of Death and Suffering in Indian Religions*, ed. Clarence O. McMullen (New Delhi: "LITHOUSE" Publications, 1983), 1–9; J. M. Sharma, "The Social Aspect of the Problem of Death and Suffering in Hinduism," in *The Problem of Death and Suffering in Indian Religions*, ed. Clarence O. McMullen, 10–19.
2. S. A. Ali, "The Problem of Suffering in Islam," in *The Problem of Death and Suffering in Indian Religions*, ed. Clarence O. McMullen, 93–102.

1:15–18A UNHINDERED ADVANCEMENT OF THE GOSPEL

Paul's words in 1:15–18a are encouragement to many Christians in Asia, including India, where occasional inter-denominational ill-feelings and disagreements have given rise to Christian leaders or groups spreading rumors about each other. Though each group preaches the gospel and teaches the Scripture according to its own denominational understanding, accusations sometimes fly thick and fast based on misunderstandings. Such activities have harmed church organizations, nevertheless some have heard about Christ through them. Hence we have reasons to rejoice. Though dark clouds of negativity may cover the sky, there can still be golden rays of light. When Christ is proclaimed at all costs, those beams of light fill our hearts with joy.

Paul witnessed a similar situation in Rome. In 1:15–18a, Paul mentions two groups of people who are preaching Christ, without identifying them specifically. He divides them into bipolar categories based on their intentions: one group preaches with ill-intent in a divisive manner; the other is praised for their goodwill towards the apostle.

Such splintered missionary engagements are not unusual in Christian mission circles, where there may be divisions based on the personality of a leader, doctrinal differences, denominational affiliations, and so on. In India today, church planting agencies in certain areas often find themselves entangled in a dirty web of infighting among Christian denominations and mission organizations. This has little to do with Christ, but is typically about other, petty reasons. Such a divided church is recognized by non-Christian neighbors, who might find Christ attractive – but not Christians.

In 1:15, the two groups indicated by "some . . . others" are introduced with specific characteristics. Interestingly, they both belong to the same stock: "the brothers and sisters" (1:14), the church, the Christian community in Rome.[18] Their common interest is to preach Christ. However, their reasons to preach Christ are contradictory. The first group preaches Christ: (1) "out of envy and rivalry" (1:15); (2) they nurture "selfish ambition" (1:17); (3) their purpose is to "stir up trouble" for Paul (1:17). In contrast, the second group preaches Christ: (1) "out of goodwill" (1:15), (2) "out of love" (1:16), and (3) out of their positive disposition towards the apostle in chains ("knowing that I am put here for the defense of the gospel," 1:16).

Interestingly, despite their contradictory opinions and attitudes towards Paul, the apostle has a great reason to cheer, for irrespective of these circumstances, "in every way, whether from false motives or true, Christ is preached. And because of this I rejoice" (1:18). In other words, the mission of making Christ known through the preaching of the gospel continues unhindered. Thus whatever happens to him – his hurts and sufferings – do not matter to him.

What do "envy and rivalry" (1:15) mean? The word *phthonos*, meaning "envy," describes the motivation behind their preaching, where there is a sense of their own inadequacy when compared with the superiority of the other, in the same way that Saul envied David (1 Macc 8:16; *TestSim* 4:5).[19] Similarly, the word *eris*, meaning "rivalry," underlines a conflict that emerges because of a difference of position on an important issue.[20] In Paul's letters, envy and rivalry are not desirable among Christians, because they disqualify one from inheriting the kingdom of God (Gal 5:21). In Galatians 5:21, the term "envy" is listed under "the acts of the flesh," and the term "rivalry" (without direct mention in the same list) is apparently associated with "discord . . . dissensions, factions" (Gal 5:20). Both "envy and rivalry" signify an existence outside of the life in Christ and are characteristic of those who are refused by God and handed over to a depraved mind (Rom 1:28; Titus 3:3).

In Philippians 1:27; 2:3, 13, 21, Paul exhorts the Philippians to be united in the spirit while preaching and to shun away from "selfish ambition" (1:17). Vincent explains the term "selfish ambition" (*eritheia*) based on its root word, *erithos*, which means "labor for hire." He observes that this term "applied to those who serve in official positions for their own selfish purposes and, to that

---

18. Hawthorne, *Philippians*, 36.
19. BDAG, 1054.
20. BDAG, 392.

end, promote party-spirit or faction."[21] If so, Paul's description of the ill-intentioned, competing preachers is very dark. Though they preached the gospel of Christ, they did so with selfish motives, which caused them to be envious of Paul and to bring rivalry and factionalism into the church.

In contrast, the second group preaches Christ "out of goodwill" (1:15) and "love" (1:16) towards Paul. "Love" is the most important characteristic that Paul encouraged among his believers in Christ, as it is the essence of the whole law (Rom 13:8, 10; Gal 5:14). In contrast to the "acts of the flesh," "love" appears at the top of the "fruit of the Spirit" (Gal 5:22). It is this "love" that Christ demonstrated upon the cross through his self-sacrificial death. The "goodwill" of those who expressed "love" towards Paul is evident in their positive attitude towards him in his moment of vulnerability ("in chains").[22] In contrast to first group's interest in stirring up trouble for Paul while he is in chains, the second group acts with "goodwill" and kindness by caring for the apostle while he is in chains. Rather than acting out of selfish ambition and hurting Paul, the second group appears to do things that comfort him in jail. While the first group deliberately hurt Paul in some ways ("supposing that they can . . ." 1:17), the latter group lovingly recognize his imprisonment and suffering as a defense of the gospel (1:16).

Paul is not specific about the identity of the people who are seeking to hurt him by their preaching. Many have speculated about various possibilities. Hansen imagines a raging competition between Paul and these ill-intentioned preachers in an attempt to amass a larger following. Now that Paul is in jail, Hansen proposes that they are taking this as an opportunity to find more converts.[23] The problem with this view is that there is no internal evidence within the letter to support such a conclusion. Similarly, Lightfoot's identification of the preachers as Judaizers[24] should be rejected, because Paul's limited positive disposition towards this group contradicts his vehement opposition to the (Christian) Judaizers elsewhere for their different gospel (e.g., Gal 1:6–9; 5:12).[25] Whatever the problem may be, it appears to be more personal in nature and less about theology.

---

21. Vincent, *Philippians*, 21.
22. Peter O'Brien's view is that their goodwill and love are directed towards Christ. However, this is unacceptable in this context, because here Paul appears to be interested in contrasting the motives of two groups based on their treatment of him. O'Brien, *Philippians*, 99–100.
23. Hansen, *Philippians*, 74.
24. Lightfoot, *Philippians*, 88–89.
25. Melick, *Philippians*, 75; Hansen, *Philippians*, 74; Hawthorne, *Philippians*, 37; Fred B. Craddock, *Philippians*, IBC (Atlanta: John Knox Press, 1985), 26.

Some suggest that these were Roman Christians who harbored a grudge against Paul because Paul's arrival in Rome threatened their aspirations to be regarded as leaders of the Roman Christian community. This appears logical. In other words, these men were members of the church in Rome. Hence, as Fee maintains, "they cannot, therefore, be related – in any direct sense, at least – to the other alleged 'opponents' who surface in this letter."[26] Melick and Vincent maintain that the lack of apostolic leadership in Rome before Paul's arrival there may have provided fertile ground for many to aspire for positions of leadership within the community. They must have faced a stiff challenge in Paul after he arrived, and so they were opposing him.[27] This position may be challenged as well, based on Paul's anticipation of securing the support of the Roman believers to go to Spain (Rom 15:28). For in all probability, he succeeded in doing that. However, in the light of the lack of concrete evidence to reconstruct the whole context in order to establish the actual identity of these ill-intentioned preachers, Melick and Vincent's proposal appears to be acceptable. Probably, many in the churches of Rome, who had earlier followed these ill-intentioned preachers, now turned to Paul to hear and learn more about their new faith. This positive response from many within the Roman church must have been influenced by his earlier letter (the letter to the Romans), which was read in public. Having grown envious of Paul's influence, these preachers may have begun to oppose him.

They could "stir up trouble" for Paul because of "envy and rivalry" by disturbing the peace in the church and projecting Paul in a false manner, as one who created problems for the Roman authorities. This could threaten Paul's desire to garner their support for his future missionary journey to Spain, which he was anticipating to receive if he were released soon (1:19–20). Moreover, this trouble could damage Paul's strong expectation of being freed from jail.

In 1:18, such apprehensions are immaterial to the apostle. It does not matter how he is affected by anyone's response towards him, for he declares: "The important thing is that in every way, whether from false motives or true, Christ is preached. And because of this I rejoice" (1:18). This is emblematic of Paul's single-minded devotion to his mission. As he goes on to display in 1:18b–26, any threat to his life does not agitate him nearly as much as the perversion of gospel which is taking place in Philippi (3:2).

---

26. Fee, *Philippians*, NICNT, 121.
27. Melick, *Philippians*, 76–77; Vincent, *Philippians*, 19.

1:18B–26 SINGLE-MINDED DEVOTION TO CHRIST

The Greek word *salla kai* (literally, "yet also"), which is translated as "[a]nd because of this" in 1:18b, is connected to the preceding expression, "in this I rejoice" (1:18a). Together, these two terms begin a new paragraph within 1:12–26 in a progressive sense. Because Christ is proclaimed in every way, Paul rejoices. Then in the same breath, Paul adds another reason for his joy (1:18b): his strong expectation of an early release from jail (1:19–20). The term *soteria* ("deliverance" 1:19) might be interpreted in three ways. First, the term could refer to eschatological salvation (Rom 1:16; 2 Cor 7:10; Phil 1:28; 1 Thess 5:8–9).[28] Second, irrespective of the outcome in the court of Caesar (whether released or martyred), Paul appears to place his hope in his final vindication (*soteria*) in the divine court by echoing in Job's words (Job 13:16).[29] Third, Paul refers to his early release from Roman imprisonment with the term *soteria*.[30]

While the first interpretation is possible in the light of its broader use elsewhere by Paul, it does not fully fit the immediate context. The second interpretation is favored by some interpreters to highlight Paul's ultimate confidence, like Job, in God's justice beyond his present suffering. However, that confidence could be used equally to support the third interpretive option. Paul's strong hope of seeing the Philippians and his desire to minister to them for their "progress and joy" (1:25) favor the third interpretation, although he is not averse to dying for Christ if the situation demands it. Further, Paul's "joy" is founded upon his personal knowledge ("for I know [*oida*]" 1:19) of his fast-approaching release from the jail. In other words, more than his hope of final vindication in the divine court – despite the fact that some accuse him for his present suffering just as Job was accused by his friends – Paul probably saw his anticipated early release from jail as God's vindicating act. Thus he reaffirms his joy.

This great cause of joy for Paul will be enabled by two vital things (1:19). First, his release will come about through the intercessory prayers of the Philippians. This is the first mention of the Philippians' partnership with Paul in prayer. However, its mention here indicates their concern for the imprisoned apostle and his well-being. This is another way, along with their material and personal support, that they are partnering with Paul in mission.

---

28. W. Foerster, "σωζω, κτλ," *TDNT* 7:993; J. Schneider, "σωζω," *NIDNTT* 3:214; Melick, *Philippians*, 81.
29. O'Brien, *Philippians*, 110.
30. Hawthorne, *Philippians*, 40.

Second, Paul's speedy release in the near future is coming by the divine "provision of the Spirit" (1:19). The relationship between the term *epichoregias*, which means "supply" (NIV translates it as "provision"), and the phrase "of the Spirit" is contentious among scholars. Based on the ambiguous grammar of "provision of the Spirit," there are two different positions: (1) the supply made available to Paul by the Spirit (subjective genitive) or (2) the supply of the Spirit as the help which Paul received (objective genitive). Although the grammatical form of the expression ("of the Spirit") may suggest such minute differentiations, Paul may not be favoring one over the other. It seems unlikely that the provision of the Spirit is to be understood as a special provision for Paul that will miraculously deliver him from jail. As Hansen observes, there is a close relationship between the Philippian believers' intercessory prayers and God's supply of the Spirit. The Spirit enables human hearts to make effective supplications before God (Rom 8:26).[31] Moreover, God's provision of the Spirit also filled Paul with eager expectation and hope for an early release from the jail (1:19). In this sense, the function of the divinely supplied Spirit is to strengthen the suffering apostle with hope for release in the near future and to effectively uphold the prayers of the saints in Philippi before God's throne for this divine intervention.

Further, the use of the second genitive, "of Jesus Christ" (1:19), which defines "the Spirit," explains the importance of Paul's experience of "the Spirit" in jail. The Spirit belongs to Jesus Christ. The expression "the Spirit of Jesus Christ" could be understood either as the Spirit supplied by Jesus Christ[32] or the Spirit as Jesus Christ himself.[33] The latter appears to be a better option in the current context. The Spirit makes the very presence of Jesus Christ real to the apostle in suffering and reminds him of the Lord's promise to rescue him from Jews and gentiles: "*I* [Jesus] will rescue you from your own people and from the Gentiles" (emphasis and bracket added, Acts 26:17).[34] Hence, the divine provision of the Spirit, which leads Paul to expect and hope in the end of his present confinement (1:20), is vital.

Undoubtedly, Paul's hope of not being put to shame in 1:20 is not unfounded or without concrete reasons. Paul's hope is not based on his wishful

---

31. Hansen, *Philippians*, 79.
32. O'Brien, *Philippians*, 112.
33. Fee, *Philippians*, NICNT, 134–135.
34. The present meaning appears to be more probable than Hansen's appeal, which similarly pairs this passage with the expectation and hope in Rom 8:19–25 in order to explain Paul's certainty about his speedy release from jail in the future. Hansen, *Philippians*, 80.

imagination but is the inevitable consequence of the prayers of the Philippian believers and the provision of the animated Jesus Christ, the Spirit, to Paul. In other words, Paul is expectant and full of hope because he is trusting in Jesus's promise that *he* will rescue him. The verb "be ashamed" (*aischunomai*) in 1:20 parallels its use in Romans 1:16, where it implies Paul's bold stand for the gospel of Christ. Now, Paul is imprisoned in Rome, being falsely accused of desecrating the purity of the temple and speaking against the Jewish religion (Acts 21:27–28). When he faces the court hearing in Rome, he expects that the truth about him and the gospel he preaches will prevail against the mischievous accusations leveled against him. This will vindicate his bold stand for the gospel.

Such a stand before the Roman court will require him to "have sufficient courage so that now as always Christ will be exalted in my body" (1:20). The term "boldness" (*parresia*, which the NIV translates as "courage") is the ability to speak freely in public with fearlessness and confidence.[35] *Parrhēsia*, in ancient Greek literature, featured a free citizen within a Greek state and later "came to denote a moral concept that was important in Cynic philosophy, related to *eleutheria*, 'freedom,' and connoting the mark of a person morally free and able to resist public attention or opposition."[36] Undoubtedly, such a bold stand by Paul for the gospel in the Roman court will glorify Christ. In Acts 4:8–17, when Peter spoke, filled with the Holy Spirit, the Jewish rulers saw his "courage" and were "astonished and they took note that these men had been with Jesus" (Acts 4:13). Perhaps Paul expects that a similar boldness displayed in his self-defense before the Roman court will exalt Christ Jesus. In fact, Paul's ultimate goal is, through his life and mission, to glorify Christ.

Even now, when he is bound in Roman chains, Paul desires to make Christ known, just as he always has in his mission. Being filled with great hope, he expects to be delivered from the jail, but that is secondary to his desire to glorify Christ Jesus in and through his life. Hence, the exact outcome of the trial in terms of "life" (i.e., release from the jail) or "death" (i.e., martyrdom) does not concern him.

Either way, his course of life will be decided during the trial. Though he expects to be released, Paul declares, "[f]or to me, to live is Christ and to die is gain" (1:21). This speaks volumes about his single-minded devotion to Christ Jesus. Viewed in the Bhakti tradition of India, Paul is not just a believer in

---

35. BDAG, 781.
36. Joseph A. Fitzmyer, *The Acts of the Apostles: A New Translation with Introduction and Commentary*, AB 31 (New York: Doubleday, 1998), 302.

Christ, but a *bhakta* (a devotee), who is saturated by undivided love and devotion to his beloved deity (*ishtadevata*) and is given over to love him, serve him, and sing his praises to all.[37] "Life" and "death" weigh equally to Paul compared to his goal of exalting Jesus always. While "life" gives him the option to preach (1:22), know (3:10), and glorify Jesus Christ (1:20), "death" allows him to be "with Christ," which is "better by far" (1:23). For Paul, a *Yesu bhakta* (devotee of Christ Jesus), there is no greater goal than to live in love of his *ishtadevata* ("beloved deity") and to be saturated by him now in his earthly existence and then to be with him in eternity.

Hence, in 1:22–23, Paul is unsure about his choice. His innermost desire is to "depart and be with Christ" (1:23). The infinitive form of *analuō*, meaning "depart," is Paul's adoption from the ancient Greek writings to make a euphemistic reference to his death.[38] His desired departure marks the end of his earthly sojourn, which is dedicated to the exaltation of Christ Jesus. However, it just marks a transfer from his life in the body to his life "with" (*syn*) Christ. In Paul's writings, the preposition *syn* is used to convey the close association or identification of a Christian with Christ.[39] Such an intimate identification begins at baptism by dying to sin and becoming alive in Christ (Rom 6:3–5). In Romans 6:5, he says, "if we have been united with him in a death like his, we will certainly also be united with him in a resurrection like his."

For South Asian readers, including Indians, it is important to understand that Paul is not teaching here about the loss of a liberated human being's individuality by merging into the ultimate reality, as in Hinduism. In Hindu *Advaitic* (Monistic) thought, an enlightened human being, upon intuitively experiencing the divine, realizes his/her salvation (*Moksha*) as a submergence into the Ultimate Being (*Brahman*). The ultimate goal of an enlightened human being is to realize complete oneness in *Brahman*, where the distinction between an enlightened human, upon being liberated from worldly entanglements, experiences complete absorption into the ultimate being. Thereby, an individual human ceases to exist.[40] For Paul, upon his departure from the body, he will be with Christ in intimate association, but he will not lose his

---

37. See Roji T. George, "Divine Grace in the Making of Paul, the *Yesu Bhakta*: Reclaiming the Role of Grace in the Self-Consciousness of Paul as a *Bhatka* in the Light of St. Tukaram's Bhakti Thought," *BTF* 45 (2013): 74–96.
38. BDAG, 67.
39. Daniel B. Wallace, *Greek Grammar Beyond the Basics: An Exegetical Syntax of the New Testament* (Grand Rapids: Zondervan, 1996), 378, 382.
40. In Hindu *Advaitic* thought, the very knowledge of separation from the Divine Being and the claim of human individuality is the effect of illusion (*Maya*) and is an unreal existence.

creatureliness. In Paul's words, the soteriological effect of Jesus' death is eternal communion with Christ Jesus: "He died for us so that, whether we are awake or asleep, *we may live together with him*" (1 Thess 5:10, emphasis added). Hence, it "is better by far" (1:23).

However, in 1:24–26, as a responsible leader and pastor who aims to safeguard the Philippian believers in Christ and encourage them to mature (1:9–11; 3:1), Paul realizes the importance of his speedy release from jail. In 1:24, Paul self-sacrificially places the needs of his believers over his own earnest inner longing to be with Jesus Christ. In this, he is modeling the ethical exhortation he gives to the Philippians in 2:3–4: "Do nothing out of selfish ambition . . . , not looking to your own interests but each of you to the interests of the others." This not only reflects his pastoral heart, but also highlights his devotion to his believers' faith journey amidst persecution (1:28–30), threats of schism and division in the church (2:1–4), and the intrusion of false teachers (3:1–2). The apostle wants to be released so that he can partner with these believers amidst their difficulties, just as they have been partnering with him during his imprisonment. In pluralistic South Asian contexts, when churches and minority Christian communities suffer violent attacks from the dominant religious and political groups, Paul teaches us, as a leader and pastor, to partner selflessly with the weak and vulnerable members of the church.

In 1:25–26, Paul mentions two issues that seem to explain his confident hope. First, continuing the thought in 1:24, his purpose in wanting to be present with the believers is so that they will "progress and joy in the faith" (1:25). Paul expresses his confidence, which is based on faith that is full of hope, that he will be able to spend some further time with them. The term *prokopē*, meaning "progress," implies the growth or expansion (1:12) of their love and knowledge (1:9), fruitfulness (1:11), and obedience (2:12).[41] The term *chara* ("joy") signifies the inner experience of gladness that comes out of faith.[42] Hansen rightly observes that the expression *tēs pisteōs* (literally, "of the faith"), which is translated as "in the faith," can be understood either as the content of their faith (1:27) or the act of faith of the individual believers (1:29). It is difficult to judge either as the single intention of Paul's meaning, because both meanings appear in the immediate context. It is probable that, in the apostle's mind, both meanings combine together as he desires to ensure their "progress and joy" by his personal presence with them.[43]

---

41. Hendrickson, *Philippians*, 79,
42. BDAG, 1077.
43. Hansen, *Philippians*, 91.

Second, he says, "so that through my being with you again your boasting in Christ Jesus will abound on account of me" (1:26). Introducing his desire to be a reason for his believers' "boasting" (*kauchēma*) with the purpose clause *hina* (literally, "so that"), Paul uses two prepositional clauses: (1) "in Christ Jesus" and (2) "in me." Since the term "boasting" (*kauchēma*) refers to the basis of boasting or taking pride,[44] we must determine whether the basis for boasting is "in Christ Jesus" or "in me." According to Hansen, "in Christ Jesus" signifies "the object of boasting," while "in me" is "the means by which boasting takes place."[45] However, O'Brien and Lightfoot propose that, while the former signifies the sphere, the latter denotes the object of their boasting.[46] It is beyond dispute that the expression "in Christ Jesus" in the letters of Paul refers to the realm of a believer's spiritual existence. Hence, the act of boasting in the imaginative space "in Christ" will be evoked by the successful return of the apostle.

---

44. BDAG, 537.
45. Hansen, *Philippians*, 91–92; Hawthorne, *Philippians*, 52.
46. O'Brien, *Philippians*, 141; Lightfoot, *Philippians*, 94.

PHILIPPIANS 1:27–2:18
LIVE A LIFE WORTHY OF THE GOSPEL

The significance of Paul's passionate call to the Christians in Philippi, urging them to pay closer attention to their good Christian testimony, cannot be overstated for any Christian community, particularly within India. Living within an environment that is predominantly non-Christian, the lives of Indian Christians ought to be fashioned according to the gospel. However, amidst opposition to the gospel in India, infighting among Christians over property, power, and position has been brought into the public sphere and has dented Christian testimony. News reports on national television during prime hours about ecclesiastical heads and priests embroiled in sex scandals has destroyed the sanctity of Christian testimony. This became even uglier when the church appeared to defend and protect the accused with the help of her political nexus, causing both agitated Christian activists as well as supporters of the victims to resort to mass protests on the streets. Such unfortunate events within the church have been used by those who oppose the advancement of the gospel, both to validate their ideological position and mobilize others to work against Christians. Paul wants his believers to understand that they must live a lifestyle that is unattested by the gospel they preach, particularly when they are experiencing persecution.

In 1:27–2:18, Paul urges his believers to pay attention to his vital ethical exhortations. He not only appreciates them for their support, but he also longs to see them living as citizens of heaven, having the mind of Christ, so that they will shine as stars in the darkness. This section reveals Paul's exemplary pastoral heart in two ways. First, his abstract theological ideas are married to the practical life of believers. Paul quotes what seems to be an early Christian christological hymn (2:6–11)[1] to teach vital ethical values for practical living that are binding for Christians. What distinguishes Christians from others in the world is not just the right theology, but the pursuit of right living. Second, the sole goal of Paul's sacrificial missionary labor is to enable his believers to shine for Jesus by being rooted in the word of God (2:16–18).

---

1. For a survey on the history of the research into the study of the hymn, see Ralph P. Martin, "Carmen Christi: Philippians II.5–11" in *Recent Interpretation and in the Setting of Early Christian Worship*, SNTSMS 4 (Cambridge: CUP, 1967), 15–95; David Alan Black, "The Authorship of Philippians 2:6–11: Some Literary-Critical Observations," *CTR* 2 (1988): 269–289; O'Brien, *Philippians*, 186–202; Hawthorne, *Philippians*, 76–79.

Hence, Paul exhorts believers about three important aspects of their life in the world. First, in 1:27–30, Paul reminds them of their heavenly citizenship, which requires them to stand in unity fearlessly amidst persecution and suffering. Second, their Christian union in Christ along with the reality of the prevailing persecution require each of them to be bound in love, putting others' interest over their own selfish ambitions (2:1–4). The supreme model of building interpersonal relationship is in the very act of incarnation (2:5–11). Third, in 2:12–18, Paul exhorts every believer to become "blameless and pure children of God" (2:15).

1:27–30 LIVE AS CITIZENS OF HEAVEN

In 1:27, the term *monon*, meaning "only,"[2] implies the importance of what Paul is going to say in the light of his desire to visit the believers in the near future (1:25–26). Paul's desire is to continue with them so that they may have "progress and joy in the faith," which is possible only through their manner of living in Philippi amidst strong opposition. In the light of its use in Galatians 2:10, the term *monon* appears to exclude everything apart from the explicitly stated purpose that is introduced by "in order that" (*hina*) in 1:27. This highlights the significance of ethical living in Paul's missionary and theological exercise.

In Greek, 1:27–28 forms one long sentence that is connected with just one imperative, *politeuesthe*, meaning "conduct yourselves."[3] It is used in the sense of "discharge your obligations as citizens,"[4] though later the term was used quite loosely.[5] Otherwise, as Brewer maintains, terms such as *peripateite* ("go about, walk around," or "conduct your lives")[6] or *zēte* ("conduct yourselves in your pattern of behavior")[7] could have been employed to exhort ethical behavior in general, without specific reference to the obligation of a citizen towards the city and corporate life in it.[8] Apart from Acts 23:1, the term *politeuesthe* is also used in 2 Maccabees 6:1 and 9:25, referring to corporate life in a city. The NIV translates it unsatisfactorily as "conduct yourselves," diluting the metaphorical sense of the term. In the light of its repeated use in 3:20, Paul probably uses the term here with a dual reference: as citizens of Philippi (and thereby of the

---

2. BDAG, 659.
3. BDAG, 846.
4. BDAG, 846.
5. Lightfoot, *Philippians*, 105.
6. BDAG, 803.
7. BDAG, 425.
8. Raymond R. Brewer, "The Meaning of *Politeuesthe* in Philippians 1:27," *JBL* 73 (1954): 77.

empire) and as citizens of heaven. The believers in Philippi are not only citizens (or at least inhabitants) of the Roman Empire, but also citizens of heaven, having joined the church by faith.

Philippi, a miniature Rome in the east, filled the hearts of its citizens with pride that required them to live responsibly by fulfilling their duty towards the colony. In this context, Paul exhorts his believers about their unique identity as both citizens of Rome and heaven by employing the idea of citizenship metaphorically. Paul does not appear to distinguish the two as mutually exclusive. The exhortation is that by living as citizens of Philippi, their conduct must be "worthy of the gospel of Christ," and for Paul, these are not contradictory. Similarly, as members of the church, they are expected to live by both individual and corporate ethical stipulations that cohere with the gospel. Hence, Paul is exhorting them to discharge their responsibilities as citizens in a manner that is worthy of the gospel of Christ.

While the adverb *axiōs* (meaning "worthily"[9]) refers to *politeuesthe* (literally, "conduct yourselves"), it is qualified by the genitive *tou euangeliou tou Christou* ("of the gospel of Christ") in 1:27. Thus the believers' citizenship must be responsibly lived out and guided by the gospel of Christ. In other words, their unity in one Spirit, striving side by side for the gospel, regarding others above themselves, having the mind of Christ, and shining among others like stars (1:27–2:18) define a life that is worthy of the gospel of Christ. In fact, these ethical actions are presupposed in the gospel that Paul is insistently preaching in partnership with the Philippian believers. Hence, as partners in advancing the gospel, they ought to pay close attention to their way of life.

Christians living in south Asian countries such as India, Pakistan, and Nepal often experience opposition from the dominant religious communities because of their faith. In Pakistan, Christians face unfair implementation of blasphemy laws and bomb attacks during their corporate worship times. In India, radical members of the dominant community have called for *Ghar Wapsi* homecoming/returning, which aims to reconvert Christians into the dominant religion. In recent years in India, Christians have been subject to verbal abuse (being referred as *Haramzade,* meaning "illegitimate children") by the elected parliamentarians of the Indian democracy in public speeches. Members of minority communities from vulnerable socioeconomic sections of Indian society have been denied government grants or job reservation after conversion. Moreover, pastors and new converts have been murdered, and

---

9. BDAG, 94.

Christian worship places have been desecrated and destroyed. Yet amidst such vulnerability, rather than being united in the mission of God to advance the gospel at every cost, the Christian testimony in India has been marred by denominational conflicts, the undercutting of each other for selfish gains, scams within churches, and division over trivial issues.

To make matters worse, in the stereotypical portrayal of Christians in Bollywood cinemas, male villains often wear crosses and have Christian or Western names, such as "Rocky" or "Tony," and immoral or evil female characters are named "Susy" or "Mona." These portrayals are, to some extent, the consequence of a pre-independent Indian perception of their British colonial masters and, to a greater extent, later Indian Christians' lifestyles. Sadly, the depiction of a good Christian family in cinemas is often interspersed with scenes of loose moral living according to the Indian social ethos (for example, showing both elders and youth consuming alcohol together at home or maintaining less distance in relationships between genders). Amidst such violent opposition and the low depiction of Christians in mass media, Paul's advice for Christians in Philippi to live responsibly as citizens worthy of the gospel of Christ is relevant for us today.

In 1:27–28 Paul's sole desire, irrespective of his actual physical presence among them, is to learn about them either through Timothy, who is soon to visit them (2:19), or by his own personal visit (1:25–26; 2:24). The Greek construction is clumsy here, but the meaning is clear. The use of *hina* (introducing the purpose) emphasizes that Paul is exhorting them about their gospel-worthy lifestyle because he wants to hear about their gospel-fashioned lifestyle in Philippi. Hence, they ought to: (1) "stand firm in the one Spirit" (1:27b) and (2) strive "together as one for the faith of the gospel" (1:27c). This second instruction is modified by the phrase "without being frightened in any way by those who oppose you" (1:28a).

The first exhortation, "stand firm in the one Spirit" (1:27b), is a call for Christian unity. However, the foundation of this unity is debated among scholars. While O'Brien, Müller, and others contend that the appropriate meaning is a human spirit united for one common purpose,[10] Fee, Moule, R. P. Martin, and others argue that the Holy Spirit is the sphere or agent of Christian unity.[11] The former group of scholars argues that Paul is referring to a corporate

---

10. O'Brien, *Philippians*, 150; Müller, *Philippians*, 68–69; F. F. Bruce, *Philippians*, GNBC (Basingstoke, Hants: Pickering & Inglis, 1983), 35; Hawthorne, *Philippians*, 56–57.
11. Fee, *Philippians*, NICNT, 163–166; H. C. G. Moule, *The Epistle to the Philippians*, TC (Grand Rapids: Baker Book House, 1981), 28; Hansen, *Philippians*, 96–97; Ralph P. Martin,

Christian unity that is experienced in the human spirit based on the parallel expression that immediately follows the exhortation: *mia psychē*, meaning "one soul." However, as Fee argues, there are other grounds for interpreting this as the Holy Spirit rather than the human spirit. First, nowhere in his letters does Paul employ *pneuma* ("spirit") to refer to a corporate unity of human minds. Second, the use of *en* ("in") can either be "locative" ("sphere") or instrumental ("agent") in its meaning, for which we find repeated evidence in Paul's letters. Third, the use of the terms "*pneuma*" and "*psychē*" again in 2:1–4 implies that the Holy Spirit is the referent. Fourth, 1 Corinthians 12:13 (compare Eph 2:18; 4:4) teaches that Christian unity is experienced in the Holy Spirit.[12]

The second exhortation strive "together as one for the faith of the gospel" (1:27c), is a call to unity by joining together in a united effort for the faith of the gospel. The term *sunathlountes* (4:3), meaning "contending/struggling along with,"[13] has been understood as a word picture with a military or athletic background. The image is either of every soldier in war fighting together in unity or of athletes competing together as a team to try to win a game.[14] This meaning of the word coheres with Paul's words in 1:28, which refer to the destruction of the opponents and the believers' salvation with God's assistance. This involves a strategic movement that is coordinated with fellow soldiers or athletes, with the intent to counter any attacks from the opposing camp.

This unity of Christian believers will be the best defense of the faith, which in an objective sense, is the body of teaching of the earliest church (1 Tim 6:20; 2 Tim 1:14). The importance of this exhortation is evident considering the historical context of the letter, where the presence of false teachers (3:2, 18) and growing in-fighting among the Philippian believers (4:2–3) were threatening the church.

In 1:28a, Paul encourages the Philippians to be fearless while facing those who oppose them. The term *antikeimenōn* ("those who oppose you") does not specify the identity of the opponents. However, as Fee observes, the Roman influence of first-century Philippi, along with the strong emphasis on the lordship and messiahship of Jesus in the letter (2:6–11), help us to deduce that the opponents were probably those who were pressurizing the believers in

---

Philippians: An Introduction and Commentary, TNTC (London: InterVarsity Press, 1959), 85.
12. Fee, *Philippians*, NICNT, 164–166.
13. BDAG, 964.
14. In the context of the term's reappearance in 2 Tim 2:5 without the prefix *sun-*, Martin finds the fight for life and death within the gladiatorial arena also suitable to understand the meaning of the term (*Philippians*, TNTC, 85–86).

Philippi to participate in the imperial cult as a mark of their loyalty to Rome and the emperor.[15] Such a charged social environment must have mounted enormous pressure on the believers, even if there was not yet state-sponsored persecution against the minority in Philippi. This pressure must have instilled fear in the hearts of the believers, who would have known the consequence of being accused of treason in the Roman Empire. Martin rightly observes that here we find "a veiled reference to mob violence," perhaps aggravated by the small group of local Jews in Philippi.[16]

Paul encourages his believers to face the challenge, however huge it might seem to be, "without being frightened in any way" (*me pturomenoi en mēdeni* 1:28). The term *pturomenoi*, which is used almost always in the passive sense, means "to let oneself be intimidated."[17] Without denying the strength of the opposition, Paul exhorts his readers not to allow themselves to be intimidated. But how is such courage possible? It is interesting to note that Paul equates their struggle with his own current situation in the jail, where he is facing a possible death sentence (1:29–30). Their standing firm in the Holy Spirit and striving fearlessly, side by side with the fellow believers, is a twofold "sign" (*endeixis* 1:28) for: (1) the *destruction* of their opponents and (2) their own *salvation* (*sotērias*) by God. In other words, the courage for the believers to face the seeming insurmountable hurdle before them is gained from the eschatological perspective that Paul himself also had (3:20–21).

Paul maintains that even if the believers' fearless encounter with persecution from their opponents leads to temporal harm, it will result in their ultimate salvation, which is in addition to their present experience of salvation by faith in Christ. Hence, they need not fear their persecutors, because they are experiencing and will experience God's preserving hands in evil days (Rom 14:4), whether by overcoming the present opposition or by their salvation in the future after suffering a violent death. Moreover, from Paul's own conversion experience, he knows that the persecution of the church in the world amounts to the persecution of Christ himself (Acts 9:4–5). Thus those who persecute believers ultimately bring destruction upon themselves through their unbelief in Christ Jesus in the present (Rom 9:32–33; compare 1 Pet 2:4, 6–8; Acts 4:11).

Finally, in 1:29–30, Paul underlines the Philippian believers' partnership in the advancement of the gospel by identifying their common experience, saying, "since you are going through the same struggle you saw I had, and

---

15. Fee, *Philippians*, NICNT, 167.
16. Martin, *Philippians*, TNTC, 87.
17. BDAG, 895.

now hear that I still have" (1:30). Paul wants the believers to understand that their suffering and pain is purposed by God and is not accidental. In 1:29, he boldly announces that "it has been granted to you on behalf of Christ not only to believe in him, but also to suffer for him." Hence, their suffering has been graciously granted (aorist tense) to them by God at a specific point of time in the past when they believed in Christ. They ought to suffer "on behalf of Christ," a phrase that parallels Paul's earlier exhortations "of the gospel of Christ" (1:26) and "for the faith of the gospel" (1:27). When the believers take a fearless position for the sake of the "gospel of Christ," they suffer for Christ. Paul has always viewed his own earlier suffering (2 Cor 11:22–33) and his present imprisonment (1:13) as suffering on behalf of Christ (Col 1:24). He even views the scars from physical attacks by those who opposed the gospel he preached as "marks of Jesus" on his body (Gal 6:17).

2:1–11 LIVE UNITED IN HUMILITY

It is not unusual to find groupism within a church, where some operate with an eye to dominate others because of pride and selfishness. This attitude often leads to quarrels and divisions within the church. The root of the problem lies in a lack of humility and in overestimating oneself. A good parallel to Paul's teaching about humility in this section is found in the words of Krishna to Arjuna. In *Bhagavad-Gita* 16.3, Krishna exhorts Arjuna that along with other virtues, such as forbearance, the "absence of self-esteem" (i.e., "*nātimānitā*" in Sanskrit) is a "mark of him, who is born with the divine gifts."[18] According to Goyandaka, *nātimānitā* ("absence of self-esteem") is the total opposite of *ātimānitā* ("overestimating oneself"). He describes *ātimānitā* as "[r]egarding oneself as superior, exalted or worthy of adoration and cherishing a special craving for honour, fame, prestige and respect etc., and feeling overjoyed on attaining these even though not hankering after them."[19] Interestingly, Paul also exhorts Philippians to practice the "absence of self-esteem" in order to stay united in Christ. In Indian terms, Paul appears to say, practice *nātimānitā* and "value other above yourselves" (2:3) just as Jesus Christ, the supreme model of *nātimānitā*, has shown you in his incarnation (2:6–8).

Having dealt with the trouble arising outside the church in 1:27–30, Paul goes on to address some pertinent issues of disunity threatening the existence

---

18. Jayadayal Goyandaka, *Srimadbhagavadgita Tattvavivecani: English Commentary* (Gorakhpur: Gita Press, 2014), 674.
19. Goyandaka, *Srimadbhagavadgita Tattvavivecani*, 674.

of the church at Philippi in 2:1–4. The current section stands in close unity with the preceding section (1:27–30), exhorting the believers in Philippi to stand firm and strive side by side. This is evident both in the use of the word "therefore" (*oun*) in 2:1 and also in the way that the command to live as citizens worthy of the gospel of Christ in 1:27 is elaborated in the intra-ecclesial context. Moreover, after Paul reminds the believers in 1:29 about the divine grace shown towards them so that they would not only believe in Christ but also suffer for him, he now banks on their relationship with Christ ("being united with Christ" 2:1), encouraging them to model Christ within the Christian community in their interpersonal relationships.

Does the apostle's call in 2:2–4, which is to live in unity and love without selfish ambition and false conceit, mirror the historical context of the Christian community in Philippi? Bruce contends that the problem of dissension in the Roman church compelled Paul to urge Philippian believers to resist from yielding to the spirit of disunity among them.[20] However, the intensity with which Paul makes a strong appeal for unity in 2:1–4, along with the intertwining of suffering and unity – the two vital themes in Philippians (especially 1:12–2:18) – both indicate that disunity was a real issue faced by the community in Philippi.[21] Further, a comparison of Philippians 1:27–2:4 with Galatians 5:6; 1 Corinthians 10:24; 13:5 and Ephesians 4:1–3 suggests that, in the context of schisms in the churches, Paul employs similar terms to make appeals for unity. Peterlin rightly concludes that "[t]hese injunctions are not mere ethical standards floating in a vacuum. They were written as a response to particular situations marked by the lack of unity . . . [Hence] it is reasonable to suggest that the similarity of the language points to the similarity in the background situation."[22]

Towards the end of the twentieth century, David Alan Black, taking a lead from Ernst Lohmeyer and J. Gnilka, explained well the masterly crafting of this literary section by dividing it into three headings: (1) the foundational basis, (2) the results, and (3) the mode of practicing Christian unity. His proposed structure of 2:1–4 is as follows (based on the NIV):

---

20. Bruce, *Philippians*, 37.
21. Peter Oakes, *Philippians: From People to Letter*, SNTSMS 110 (Cambridge: Cambridge University Press, 2001), 175–176.
22. Davorin Peterlin, *Paul's Letter to the Philippians in the Light of Disunity in the Church*, NovTSup 79 (Leiden/New York/Köln: E. J. Brill, 1995), 62.

1. **A** Therefore if you have any encouragement from being united with Christ,

   B if any comfort from his love,

   C if any common sharing in the Spirit,

   D if any tenderness and compassion, (v. 1)

2. **A** [T]hen make my joy complete by being like-minded,

   B having the same love,

   B being one in spirit

   A and of one mind. (v. 2)

3. **A** Do nothing out of selfish ambition or vain conceit,

   B [R]ather, in humility value others above yourselves, (v. 3)

   A not looking to your own interests

   B but each of you to the interests of the others. (v. 4)[23]

2:1–4 United in Mind by Serving Others' Interests

This short but important section begins with a series of four "if" (*ei*) clauses (2:1). Rather than "if" referring to a doubtful condition, it represents an affirmation of a present reality.[24] These four statements about present realities form the foundation of Paul's appeal to build unity, and they are part of every Christian's experience in Philippi: "comfort" (*paraklēsis*), "love" (*agapē*), "common sharing in the Spirit" (*koinonia pneumatos*, or literally fellowship of/in the Spirit), and "tenderness and compassion" (*splanchna kai oiktirmoi*). Because of these present realties, the Philippian believers must heed to the vital exhortations of the apostle in 2:2–4.

2:1 Four foundations for Christian unity

The specific meaning of *paraklēsis*, translated as "encouragement" in 2:1, is disputed among the scholars. The majority of scholars prefer to translate it as "encouragement,"[25] while others, for more persuasive reasons, understand it as "comfort."[26] The former camp prefers "encouragement" because the apostle

---

23. David Alan Black, "Paul and Christian Unity: A Formal Analysis of Philippians 2:1–4," *JETS* 28 (1985): 301.
24. Ben Witherington III, *Friendship and Finances in Philippi: The Letter of Paul to the Philippians* (Valley Forge, PA: Trinity Press International, 1994), 61; Hawthorne, *Philippians*, 64. Hawthorne explains its meaning as equivalent to saying, "Since there is . . . "
25. Hawthorne, *Philippians*, 65; Müller, *Philippians*, 72; Martin, *Philippians*, TNTC, 90.
26. Hansen, *Philippians*, 108; O'Brien, *Philippians*, 170.

repeatedly uses this term for the exhortations he gives elsewhere (Phil 4:2; Rom 12:1; 15:30; 1 Thess 2:11–12).[27] Hence, "encouragement" refers to the encouragement they receive from being one in Christ. The latter camp argues for "comfort" based on its close connection to the assurance of sharing in suffering for Christ's sake as God's favor to them (1:29). Amidst suffering and pain, they can be comforted because: (1) God is their vindicator (1:28); (2) they share with Paul in his suffering for the gospel (2 Cor 1:5–7); and (3) Jesus Christ himself has gone ahead in suffering for them (2:8).[28] In this light, it is preferable to understand the term *paraklēsis* as the "comfort" that is available to all in the church in Philippi (1:1) because they are united in Christ (*en Christō*).

The meaning of the first "if" clause is further explained in the second "if" clause (2:1b). After reminding the believers about the comfort that is available to them because they are spiritually united to Christ, Paul specifies the source of that "comfort," which is "of [his] love" (*agapēs*; note the subjective genitive form). Witherington is wrong in interpreting this as God's love[29] for two reasons: (1) the context does not suggest God, as "love" stands in close relation to the second "if" clause, where Christ is mentioned; and (2) Hawthorne points out that "consolation"[30] (*paramuthion*) and its related forms are used in the NT only to describe human action and never God (John 11:19, 31; 1 Cor 14:3; 1 Thess 2:12; 5:14).[31] Witherington's understanding adds novelty to his interpretation, as he finds the agency of Trinity implicitly appealed to by Paul in 2:1, identifying the three persons of the Trinity in the first three "if" clauses. However, his position is unwarranted in the present context. Similarly, the limited understanding of "love" as Paul's love would be mistaken.[32] The source of love experienced by the Philippians is the love of Christ (1:8; 2:1a), which Paul and his believers not only share, but also demonstrate towards each other (1:9, 16).[33]

The third "if" clause adds another dimension to the foundation of unity among the Philippian believers by appealing to their "sharing in the Spirit" (2:1c). The genitive *pneumatos* signifies the agent who forms the mutual participation of the believers (2 Cor 13:13) in the body of Christ. The *koinonia*

---

27. Hawthorne, *Philippians*, 65.
28. Hansen, *Philippians*, 107–108.
29. Witherington, *Friendship and Finance*, 61.
30. BDAG, 769.
31. Hawthorne, *Philippians*, 65.
32. Hawthorne, 65.
33. Hansen, *Philippians*, 108–109; Martin, *Philippians*, TNTC, 91.

is in "one Spirit in whom they all share by virtue of that incorporation into Christ and in their access to the Father (Eph. ii.18)."[34] Thus, the Philippian believers have fellowship with the apostle in preaching the gospel (1:5) and for Paul that exists in the Holy Spirit (2:1c). In 1:27, Paul expresses his sole desire for them that, whether by learning in person or by hearing about them from afar, he wishes to hear that they are striving side by side in one Spirit.

As Hawthorne rightly contends, the final "if" clause in 2:1 refers to divine "tenderness and compassion" (*splanchna kai oiktirmoi*) rather than the human emotions.[35] Earlier, in 1:8, Paul uses the term *splanchna*, meaning "tenderness," to speak about his strong emotions towards the Philippian believers. The second term *oiktirmoi*, meaning "mercy" or "compassion,"[36] is used by Paul to describe God's mercies in Romans 12:1 and 2 Corinthians 1:3. In all probability, these terms are used here for God's tenderness and compassion towards the believers in Philippi.

2:2 Fourfold response for Christian unity

Paul structures 2:2 as part of a chiastic structure, as indicated within the structure outline above. Paul's overarching concern is to see the Philippian Christian community united because of the reasons mentioned in 2:1. But he personalizes this ultimate goal by commanding them to "make my joy complete" (2:2a). The flip side of this command is a message to the Philippian believers about the pain and sadness he experiences because of the division among them. Hence, he requires his partners in mission to complete his joy, for which he thanks God in 1:5. Paul's well-being and joy in suffering for the gospel is directly connected to his believers' unity with Christ, which is facilitated in the Spirit.

Thus Paul gives clear directives concerning what needs to be done: (1) be "like-minded," (2) "having the same love," (3) "being one in spirit," and (4) "of one mind" (2:2). These four directives are connected to the former four foundational bases for Christian unity mentioned in 2:1. There are ten references made to being "like-minded" (one time each in 1:7; 2:5; 3:19; 4:2, two times each in 2:2; 3:15; 4:10), which go beyond merely intellectual aspects of thinking, but rather "[incorporate] the will and emotions into a comprehensive outlook which affects the attitude."[37] In other words, being like-minded describes

---

34. Martin, *Philippians*, TNTC, 91.
35. Hawthorne, *Philippians*, 66–67.
36. BDAG, 700.
37. Melick, *Philippians*, 94.

"the dominant attitude and settled disposition of the entire person,"[38] which is further defined by the next phrase: "having the same love." (2:2)

In Greek, the phrase *tē nautēn agapēn* ("the same love") points back to the "love" that they experience by being united with Christ (2:1). This is the same comforting love that the Philippian believers are exhorted to demonstrate towards one another, which will comfort them amidst persecution. Undoubtedly, sharing this love is an effective step towards forming unity. Without uniting in the love of Christ, there can be no unity in the Spirit among them.

Further, harkening back to the fervent call in 1:28 for the believers to strive side by side, Paul employs two important words in 2:2, "soul" (*psychē*) and "mind" (*phronein*), in order to highlight the nature of their actual visible unity. While the term *phronein* (meaning "to think"[39]) is repeated again in 2:2, demonstrating the vitality of the same disposition among Christians to live as a community, the term *psychē* ("soul") refers back to the faith of the gospel for which they need to come together and work actively (1:27). This exhortation sets the stage for Paul's appeal for their selfless living in 2:3–4.

2:3–4 Humbly put others' interests over self-ambition

By using the word *mēden* ([do] "nothing") in 2:3, Paul empowers his words with "the force of a moral imperative."[40] In the clauses that follow this imperative, he mentions the negative behaviors of the Philippians that jeopardize Christian unity. He counterbalances these negative behaviors with the opposite positive responses that they need to practice consciously in order to forge unity in the church. The pairs of contradictory behaviors, both negative and positive, are: (1) "selfish ambition or vain conceit" versus "humility" (2:3) and (2) "not looking to your own interests" versus looking to "the interests of the others" (2:4).

The word *eritheia*, meaning "selfish ambition," when used in ancient Greek writings denotes "a self-seeking pursuit of political office by unfair means."[41] Paul lists it among the vices in Galatians 5:20. Earlier in 1:17, it characterizes those who preach Christ in order to increase the pain of the apostle. Paul, based on his knowledge of the current situation within the church in Philippi, is concerned about factionalism, which has been exacerbated by the selfishness of the leaders in the church. This situation within the church is further

---

38. Hansen, *Philippians*, 111–112.
39. BDAG, 1065.
40. Hansen, *Philippians*, 113.
41. BDAG, 392.

complicated by *kenodoxia,* meaning "a vain or exaggerated self-evaluation."[42] Interestingly, this term only appears here in the entire NT, which gives it a particular significance. The former term, "selfish ambition," reflects the problem plaguing the church, while the latter term, "exaggerated self-evaluation," identifies the cause of the problem.

Hence, Paul's solution to the existing problem is to encourage the believers to value others above themselves with humility. The exhortation to "value others above yourselves" places others' interests higher in priority.[43] In a strife-ridden context, fulfilling Paul's exhortation will require the believers to embrace an other-worldly, counter-cultural ethic. Paul rightly describes this ethic as "humility," which is a total reversal of normal social behavior in a Hellenistic context, though not necessarily a Jewish context. It is evident that ancient Hellenistic writers did not esteem humility as a desirable virtue, but rather viewed it with disdain,[44] whereas in the OT, God approves of humility (Prov 3:34). Similarly, the teachings of Jesus (Matt 5:5; 11:29) as well as other canonical Christian writers encourage humility among Christians (1 Pet 5:5–6).

The second part of the ethical exhortation in 2:4 describes the mental disposition of a person. Martin maintains that the term *skopein* (meaning "to pay careful attention to"[45]) is used in a sense of making it one's own goal. However, it is unclear what that goal entails. Martin maintains that it means to take note of "good points and qualities in one's fellow-Christians" and to emulate them in our lives.[46] The conclusion appears to be acceptable in the light of the term's repeated use in Philippians 3:17. In this sense, it is fitting for Paul to shift his attention suddenly in 2:6–8 to the example of Christ as a model for Christians in Philippi to emulate. However, the term *skopein* can also mean bearing a burden, and Paul writes about bearing each other's burdens in Galatians 6:1–2. In the context of persecution and strife, Philippian believers need to share each other's burdens while also seeking to emulate in public the good qualities in the lives of fellow-believers in order to help prevent the church from falling apart.

---

42. BDAG, 538.
43. Hansen, *Philippians,* 116.
44. W. Grundmann, "ταπεινος," *TDNT* 8:1–27.
45. BDAG, 931.
46. Martin, *Philippians,* TNTC, 94.

2:5–11 Christ Jesus, the Supreme Model of Humility

2:5 Purpose for citing the ancient christological hymn

In 2:5, Paul identifies his purpose for citing the ancient christological hymn in 2:6–11. Paul commands his readers by saying, "Think this among you" (*touto phroneite en humin*). Paul is saying that the believers ought to have among themselves a certain frame of mind or attitude, which he referred to earlier in 2:2 as a mental disposition that will yield Christian unity. While the meaning of the first part of 2:5 is clear, the interpretation of the second clause (*ho kai en Christō Iēsou*), which lacks a verb, is debated among scholars. Does the second clause mean that their frame of mind (*touto phroeite*) should be modeled after the example visible in Christ Jesus (ethical emphasis),[47] or is it to be founded on the reality of their union in Christ (doctrinal emphasis)?[48] The latter camp views 2:5 as detached from 2:4.[49] Arguing in favor of the latter position, Martin maintains that this "interpretation gives to 'in Christ Jesus' the regular Pauline meaning of 'in union with Christ,' which is often tantamount to 'in the fellowship of His people'."[50] Arguing for the first position, Keener observes that "[t]he call to have Jesus's frame of mind (2:5) appeals to Jesus's example of service (2:6–8), which thereby summons the Philippian believers to unity."[51] Keener's position appears to be a better option for the following reasons. First, it is grammatically sound because it supplies the verb "think" from the first clause (instead of "was," which is a "to be" verb) to the second clause, which maintains parallelism between the two clauses. Second, Paul's purpose in drawing on the hymn should not be reduced to a narrow ethical purpose based on the example seen in Christ Jesus. Rather, he teaches that Christian conduct is energized by the fact of a Christian's union in him. Third, the striking similarity between 2:5 and 4:2 follows the thought of our union with Christ.[52]

However, this does not mean that we should view the former position as mistaken. It is still possible to see the ethical emphasis in Paul's use of the ancient Christian hymn. First, the term "this" (*touto*) in the beginning of 2:5 refers not to 2:6–8, but back to 2:2–3, where Paul exhorts the believers

---

47. O'Brien, *Philippians*, 204–205; Hansen, *Philippians*, 119–122; Müller, *Philippians*, 77–78.
48. Martin, *Philippians*, 95–96.
49. Martin, *Carmen Christi*, xii–xix.
50. Martin, *Philippians*, TNTC, 95.
51. Craig S. Keener, *The Mind of the Spirit: Paul's Approach to Transformed Thinking* (Grand Rapids: Baker Academic, 2016), 231.
52. Hansen, *Philippians*, 119–121.

on similar lines. Second, Hansen's interpretation of 2:5 appears to be much more balanced and convincing. Without denying the doctrinal interpretation, Hansen maintains that the ethical interpretation is still possible. He argues that Paul does not dichotomize the doctrinal from the ethical interpretation, because his ethical logic regards the doctrinal facts as foundational to the ethical imperatives.[53] Hence, their union in Christ is foundational to their ethical behavior as they emulate him who is the paramount model for their imitation. The humility characterizing their interpersonal relationships is modeled after the pattern of behavior exemplified in the event of the incarnation.

2:6–8 Paramount model of humility

Paul seems to be quoting a first-century Christian hymn to encourage a particular attitude or mindset among the Philippians. The hymn begins (2:6) with a relative pronoun, "who" (*hos*), which refers back to "Christ Jesus" in 2:5. The pronoun connects the historical Jesus with the following christological confession (2:6–11) and its ethical implication for the Philippians. The historical Christ Jesus is preexistent, equal with God, and not grabbing that equality for "his own advantage" (2:6).[54]

Our understanding of the entire hymn (2:6–11) depends upon the position from which we interpret 2:6 based on a shroud of ambiguity. The meaning of the terms used in 2:6–8 are disputed, with interpretations varying according to the background assumed for the hymn. Here, these terms do not bear the exact meaning which they acquire elsewhere in Paul's theological discussion if they are viewed in relation to other terms in their respective immediate contexts. So on three crucial accounts in 2:6, a commentator must display consistency and clarity of thought in interpreting the lines of the hymn based on the assumed interpretive position. These three accounts are as follows: (1) the meaning of the expression *en morphē Theou hyparchōn* ("being in very nature of God"); (2) the meaning of the words *morphē* ("form") and *hyparchōn* ("be"); (3) the meaning of *harpagmon* (translated as "something to be used to his own advantage," NIV).

Beginning with the first interpretive question, the participle verb *hyparchōn*, translated as "being" (NIV), seems to refer to the preexistent state of Christ Jesus. However, as Hansen argues, the term can also be understood as referring to Christ's preexistent state by reading it in relation to "an aorist finite verb,

---

53. Hansen, 121.
54. Roji T. George, "'God Sent His Son, Born of a Woman' (Gal. 4:4): The Idea of Incarnation, Its Antecedents, and Significance in Paul's Theology," *DTJ* 5 (2008): 77–78.

he emptied, which is modified by two aorist participles, *taking* and *becoming*."[55] Even though the hymn does not say explicitly that Christ Jesus is God, these three words – *empty, taking,* and *becoming* – assume the preexistence of Christ. If so, while the participle verb *hyparchōn* refers to the preexistent state of Jesus, the expression "being in very nature of God" (*en morphē Theou hyparchōn*) speaks about the location (note the use of *en,* meaning "in") in which Christ Jesus existed prior to incarnation. In the light of similar usage in Luke 7:25, the expression seems to mean that "he was wrapped or covered in the *morphē* of God."[56] This leads us to the second interpretive question regarding the term "form" about which scholars and theologians have disputed vehemently.[57] The basic meaning of the term refers to the "object's perceptibility and visibility"[58] with regard to its appearance. In this sense, the term must refer to Christ Jesus, who existed in the being of the God of Israel that is known only through his visibility. Both in the OT (LXX) and NT, the "form" of God, in the sense of his visibility to humans, is understood as God's glory (Exod 16:10; 24:16–17; 33:17–23; 2 Macc 2:8; 3 Macc 4:18; 1 Enoch 14:21; Rom 1:23; 1 Cor 11:7; 2 Cor 3:18; 4:6). Conceptually, the invisible God of the OT manifests himself to us in his glory. This way of understanding the preexistent divine state of Christ Jesus, as existing in the glory of God, echoes the word of Jesus in John 17:5.[59] In other words, the term "form" implies that Christ, in his preexistent state, was wrapped in the glory of God. Thus Hansen argues that if "*the form of God* means the glory of God and the glory of God is intimately related with the being of God, then we will also conclude that that phrase *existing in the form of God* points to Christ's *being in very nature of God*."[60] If so, then Christ shares in the essential character of God, which is not limited to what humans can see, but this essential character of God is only recognizable to humans by the manifestation of his glory before people.[61]

The idea of Christ being in the form of God is further underlined in the expression that relates to our third interpretive question: he "did not consider equality with God something to be used to his own advantage" (2:6). The expression "equality with God" refers to the pre-incarnate state of Jesus Christ,

---

55. Hansen, *Philippians*, 134 (emphasis original).
56. Hawthorne, *Philippians*, 81; Hansen, *Philippians*, 134–135.
57. For an overview of various proposals regarding its meaning, see Hawthorne, *Philippians*, 81–84.
58. Stephen E. Fowl, *Philippians*, THNTC (Grand Rapids: Eerdmans, 2005), 91.
59. Fowl, *Philippians*, 91–92; Hansen, *Philippians*, 135–137.
60. Hansen, *Philippians*, 138 (emphasis original).
61. Hawthorne, *Philippians*, 84; Lightfoot, *Philippians*, 110.

where he shared equally in the very glory of God and is therefore a parallel expression to "the form of God." Together, these expressions point to the same reality, which is that, in Christ's preexistent state, he was God himself.

This interpretation requires us to understand the term *harpagmon* as Christ's refusal to grab his equality with God for his own advantage, although the meaning of the term *harpagmon* (implying "something to which one can claim or assert title by gripping or grasping")[62] is difficult to explain. It does not appear elsewhere in the OT (LXX) or the NT, and it is not commonly found in other Greek writings.[63] Scholars have widely disputed the exact meaning of the term and its hermeneutical bearing upon the meaning of the hymn, particularly 2:6.[64] However, as Fowl maintains, "it now appears that here is a consensus emerging, which is that in contexts such as this one we should understand the word indicating something that is used for one's own advantage."[65] The wording implies that Christ, in his pre-incarnate state, was equal in status with God, and so Christ had legitimate authority to cling to God for his advantage. However, Christ acted selflessly, relinquishing what was legitimately his own in order to fulfill the salvific purpose of God.

The fuller significance of the theological assertion in 2:5, which introduces the desired ethical pattern of behavior for the Philippian believers in 2:6, is further amplified by contrasting the pre-incarnate and incarnate states of Christ's existence. While 2:6 speaks about Christ choosing not to do something, 2:7–8 speak about what Christ chooses to do. The act of not grabbing his equality with God for his advantage (2:6) is explained by the word that introduces 2:7, *alla,* which means "but," and contrasts the fact that "he made himself nothing by taking the very nature of a servant and being made in human likeness" (2:7). The use of *heauton* in the emphatic position "points to the humiliation of our Lord as *voluntary, self-imposed.*"[66] Christ Jesus emptied himself (*ekenōsen*) voluntarily of all divine privileges and "made himself nothing" (2:7).

---

62. BDAG, 133.
63. Hansen, *Philippians*, 142.
64. For a detailed discussion on multiple positions, see Hansen, 142–146; Hawthorne, *Philippians*, 84–85.
65. Fowl, *Philippians*, 94. Fowl depends upon the study of Hoover for the term *Harpagmos*. Roy W. Hoover, "The *Harpagmos* Enigma: A Philological Solution," *HTR* 64 (1971): 95–119.
66. Lightfoot, *Philippians*, 112.

But what does this self-emptying (*alla heauton ekenōsen*, meaning "made himself nothing," 2:7a) entail? Some, such as Kärkkäinen[67] and Schreiner,[68] reject that it means a disavowal of his deity in incarnation, arguing that its meaning is added to the "likeness of a man." Nevertheless, taking a cue from the word *kenoun*, meaning "to pour out," Hawthorne argues that it must be viewed as a poetic way of expressing "Christ pouring out himself, putting himself totally at the disposal of people (compare 1 John 3:16), that Christ became poor that he might make many rich (2 Cor 8:9; Eph 1:23; 4:10)." On two accounts, this meaning appears to be more acceptable. First, the classical Hellenistic and patristic writings use the term to imply spending wealth for the poor. Second, the wordplay between *kenodoxia*, meaning "a vain or exaggerated self-evaluation,"[69] in 2:3 and *kenoun*, meaning "to pour out," in 2:7 contrasts the behavior of those who insist on pressing their way upon others with the behavior of Christ, who relinquished all privileges to benefit others.[70]

Further, the terms "taking" (*labōn*) and "becoming" (*genomenos*) in 2:7 narrowly define the broader act of self-emptying. According to Schreiner, "[b]oth of these participles should be understood instrumentally, in that they describe the manner in which Christ emptied himself."[71] Paul says that he emptied himself by "taking the very nature of a servant, being made in human likeness" (2:7). It is evident that Christ assumed the "form" (*morphē*) of a slave in his incarnation. Fee argues that the phrase "taking the form of a slave" is a modal participle, which expresses the act of self-emptying as a pouring out of himself.[72] Mark 10:45 attests to such an understanding: "the Son of Man did not come to be served, but to serve, and to give his life a ransom for many." In other words, the visibility of Christ's slave "form" (*morphē*), which is similar to his being in the "form" (*morphē*) of God in 2:6, does not suggest that he belongs to the class of slaves in the Roman or Jewish society, but that in essence he fulfills the role of a slave before others.

In John 13:3–5, Jesus takes the form of a slave before his disciples when he voluntarily takes a basin of water and begins to wash their feet. This intentional act denies his privilege as a master before his disciples. In this way,

---

67. Veli-Matti Kärkkäinen, *Christology: A Global Introduction* (Grand Rapids: Baker Academic, 2003), 55.
68. Thomas R. Schreiner, *Paul Apostle of God's Glory in Christ: A Pauline Theology*, 1st Indian ed. (Secunderabad: OM Books, 2003), 172.
69. Schreiner, *Paul Apostle of God's Glory in Christ*, 538.
70. Hawthorne, *Philippians*, 85–86.
71. Schreiner, *Paul*, 172.
72. Fee, *Philippians*, NICNT, 210.

Jesus not only demonstrates his slave "form" through his incarnation, but he also sets the right model of conduct before his disciples. Similarly, by using the slave image of Jesus in 2:7, Paul speaks simultaneously of two ideas: (1) Jesus's voluntary relinquishment of his rights when he assumes the *morphē* of a slave; (2) Paul's exhortation to divide believers in Philippi to imitate the mindset of Christ by behaving without selfishness and seeking to act in the interests of others before their own.

Similarly, "becoming" (*genomenos* in 2:7) indicates a fresh beginning, which contrasts with *hyparchōn* ("being") in 2:6, referring to Christ's preexistence. Hansen maintains that "[w]hile the hymn does not offer a narrative of the birth and infancy of Christ, it does contemplate the entrance of Christ into human history."[73] The earthly existence of Christ Jesus is summarized in the expression "in human likeness" (*en homoiōmati anthrōpōn*, 2:7). The term "likeness" (*homoiōmati*) is also used in Roman 8:3, where it "indicates that Jesus did not participate in the sinfulness of human flesh."[74] For Dunn, "it denotes a 'likeness' which embodies the reality 'enlikened' so far as that is possible, as we would say, 'a mirror,' an exact replica . . . flesh not sinful in itself, but flesh in its weakness and corruptibility, vulnerable to and in the event dominated by the power of sin."[75] In Philippians 2:7, the term "likeness" reveals that Christ fully identified with humanity and that in Christ, God was living out a truly human life.[76] So Christ's incarnation was perfectly real, for his likeness was identical to human physical nature, and yet his flesh was without any stain of sin.[77] The term "appearance" (*schēmati*) in 2:7 (2:8 in NIV), along with the phrases "form of a slave" (*morphēn*) and "likeness of men" (*homoiōmati*) further expand the idea of the incarnation. According to Hawthorne, these three ideas make a "threefold reiteration of the one fundamentally important idea, that Christ in the incarnation fully identified himself with humanity."[78] In 2:8, the very act of "being found in the appearance of a man" is stated as Christ "humbled himself" and became "obedient to death" in incarnation. Because Paul is presenting Christ as a model for the Philippians to follow in their ethical conduct within their context, the reference to Christ humbling

---

73. Hansen, *Philippians*, 152.
74. Ben Witherington III, *Paul's Narrative Thought World: The Tapestry of Tragedy and Triumph* (Louisville, KY: Westminster/John Knox, 1994), 139.
75. J. D. G. Dunn, *The Theology of Paul the Apostle* (Grand Rapids: Eerdmans, 1998), 202.
76. Fee, *Philippians*, NICNT, 213.
77. C. K. Barrett, *The Epistle to the Romans*, BNTC, rev. ed. (London: Hendrickson, 1991), 147 (emphasis original).
78. Hawthorne, *Philippians*, 87–88.

himself and being obedient to God unto death on a cross are two essential virtues of which they must take notice.

The act of Christ humbling himself implies that "his whole life was characterized by self-surrender, self-renunciation and self-sacrifice."[79] Although some have found echoes here of Isaiah's servant song,[80] there is no evidence to prove that the "hymn is consciously using the model of Isaiah's servant," because the hymn neither mentions how Christ was obedient, nor does it speak of the soteriological value of his obedience.[81] Further, in Isaiah's servant song, the title "'my servant' connotes a position of honor," and yet the reference to a servant in the hymn states a position of dishonor.[82] Martin suggests that the act of Christ humbling himself is not what Paul had in mind as a virtue for imitation by the Philippians.[83] However, this is not convincing, because the hymn noticeably "echoes the language of 2:3–4," which articulates the desired pattern of behavior among his readers.[84] Undoubtedly, "Paul does draw a parallel between the ethical behavior of the church and the life of Christ by first requiring the church to practice humility and then pointing to the precedent for their behavior in the self-humbling obedience of Christ."[85]

The imitation of Christ's humiliation is further highlighted by the reference in 2:8 to Christ's obedience unto death on a cross. According to Bruce, this "forms the climax of the first part of the hymn."[86] The humbling of Christ was self-inflicted and not against his will, for it was the direct consequence of his perfect obedience to the will of the Father. The full extent of his obedience is embedded in the phrase, "even death on a cross" (2:8). During the Roman time, crucifixion was a cruel and humiliating imperial punishment for those who were considered a threat to the empire or were slaves.[87] Bruce states that in "polite Roman society the word 'cross' was an obscenity, not to be uttered in conversation. Even when a man was being sentenced to death by crucifixion,

---

79. Hawthorne, 89.
80. Hansen contends that despite difference between Isaiah's servant and the servant in the hymn, the latter does identify Jesus with the servant figure in the former passages (*Philippians*, 155).
81. Ralph P. Martin, *Philippians*, NCBC (Grand Rapids: Eerdmans/London: Marshall, Morgan & Scott, 1980), 98.
82. Hansen, *Philippians*, 154–155.
83. Martin, *Philippians*, NCBC, 99.
84. Fowl, *Philippians*, 99.
85. Hansen, *Philippians*, 155–156.
86. Bruce, *Philippians*, 54.
87. Martin Hengel, *Crucifixion: In the Ancient World and the Folly of the Message of the Cross* (Philadelphia: Fortress Press, 1977), 46–63.

an archaic formula was used that avoided the pronouncing of this four-letter word – as it was in Latin (*crux*)."[88] Among Jews, death by crucifixion was considered to be God's curse (Deut 21:22–23). In fact, mentioning "death on a cross," as the extreme extent of Jesus's obedience to God the Father, stands in absolute contrast to the equality of Christ with God in his preexistent state. The descent from the divine stage to the most loathsome death is an apt description of the humiliation that Christ endured in his incarnation.

2:9–11 Humility leading to exaltation

In 2:9a, Christ Jesus's humiliation through his self-abasement is contrasted with God's initiative to reverse Christ's humiliation into his glorification. God exalted him to the "highest place," giving him a name "above every name" and causing others to confess Jesus Christ as "Lord." In 2:6–8, Christ is the subject of every verb, but in 2:9–11, God is the subject of every verb. The reversal of Christ's humiliation through his death on a cross is introduced by an inferential conjunction, "therefore" (*dio*), but the use of *kai* (literally, "also" or "and") in 2:9a underlines the divine reciprocity. In other words, the reason that God exalts Christ is based on his self-abasement, which is mentioned in the earlier part of the hymn (2:6–8). Jesus taught the same kingdom principle in Matthew 23:11. However, one must be cautious not to consider God's reciprocity as a reward for Christ's obedience to death on a cross. Instead, as Fee contends, "it asserts the divine vindication of Christ's emptying himself and humbling himself in obedience by dying on a cross."[89]

The unusual compound verb, "exalt," prefixed with *hyper,* meaning "above," does not imply that Christ Jesus is lifted (2:9a) to a higher position than before. Rather, Fee understands it as an intensification of the term, suggesting Christ's exaltation "to the highest possible degree."[90] To put it differently, Christ's exaltation is not regarding his position within the Godhead, but "as ascription to Him of what could only be His after the submission and sacrifice of His earthly life."[91] The same verb is used in Psalm 97:9, emphasizing Yahweh's exaltation as his incomparability to any other gods. Isaiah 52:13 uses the verb (without prefix) to speak of the glorification of the servant of the Lord.

The exaltation is further explained as God giving (*echarisato,* "gave") Christ Jesus "the name that is above every name" (2:9b). At first, God "gave"

---

88. Bruce, *Philippians*, 47.
89. Fee, *Philippians*, NICNT, 220.
90. Fee, 221.
91. Martin, *Philippians*, TNTC, 104.

(*echarisato*) indicates that, just as the Philippians are given a gift by grace to believe and suffer for Christ, so the majestic name "Lord" is a gracious gift to Jesus in 2:9.[92] Although "Jesus" could also be considered as "the name that is above every name," there is a broad consensus among scholars that the name given to the exalted Christ is "Lord" (*kurios* 2:11). In support of the latter proposal, the Greek OT (LXX) uses this title for Yahweh, denoting "rulership based upon competent and authoritative power, the ability to dispose of what one possesses."[93] Moreover, in Isaiah 45:23, before Yahweh, every knee shall bow, and every tongue shall confess his righteousness. Within the context of the hymn, it is interesting to notice that the circumlocutory expression, "the name that is above every name," in 2:9b later climaxes as "Lord" in 2:11. Hence, Paul most probably had "Lord" in his mind when he was thinking about the name "that is above every name." If so, Paul ascribes the name "Lord" to Jesus within the hymn. Within the Roman imperial context, ascribing a title of such honor to Jesus, who was crucified under Roman imperial law, subverts the absolute claim of Caesar for the title of "Lord" throughout the empire. Paul dares to address Jesus as "Lord" while writing to Philippi, a leading Roman city, where all must have been familiar with it as a high imperial title.

In 2:10–11, the hymn explains God's purpose in exalting Christ by using two important verbs: "bow" and "acknowledge." Both these verbs allude to Isaiah 45:23, where the zealous God claims not to share his glory with any other being. At first, the expression "at the name *of* Jesus" (emphasis added) indicates that the name implied is not "Jesus," but the name that belongs to him, which is "Lord." Hence, the lordship of the historical figure of Jesus is central.

The universal lordship of Jesus is absolute because he was obedient to God even unto death on a cross. Just as Christ rendered obedience to God unquestioningly in his incarnation, so now all believers must submit to him. There is nothing within the created order, visible or invisible, that is exempted from the scope of Christ's authority. The universal authority of Jesus, the Lord, is to be acknowledged by every intelligent being in all three layers of existence: "in heaven," "on earth," and "under the earth." Martin states that "[i]t is a universal acclamation in which angels, men and devils join to proclaim the cosmic victory and authority of the obedient One who receives the worship and homage which, according to rabbinic thought, the first Adam had, and

---

92. Fowl, *Philippians*, 102.
93. Martin, *Philippians*, TNTC, 104–105.

later forfeited because of his vain designs to rival God."[94] Now, by his perfect obedience and total submission to God unto death on a cross, Christ Jesus reverses the failure of the first Adam.

The act of bowing one's knees before a superior reflects absolute submission and an attitude of worship.[95] In Revelation 5:6–14, all the heavenly beings fall at the feet of the Lamb in worship, which suggests that the first-century Christians accepted Jesus, the Lamb of God, as worthy of receiving the same homage that Yahweh claims for himself alone in Isaiah 45:23. He, the Lord, is exalted and worthy of receiving the submission of everything in the sphere of heaven in ancient cosmology.[96] Similarly, in Philippians 2:10–11, all – without exception, believing or unbelieving – will have to bow their knees in confessing the sovereignty of Christ Jesus. It is interesting to notice that Paul, as a Jew, could confess Jesus as the worthy recipient of homage reserved for Yahweh alone. Exodus 20:5 commands, "You shall not bow down to them or worship them; for I the Lord your God, am a jealous God." The first-century Christians found no contradiction between their monotheistic faith and their confession of Jesus as the sovereign "Lord."

In 2:11, the second aspect of God's purpose is stated as a cosmic confession of Christ's lordship: "Jesus is Lord." This is climactic to all that has been said earlier about Christ. The hymn seems to complete a full circle – Jesus's divine preexistent status (2:6), his incarnate state of self-abasement (2:7–8), and God's exaltation of him to the highest position, worthy of worship, under whom the whole cosmos is brought into submission (2:9–11). By God's gracious act, the one who, being in the very nature of God, humbled himself in obedience is reinstated to his highest position. Elsewhere in Paul's letters, the confession, "Jesus Christ is Lord," is characteristic of Christian believers who are aided by the Spirit (1 Cor 12:3).[97] However, in 2:11a, "every tongue" (*pasaglōssa*) is a blanket expression that exempts none – living or dead, believing or unbelieving – from confessing Christ's lordship in the eschatological time. Every creature is destined to acknowledge the sovereignty of Christ. Hansen maintains that "[b]y placing Lord first in this acclamation, the Greek text puts the emphasis on that name. That name is dramatically withheld until every tongue in the whole creation reveals that name."[98]

---

94. Martin, 105.
95. H. Schlier, "γονυ," *TDNT* 1:738.
96. Hansen, *Philippians*, 164–165.
97. Fee, *Philippians*, NICNT, 225.
98. Hansen, *Philippians*, 166.

Within the Roman context of Philippi, "every tongue" (*pasaglōssa*) would be heard as including the entire imperial bureaucracy, from the emperor at the top to the lowest official, along with the colonized subjects in the socio-political hierarchy. This means that the unbelieving and persecuting majority populace in Philippi will, at the eschatological time, join humbly with the persecuted minority of Philippian Christians to acknowledge the sovereignty of Jesus, the one crucified under the Roman law. Their present ability to resist the gospel by aligning with the human powers does not alter this inevitable submission.

Finally, Paul makes it absolutely clear that the ultimate exaltation of Jesus Christ with the bestowal of the ultimate name, "Lord," and through the confession by every creature that "Jesus is Lord," does not threaten his monotheistic faith. There is a reciprocal relationship between God, the Father, and Jesus Christ, the Son: "When the Son is honored, the Father is glorified; for none can bestow on the Son higher honors than the Father himself has bestowed."[99] Thus the final expression, "to the glory of God the Father," preserves Paul's faith in one God, one Lord (1 Cor 8:6).[100] There appear to be two reasons for placing this expression at the very end of the hymn (2:6–11): (1) "to focus on Christ himself" and (2) to "point to him as the ultimate model of the self-sacrificing love to which he is calling the Philippians" (i.e., obedience by self-abasement).[101]

In short, although the content of this early Christian hymn is highly theological, its literary function within the letter is mainly ethical, presenting Christ himself as the model for imitation. By citing the hymn, Paul exhorts the virtues of obedience and self-abasement to the Philippian believers.

2:12–18 WORK OUT YOUR SALVATION

The following quote has been repeatedly attributed to Mahatma Gandhi: "I like your Christ. I do not like your Christians. Your Christians are so unlike your Christ." Whether Ghandi actually said this or not, it reflects the sharp critique of someone who loved Christ for his life and teachings but found Christians completely failing to replicate their Lord. In writing to the Philippian believers, Paul appears to have anticipated such duplicity becoming real among Christians unless they consciously made it their point to emulate Christ in their day-to-day lives, working out their salvation.

---

99. Bruce, *Philippians*, 51.
100. Fee, *Philippians*, NICNT, 226.
101. Fee, 226.

Paul's earnest appeal in 2:1–4 to live in unity and to be without selfish ambition is reinforced by calling the believers to emulate Christlike obedience for all to see while working out their salvation (2:12–16). In fact, the apostle himself is a concrete example before the Philippian believers of selflessness and humility (2:17–18). He instructs them to live in obedience to God, conducting themselves in a manner that is worthy of the gospel of Christ by walking blamelessly and shining as stars before others (2:15). Hence, the flow of the apostle's thought within 2:12–18 appears to move at three levels. First, the Philippian believers ought to walk in obedience and work out their salvation with caution (2:12–13). Second, they must shed all negativity found among them and shine like stars among a crooked generation (2:14–16). Third, they ought to rejoice upon hearing Paul's heartfelt desire to be poured out in order to complete their sacrifice (2:17–18).[102]

2:12–13 Walk in Obedience

In 2:12, Paul begins his exhortation by reminding his converts of the strong relationship he shared with them in Philippi, addressing them as "my beloved." According to Martin, this is "the loving expression of his pastoral heart."[103] If so, this loving relationship reflects a very important aspect of Paul as a pastor. Amidst external pressure, when some within the church in Philippi are falling away from living a life that is worthy of the gospel, he banks on the strength of his intimate relationship with them. He appreciates their faith journey in the past, saying, "as you have always obeyed" (compare Acts 16:14, 32–33), but then he quickly commands them to continue "to work out" their "salvation with fear and trembling" (2:12). Elsewhere, Paul's pastoral strategy is to appreciate his readers (Rom 1:8; 6:17) while also expecting them to continue in obedience (2 Cor 7:15; 10:6; Phlm 21). This implies that Paul has not been totally negative about the Philippian believers' faith journey since the day of their conversion, but he expects them to take care and do better in the light of the eschatological day.

In 2:12, Paul exhorts them to obey, whether he is present among them or absent. Since their careful obedience to God during the apostle's presence among them proves his apostolic authority over them, the question of whether Paul is making particular reference to his presence among them in the past

---
102. Melick, *Philippians*, 109.
103. Martin, *Philippians*, TNTC, 110.

or his anticipated presence with them in future is insignificant.[104] Paul does not use a verb here that specifies his presence at any particular point of time. Rather, his concern is the need for their consistent obedience to God. They ought to obey God all the more carefully when Paul is absent from them, because they are troubled by internal discord and strife (2:1–4) as well as external opposition from non-Christians (1:28). As a pastor, Paul appears worried, recognizing that the situation could be detrimental both to their individual and corporate existence. Hence, he exhorts them to "work out [their] salvation with fear and trembling" (2:12).

In the light of Paul's absence, the believers need to take initiative and consciously exert energy "to live in accord with their salvation, letting the implications of their relationship with Christ transform their social relationships."[105] The Greek term *katergadzesthe*, an imperative, means "cause a state or condition, bring about, produce, or create."[106] It implies a *"continuous, sustained, strenuous effort"* to "carry it to its conclusion" on the eschatological day.[107] Scholars are divided about the significance and scope of Paul's command to "work out your salvation" (2:12). While many, including Martin, Hawthorne and Bruce, argue for understanding *sōtēria* ("salvation") as the "well-being" of the community of the believers (sociological sense),[108] others, including O'Brien, Müller, Melick, and Hendricksen, argue that Paul is exhorting individual believers to pay careful attention to their personal salvation (theological sense).[109] The former camp's arguments include the following: (1) *en humin* in 2:13, being plural, should be translated as "among you" rather than "in you"; (2) understanding *sōtēria* in a sociological sense coheres well with the spirit of Paul's exhortation in 2:1–4; (3) the plural forms of *katergadzesthe* (verb) and *heautōn* (reflexive pronoun) overrule the idea of an individual's salvation in Paul's mind.[110] In contrast, the latter camp's arguments for the theological meaning of *sōtērian* include the following: (1) in line with the apostle's use of the term in 1:19, 28, personal eschatological salvation appears to be intended

---

104. While Hawthorne contends that Paul is speaking about the future visit to them (*Philippians*, 99), most other scholars consider it a reference to the past, when Paul's presence among them evoked obedience among the Philippians believers. E.g., Hendriksen, *Philippians*, 119; Müller, *Philippians*, 90.
105. Melick, *Philippians*, 110.
106. BDAG, 531.
107. Hendricksen, *Philippians*, 120.
108. Hawthorne, *Philippians*, 98–99; Martin, *Philippians*, TNTC, 111; Bruce, *Philippians*, 56.
109. O'Brien, *Philippians*, 278–280; Hendricksen, *Philippians*, 120; Müller, *Philippians*, 90; Melick, *Philippians*, 110; Silva, *Philippians*, WEC, 136–137.
110. Hawthorne, *Philippians*, 98.

in 2:12; (2) the plural forms of *katergadzesthe* (verb) and *heautōn* (reflexive pronoun) merely underline the fact that the exhortation is intended for all the believers individually; (3) Paul's interest in 2:12 is different from 2:1–4, and therefore the two do not need to mean the same thing.[111]

However, one need not understand the sociological and theological meanings of the term *sōtēria* ("salvation") in exclusive terms. It is possible to understand both the meanings as interconnected and coexisting in Paul's exhortation in 2:12. Hansen maintains that Paul wants his believers in Philippi to live out practically their heavenly citizenship before others in the city.[112] Rightly, Fee states:

> A great deal of unnecessary ink has been spilt over this passage, as to whether "salvation" has to do with the individual believer or with the corporate life of the community. But that is a false dichotomy. The context makes it clear that this is not a soteriological text per se, dealing with "people getting saved" or "saved people persevering." Rather it is an ethical text, dealing with "how saved people live out their salvation" in the context of the believing community and the world. What Paul is referring to, therefore, is the *present* "outworking" of their *eschatological salvation* within the *believing community* in Philippi.[113]

Further, Paul qualifies the manner of working out their salvation with the prepositional phrase, "with fear and trembling" (compare 1 Cor 2:3; 2 Cor 7:15; Eph 6:5). Though the terms employed could sometimes be understood in a negative sense, the sense in which they appear here underlines the positive human attitudes of humility, reverence towards God, and submission to God's will.[114] This does not mean that Philippian believers had to work to earn their justification on the last day, for Paul is teaching them "the absolute necessity of the empowering presence of God not only to do any work but also to have a desire to do the work."[115] They are assured that God is at work in them while they are working out their salvation. In the light of Paul's later reference to the believers' status as children of God (2:15), the idea of the indwelling presence of the Spirit is probably present at the back of his mind. In Galatians 4:6,

---

111. O'Brien, *Philippians*, 278–280.
112. Hansen, *Philippians*, 174.
113. Fee, *Philippians*, NICNT, 235, emphases in the original.
114. O'Brien, *Philippians*, 283–284; Hansen, *Philippians*, 175–176.
115. Hansen, *Philippians*, 177.

Paul says that as sons and daughters, the believers are given "the Spirit of his Son into our hearts." Similarly, in Romans 8:14, Paul teaches that "those who are led by the Spirit of God are the children of God." In short, it is not just a human effort but God (through the Spirit) who is said to be (literally) "the one who energizes" (*ho energōn*, a participle form) the believers both to will and to act in working out their salvation (2:13). Through God's assistance, all believers can fulfill the task of working out their own personal salvation with fear and trembling. Moreover, the formation of the community of God on the earth is also the result of God's activity. The Philippian community's attitude of reverence and humility before God is also due to the work of God in them, which leaves no room for anyone to boast, compete, or seek their own interests within the church.

According to Paul, the explicit purpose of divine activity in us is "to fulfill his good purpose [*eudokias*]" (2:13). The term *eudokia* generally relates to the ultimate will of God (see Eph 1:5, 9), his own glory.[116] Silva maintains that the expression is "roughly equivalent" to "the glory of God."[117] Paul wants the Philippians to stay humble and submissive before God, because God is at work in them to bring about, for his own glory, his universal plan of salvation. Although the Greek text in 2:13 is missing the pronoun "his" (referring to God), it is clear that Paul means God's "good purpose" here because God is the subject – "the one working" (*ho energōn*). God is the one who activates us "to will and to act." Interestingly, God is the ultimate cause of every human action that falls in line with his sovereign purpose. Even our human will to act in tune with his "good purpose" is a divine initiative. He does things in order to accomplish his *eudokia*, "good purpose," *in* and *through* us *for* us and *for* the church, as in Philippi. Both human volition and the action of believers obedient to God's sovereignty over their own lives – like Jesus, who humbled himself and became obedient to God even unto death on the cross (2:7–8) – are God's fields of action to perform his "good purpose." Such God-energized obedience on an individual's part is sure to lead a believer to exaltation, despite momentary pain and loss (2: 9). In fact, the Philippians have already been told about Paul's confidence, based on their partnership with him in his mission, that God "who began a good work in you will carry it on to completion until the day of Christ Jesus" (1:6).

---

116. Melick, *Philippians*, 111.
117. Silva, *Philippians*, WEC, 142.

2:14–16 Shine Like Stars among a Crooked Generation

In 2:14–16, Paul instructs the believers about the manner in which they need to work out their salvation in both personal and corporate life. He begins with a general command with a negative modification: "Do everything without grumbling and arguing" (2:14). In his letter to the Colossians, Paul exhorts his readers to render all their social responsibilities "in the name of the Lord Jesus, giving thanks to God the Father through him" (Col 3:17). In the light of this exhortation, Paul's all-encompassing command to the Philippians, "Do everything," would include their every word and deed. This perspective does not warrant the mistaken modern dichotomy that divides human life into spiritual and secular aspects, for the ultimate goal of every Christian's will or act, word or deed is to glorify God (1 Cor 10:31). In other words, they must not be concerned about to whom they are rendering service on the earth, but in all things must consider themselves as "working for the Lord" (Col 3:23).

Now, this noble attitude about everything that they do must be supported by acting "without grumbling and arguing" (2:14). While "grumbling" refers to grudging and quietly speaking ill,[118] "arguing" could refer to a quarrelsome exchange of opinions[119] (see reference to Euodia and Syntyche [4:2]). The Philippian believers have a striking example for understanding the negative consequences of grumbling in the life of the Israelites in the wilderness (Num 11:1–6; 14:1–26).[120] A few years earlier, in his letter to the Corinthians, Paul used the story of the Israelites to provide a warning (1 Cor 10:1–11). The underlying truth that the believers in Philippi ought to understand is that, as a Christian living and working in this world, there is no room for negativity in whatever they do. Even though there are things they could complain about while working out their salvation (2:12) and living "blameless and pure" to shine "like stars in the sky" (2:15), they must remain positive and act in the name of the Lord Jesus, because God is always at work in them to "fulfill his good purpose" (2:13).

In 2:15, the *hina* ("so that") introduces a purpose clause that explains the purpose of Paul's exhortation that they ought to "become" (*ginomai*) "blameless and pure." In 2:7, the term employed for Christ signifies him taking up human form. Similarly, in 1 Corinthians 9:19–22, Paul acknowledges that he has become more than a Jew without ceasing to be a Jew. In this sense,

---

118. K. H. Rengstorf, "γογγυσμος," *TDNT* 1:735–736.
119. G. Schrenk, "διαλογισμος," *TDNT* 2:97.
120. Bruce, *Philippians*, 59.

the Philippian believers must become "blameless and pure" without ceasing to be a citizen of Philippi, so that they shine "like stars in the sky" (2:15) as "children of God" within their own cultural context.

Paul admonishes his audience to be "blameless" (*amemptos*) before God because, as Grudmann states, it is the actual goal of one's Christian life. As the opposite of *memphomai,* which means "to blame,"[121] becoming "blameless" (*amemptos*) suggests a life that is beyond accusation. This is further clarified by the word "pure" (*akeraios*), which is associated with the word *kerannumi,* meaning "to mix components, mostly of water with wine," in order to dilute its "high alcoholic strength."[122] The term "pure" (*akeraios*) is always used in the NT in a figurative sense, where it refers to "that which is still in its original state of intactness, totality or moral innocence."[123] In Asian countries, we often encounter milkmen who mix additional water into pure milk to increase its quantity for sale, or goldsmiths who produce impure gold by adding other metals to pure gold. In India, a Hindi word used for adulteration is "*milavat,*" which is the opposite of *shudha* ("pure," "unadulterated"). Paul reminds the believers that they ought to lead an undiluted and unadulterated life – one that cannot be accused of anything impure and is uncorrupted by sin.

Further, quoting Deuteronomy, Paul reminds his audience that they are "Children of God without fault [*amōmos*] in a warped and crooked generation" (2:15). Whereas Moses spoke of the Israelites as "corrupt and not his children . . . a warped and crooked generation" (Deut 32:5), Paul exhorts the Philippian believers that by working out their salvation in complete obedience to God and allowing him to work in them, they will become God's children, who are blameless, pure, and without fault. Paul emphasizes that they are in a position to share a new, intimate relationship with God as his children, having been born into the family of God and receiving the privilege of addressing God as "*Abba,* Father" (Gal 4:6; Rom 8:15).

For Paul, the lives of the believers will reflect their identity as "children of God," causing them to shine forth as "stars in the sky" as they "hold firmly the word of life" (2:15b–16). He draws an intense contrast between the Philippian believers as "children of God" and others as a "warped and crooked generation." Like the celestial bodies – sun, moon and stars – the believers lighten the dark places. Though Jesus addresses his audience as the "light of the world" (Matt 5:14–16), such brilliance is not inherent to the believers, but to the

---

121. W. Grudmann, "μεμφομαι," *TDNT* 4:571–573.
122. BDAG, 540.
123. Gerhard Kittel, "ἀκεραιος," *TDNT* 1:209.

"word of life" that they "grasp."[124] For Paul, "the word" is synonymous to the gospel he preached (1 Thess 2:13; 1 Cor 1:18; 2:4), which the believers are daringly and fearlessly proclaiming amidst opposition (Phil 1:14). Although the expression "the word of life" is used only here, the idea corresponds to 2 Corinthians 2:16, where the gospel of Christ yields life to those who accept it and are saved. By boldly proclaiming and practicing the gospel blamelessly, purely, and without fault, the believers in Philippi are actually shining forth before unbelievers the good purpose of God. In short, the activity of God in their personal and corporate lives, along with their firm grip upon the "word of life," will ensure their salvation, both in the present and on the eschatological day. The divine activity will transform them into children of God, shining forth in a dark world.

Interestingly, Paul identifies his eternal reward on the last day based on the real transformation happening in the life of his audience: "And then I will be able to boast on the day of Christ that I did not run or labor in vain" (2:16b). The test of Paul's success in ministry is not the length and breadth of the Roman Empire that he has crisscrossed with the gospel, but the transformation that he is able to bring in the life of the believers. Paul's boasting is not in his personal success, but in seeking the interests of others (2:4). In other words, Paul's boasting is not in his own preaching or teaching, but in his encouragement to others to be united in Christ (2:1) and saved at the last as the children of God. Hansen maintains that Paul's boasting seems somewhat strange within a parenaetic section exhorting others to be humble, but it is nevertheless coherent with his understanding of boasting in other letters (i.e., boasting in the Lord in 1 Cor 1:31; Phil 3:3 and boasting in the cross of Christ in Gal 6:14).[125]

Hence, Paul lives in eager expectation of "the day of the Lord" (2:16). In 2 Corinthians 5:1–10, Paul expresses his innermost groaning for the day of the Lord, when all must appear before the throne of judgment. Because he is under a burden to give an account of his work on the day of the Lord, Paul persuades others (2 Cor 5:11). In Philippians 2:16, Paul desires to boast about the birth of his audience into the family of God ("children of God"), but in 2 Corinthians 5:12, his manner of conducting his ministry gives others a reason to take pride in him and his companions.

---

124. BDAG, 362.
125. Hansen, *Philippians*, 185.

Paul uses two metaphors to describe his apostolic ministry: "run" (from athletics) and "labor" (from handicraft). As an athlete runs undistracted towards the finish line in order to win the prize, Paul later pictures his ministry as pressing "on towards the goal to win the prize for which God has called" him (3:14; compare 2 Tim 4:7). Deissmann suggests that Paul's second metaphor, "labor in vain," comes from his knowledge of weaving, where badly stitched cloth would be rejected without remuneration.[126] Both the metaphors exhort readers to be careful and diligent in expending their energy while focusing clearly on the ultimate goal of earning a reward or profit in the end. Paul's eschatological orientation enables him to envision his apostolic labor with a clear goal to press towards always before him.

2:17–18 Mutual Celebration of Sacrifices

Finally, at the end of the parenaetic section on ethical exhortation (1:27–2:18), Paul pours out his heart before his audience and presents himself as a concrete model of the Christ-based ethical teachings he has imparted so far. He builds upon the previous two metaphors regarding his single-minded hard labor (2:16) by depicting suffering in ministry – possibly even martyrdom – as the ultimate offering ("libation") upon the sacrifices of others. Philippians 2:17 begins with a conditional clause, "But even if" (*alla ei kai*), suggesting that the threat of impending death is present in Paul's mind, although he is hopeful of a positive outcome at the end of the trial in Rome (1:25–26; 2:23–24). He does not regret his tireless ministry among his converts for the glory of God. In fact, he wants his believers in Philippi to recognize his willingness to "pour out" his life as a "libation" through martyrdom (2 Tim 4:6), if required, in order to complete the sacrifices they are offering unto God.

In the light of the self-sacrificial death of Jesus, Paul views himself as willing to be poured out like a drink offering. Hansen maintains that the practice of pouring out a drink offering was common both in Jewish and Greek sacrificial systems. Among Greeks, the practice of offering a small drink to Zeus was common. Out of this context, the Septuagint borrows the same verb to speak about pouring out a drink offering to God.[127] Hawthorne observes that in ancient Greek and Jewish sacrificial systems, a drink offering was offered at the end of a sacrifice, either on the top or at the foot of the altar (2 Kgs

---

126. Adolf Deissmann, *Light from the Ancient East*, 4th ed. (New York, 1927), 317, quoted by Martin, *Philippians*, TNTC, 118.
127. Hansen, *Philippians*, 187.

16:13; Jer 7:18; Hos 9:4).[128] An important point to remember is that Paul values the Philippian believers' financial assistance through Epaphroditus and their partnership with him in ministry as a sacrifice (4:14–18). He maintains that their sacrificial financial contribution and their service in partnership to preach the gospel boldly are the results of their faith, and their efforts are more important than his own. Melick states that "[t]he use of this terminology reveals Paul's humility about his own importance. In the ritual, the sacrifice was primary; the drink offering was secondary. If Paul placed himself in the position of the drink offering, he saw their gift as the primary matter and his own circumstances as secondary."[129] Thus in 2:17, Paul humbly counts the efforts of his believers as more important than his own, while in 2:16 he speaks about his desire to boast on "the day of the Lord" about their eternal benefit.

Hence in 2:17b–18, Paul calls for a mutual celebration of sacrifices made to fulfill God's "good purpose" (2:13): "I am glad and rejoice with all of you. So, you too should be glad and rejoice with me." In sacrifices made by faith, there is no room for sorrow or mourning. Paul repeats two words, *chairō* and *sunchairō*, in two sets in 2:17b–18: the first set expresses his own emotion, while the second set exhorts his partners in mission to be of the same mind. Neither his own imprisonment, nor the struggles of the believers in Philippi, is to be viewed negatively, because Paul trusts that God is working in them at all times.

---

128. Hawthorne, *Philippians*, 105.
129. Melick, *Philippians*, 115.

PHILIPPIANS 2:19–30
PAUL'S COMMENDATION OF
THE FELLOW WORKERS

In the ancient Indian education system, disciples lived with their *guru* (master) and learned at his feet. In addition, they served the *guru* in times of need or till his deathbed. In fact, a disciple's faithfulness and gratitude towards his *guru* was measured by the sacrificial service he rendered to the *guru*. Yet only the disciple whom the *guru* loved the most was kept with the *guru* to serve him till the end. A similar story is playing out in the background of 2:19–30. Paul, in his imprisonment, requires the support of Timothy, who is perhaps his most trusted and loved disciple, and Epaphroditus, who is a representative of the Philippian church. They gladly serve Paul in the jail. In fact, at Paul's will, Timothy stays back with him in jail until the final verdict concerning the apostle's future is declared in Rome. Owing to their sacrificial service, Paul commends both and presents them as good models of Christian conduct before the Philippian believers.

According to F. W. Beare, Paul seems to be concluding the letter on a personal note, stating his intention to send Timothy and Epaphroditus to Philippi very soon.[1] However, a closer reading of 2:19–30 suggests that it is placed strategically in the middle of the letter.[2] Paul is not merely stating his plans about the future visit of his companions to the believers in Philippi, but he is also identifying these companions as models of Christlike living, along with the apostle. In fact, their gospel-worthy lifestyles and eagerness to serve others' interests as their priority in ministry sets them apart as legitimate models of imitating Christ (3:17).[3] Stephen Fowl observes that they model the

---

1. F. W. Beare maintains that Paul, in writing 2:19–30, was concluding his letter and had no intention of adding anything further by way of warning and exhortation (*The Epistle to the Philippians*, BNTC, 2nd ed. [London: Adam & Charles Black, 1959], 95).
2. Hansen maintains that the mention of future travel plans, not as part of concluding a letter, is normal for Paul (1 Cor 4:14–21; Gal 4:12–20; 1 Thess 2:17–3:11), with the goal of sending a word of recommendation for his emissary and informing his readers about his plans to undertake a personal visit to them in the near future (*Philippians*, 191, fn. 387, 388). However, T. Y. Mullins sees greater value of the travelogue in the letter and maintains that, in the light of other letters, Paul's talk about future visits is a theme along with other themes ("A Visit Talk in New Testament Letters," *CBQ* 35 [1973]: 350–358).
3. Roji T. George, "'Join Together with Me in Imitating My Example': Reflection on Paul's Call to Imitate in the Letter to the Philippians," in *Bible, Mission, and Theology: A Festschrift in*

teachings Paul imparted in 1:27–2:18 by regularly "attending to the concerns of others above one's own concerns," that is "as manifestations of the specific command to display the practical reasoning found in Christ Jesus (2:5)."[4]

This section can be divided into two parts. First, Paul commends Timothy and plans to send him to Philippi soon (2:19–24). Second, Paul showers words of appreciation on Epaphroditus for his self-sacrificial service. In sending him back, Paul is placing the interests of the Philippians (their joy in seeing him) above his need in the jail (2:25–30).

Timothy is a faithful companion and a spiritual son (2:22) of Paul, and he is mentioned repeatedly in Paul's other letters (2 Cor 1:1; 1 Thess 1:1; compare Acts 16:1–5; 17:14–15; 18:5; 19:22; 20:4). On two occasions in 1 Corinthians, Paul mentions him not merely as his faithful emissary, but rather as the one who is actually "carrying on the work of the Lord, just as I [Paul] am" (1 Cor 16:10). He is a reliable tutor of the way of life lived and preached by Paul (1 Cor 4:17), an encourager of others in faith (1 Thess 3:2), and a valued bearer of reports from churches to Paul (1 Thess 3:6). He is important to Paul because he works without self-interest (2:21), and so Paul depends upon Timothy to serve his believers (compare 2:20).

Similarly, Epaphroditus also embodies important virtues based on the Christ model mentioned in 2:6–11. His name allows us to conclude that he is a gentile convert.[5] We also know that he is a representative of the believers in Philippi who carries a gift to Paul (4:18) and serves him in jail. In 2:25–30, Paul gives two reasons for sending Epaphroditus back to Philippi. First, Paul says that he earnestly desires to see his people in Philippi (2:26). Second, the Philippian believers have heard about Epaphroditus's illness and are anxious. Seeing Epaphroditus safely back among them at the earliest opportunity will surely make them glad (2:26, 28). Further, reading between the lines, we can also see how Paul, as the senior leader, guards the honor of his fellow companion before his people. The heap of praiseworthy terms, such as "my brother, coworker, and fellow soldier" (2:25, which are not used for Timothy), indicate the apostle's farsightedness, care, and provision for this team member. Paul does not express disappointment about the sad turn of events, where Epaphroditus – who came to serve the apostle during his imprisonment – instead requires

---

Honor of Rev. Dr. Simon Samuel, ed. P. V. Joseph (Dehradun: Luther W. New Jr. Theological College/Delhi: ISPCK, 2018), 99–111.
4. Fowl, *Philippians*, 131.
5. Thompson observes that the name is derived from the name of the Greek goddess, Aphrodite, which proves his non-Jewish identity (*Philippians*, 85).

attention, care, and service in order to survive his own serious illness. Rather, Paul appreciates Epaphroditus's devotion and the fact that he risked his life in order to complete the work that was assigned to him (2:30). However, Epaphroditus's illness compels Paul to send him away immediately before hearing about the outcome of Paul's trial in Rome. Hence, Epaphroditus seems to have departed ahead of Timothy, possibly carrying this letter along with him.

2:19–24 COMMENDATION OF TIMOTHY

Speaking about his future plan to send Timothy, Paul speaks with confidence "in the Lord Jesus" (2:19). The Greek word *elpidzō* is generally translated as "I hope," but suggests a high and reasonable level of confidence about things that will happen in the future. Hawthorne deduces that the use of this term in 2:19, when compared with the term used in 2:24 (*pepoitha*, meaning "I am confident") about his own hope to come to them, suggests that Paul sees the possibility of Timothy coming to them as less likely than his own personal visit to them later.[6] However, this conclusion is unnecessary, because Paul hopes "in the Lord Jesus," who is the sovereign Lord (2:11) and directs Paul's future, whether in the ongoing legal course before the emperor or in his missional plans. In this case, Timothy's and Paul's future plans to travel are subject to divine, not human, approval, and this gives Paul confidence about their fulfillment.

The term "soon" (*tacheōs*) in 2:19 implies brevity between two particular events, but not immediacy or swiftness of the action.[7] In the light of the use of the same term *tacheōs* by Paul in 2:23, the two particular events are: (1) the time when Paul comes to know the final verdict that will decide his future in the ongoing case before the emperor, and (2) the time when Timothy will undertake his journey to Philippi. Although Paul is unsure about the outcome of the case, he is hoping for a speedy release from the jail, and so assumes that the duration of the interval will be short.

Paul has two purposes for sending Timothy to Philippi. First, it is for Paul's and the Philippians' mutual benefit, which is implied by the term *kagō* (literally, "I also") in 2:19. When Paul says, "that I *also* may be cheered when I receive news about you," he is implying that the spirit of the Philippians will be cheered when they get the actual report about Paul's condition in jail. In other words, Timothy's travel to Philippi is mutually enriching for both Paul

---

6. BDAG, 319.
7. BDAG, 992.

and his mission partners, the believers in Philippi. Hansen observes that Paul's concern for the church would have the effect of persuading the believers to be united in one spirit and mind (2:2), because by that alone can they bring joy to the apostle, who is a bit wary about the disharmony among them.[8]

Second, in 2:20–21, Timothy's unique quality of showing genuine concern for the welfare of others makes him best suited as Paul's emissary. Underlining this in 2:20, Paul concedes, "I have no one else like him," using the adjective *isopsychos* ("equal soul"). This is not an absolute statement about Timothy being unique among all others, for the adjective *isopsychos* ("equal soul") does not reflect Timothy's uniqueness from every other person, but that he has feelings in common with Paul, or "likemindedness *with Paul*,"[9] and therefore for the believers in Philippi.[10] This statement authorizes Timothy to speak and act with authority on behalf of Paul because he knows the mind of Paul better than anyone else concerning the Philippian believers.[11] In a community struggling with strife and discord, Timothy, Paul's spiritual son (compare 2:23), understands Paul's heart for their unity. The believers can depend on Timothy's role in securing their communal well-being by inculcating the one mind of Christ among them (John 17:20–21). From his initial mission trip to Philippi (Acts 16), Timothy has suffered along with Paul, and the Philippian believers have witnessed this and know that his loyalty and filial bonding with Paul has never diminished. Thus Paul appeals to their personal knowledge of this relationship, saying, "you know that Timothy has proved himself, because as a son with his father he has served with me in the work of the gospel" (2:22). Even at present, Timothy's willingness to go on behalf of Paul to Philippi amidst a difficult situation reflects his dedication to serve with Paul in the work of the gospel.

However, in 2:21, Paul appears to be contrasting others uncharitably with Timothy's importance in mission: "For everyone looks out for their own interest, not those of Jesus Christ." Paul's words are difficult to interpret with confidence without actual knowledge about the situation in Rome at that time. We are unsure about whom Paul is speaking in these words. Philemon 23–24 and Colossians 4:10, 14 inform us that, during Paul's imprisonment in Rome, Luke, Aristarchus, Epaphras, and Mark were with him. So is Paul referring to these close associates or the larger community in Rome? Does Paul, in order to commend his favorite (i.e., Timothy), become uncharitable

---

8. Hansen, *Philippians*, 194.
9. Silva, *Philippians*, WEC, 158.
10. Compare BDAG, 481.
11. Compare Hawthorne, *Philippians*, 194.

Philippians 2:19–30

towards his other fellow companions or believers in Rome? Most likely, Paul is not referring to his close companions because, despite other letters that give the impression that they were present with Paul in prison, the absence of any mention of them along with Timothy in Paul's greetings to the Philippian readers suggests their absence from the jail at this time. It is probable that they were busy tending mission in some other place. It also seems highly unlikely that Paul has become uncharitable towards his friends in Rome. In 1:14 and 4:21–22, Paul mentions that these companions have been emboldened to preach Christ because of his chains (1:14).

However, this does not resolve the problem of identifying those who appear to act out of selfish interest rather than the interest of Jesus Christ in 2:21. A general consensus among scholars, though not conclusive or without problems, is that Paul is contrasting Timothy's concern for the well-being of his readers with those who have been preaching Jesus Christ out of envy and wrong motives (1:15).[12] However, Hendrickson maintains that Paul's reference to his "first defense" (2 Tim 4:16), during which he was deserted by all, surely connects with the "first imprisonment of Paul" in Rome, and so those who are acting out of selfish interests are those who "offered excuses or upon further reflection were simply dismissed from the apostle's mind as spiritually unqualified."[13] Hence, Paul's reference to "everyone" is not all-encompassing in Rome, but is limited to some who either deserted Paul or were unwilling to share Paul's concern for the believers in Philippi. For Paul, their unwillingness to prioritize others' interests above their own is selfish and does not reflect the concerns of Jesus Christ (2:3, 6–8). Hence, in 2:23, Paul repeats his intention to send Timothy to them as early as possible after hearing how things go for him in Rome.

Even so, in 2:24, Paul expresses his complete assurance that what happens in Rome will not hinder him from visiting them. Paul emphasizes his personal visit, saying, "*I myself* will come soon," indicating the gravity of the issue that cannot be left to Timothy alone to handle. Paul expresses even greater confidence about his visit, using the word *pepoitha*, meaning "I am confident," to convey his complete trust in the Lord (from 2:19) so that certain quarreling, selfish believers in Philippi will not take his words or Timothy, his emissary, lightly. Just like his hope "in the Lord" (2:19) who directs everything, including Timothy's visit, Paul is even more confident that his personal dilemma

---

12. Fowl, *Philippians*, 133; Hansen, *Philippians*, 195.
13. Hendrickson, *Philippians*, 135–136.

(1:20–24) concerning the final outcome of the legal procedure in Rome will not hinder the divine initiative in guaranteeing his freedom very soon. Paul's choice of words here contributes to his authoritative demand for an appropriate pattern of behavior in their corporate life.

2:25–30 COMMENDATION OF EPAPHRODITUS

In many Asian societies, including India, the divide between the sacred and secular is well-defined, and the practice of spirituality and service to God is specifically ritualistic in nature. In contrast, Paul commends his fellow workers, Timothy and Epaphroditus, as authentic models who emanate Christian virtues, and so in some sense, he sees their sacrificial service and genuine concern for others as a spiritual service. After endorsing Timothy, the apostle proceeds to guard the honor of his fellow companion, Epaphroditus, who is being sent back on account of his serious illness. A careful reading of this short section allows us to see Paul's farsighted, compassionate, mature leader's heart for a vulnerable member of the team who may be misunderstood by others.

In 2:25, Paul begins by stating the circumstances that are forcing him to send Epaphroditus back to Philippi. Paul delayed Timothy's travel to Philippi and chose to send Epaphroditus first, who was sent to serve him in his need (2:25). Based on 2:26, Paul's words, "it is necessary," are often understood to imply a circumstantial compulsion arising out of Epaphroditus's intense (and not entirely appropriate) desire to return.[14] On that basis, it is argued that Paul speaks highly of him in an attempt to limit his loss of honor in the eyes of the Philippian believers. But such a reconstruction of the situation is unnecessary and indeed irreconcilable with Paul's extraordinarily positive commendation of Epaphroditus, where there is not even a hint of failure. Rather, Paul appears to be fully satisfied with his efforts in accomplishing his mission. A more justified assumption would be that Paul understands the concerns of both the believers in Philippi and Epaphroditus because of his serious illness (2:36, 28) and therefore is confident that it is right to send him back in good spirit and with full respect. In 2:26, Paul uses the same word (*epipothōn*, literally meaning "longing after") to describe Epaphroditus's longing as he uses in 1:8 to describe his own longing for the Philippians.

In support of the decision to send Epaphroditus back, Paul says, "[b]ut *I* think" (2:25 emphasis added). Then he employs three important terms to

---

14. Hawthorne, *Philippians*, 115.

define his relationship with Epaphroditus: "my brother, coworker, and fellow soldier" (2:25). The pronoun "my" indicates his personal relationship with Epaphroditus and the closeness Paul felt with him. First, as a leader, Paul uses the familial term "brother" to describe other team members elsewhere (Timothy in 1 Thess 3:2 and also "child" in 1 Cor 4:17; Tychicus in Col 4:7 and Eph 6:21). This term reflects the spiritual bonding that characterizes their relationship, for they now belong to the same family of God.

Second, Paul uses the term "coworker" for those who partner with him in spreading the gospel.[15] He treats his fellow workers as being on an equal footing with him in God's mission. Hawthorne assumes that this term signifies that Epaphroditus had a role alongside Paul in founding the church in Philippi. Though this is possible, we do not have any positive evidence to prove it within the text.[16] Paul's wording may simply reflect his positive disposition towards Epaphroditus because of the sacrificial service he rendered to Paul (2:30), despite his physical weaknesses. Whether Paul knew him earlier or not, it is evident that his sacrificial service qualifies him as a minister of God equal to the apostle of Christ.

Third, the term "fellow soldier" is used rarely. Here, Paul employs this military term to characterize their common mission amidst conflict. Paul is imprisoned in Rome (1:13), while Epaphroditus belongs to a community in Philippi that is facing opponents of the gospel (1:29), and he has also suffered nearly to death, similar to a soldier in accomplishing his mission on a battlefield (2:27). Fowl is right in observing that by addressing Epaphroditus as a "fellow soldier," especially in the Roman colony of Philippi, Paul draws a contrast between the soldiers of God and those of Caesar.[17] Although soldiers of God may suffer at present, they belong to the army of him who is the sovereign Lord (2:11). Judge's study on the origin and meaning of the term "Christian," meaning "the soldiers of Christ" among Latin-speaking Syrian Antiochians,[18] suggests that the residents of Philippi, a Latinized Roman colony, would have understood the gravity of the designation. Such a highly prized contextual accolade might have highlighted their disciplined lifestyle "worthy of the gospel" (1:27), their willingness to suffer unto death in the mission of God, and

---

15. Georg Bertram, "συνεργός," *TDNT* 7:871–876.
16. Hawthorne, *Philippians*, 116.
17. Fowl, *Philippians*, 135.
18. Edward A. Judge, "Judaism and the Rise of Christianity: A Roman Perspective," *TynBul* 45 (1994): 362–366. See David G. Horrell, "The Label Χριστιανός: 1 Peter 4:16 and the Formation of Christian Identity," *JBL* 126 (2007): 362–367; Thomas Scott Caulley, "The Title *Christianos* and Roman Imperial Cult," *ResQ* 53 (2011): 194.

their devotion to a self-sacrificial life for the sake of others (1:20–23; 2:17, 27). These are the same virtues that Paul demonstrated personally before the Philippian believers in jail (1:12–28) and exhorted them to practice diligently (1:27–2:18).

Further, the additional two terms, "apostle" and "minister" (2:25), explain Epaphroditus's designation in relation to the Philippian community. The former, *Apostolos* ("apostle" or "messenger") (2:25), is not used in a technical sense to refer to an office, as it is used in later ecclesiastical tradition, but it refers to Epaphroditus's position as the official representative of the church in Philippi from whom he was commissioned to carry gifts to Paul (4:18) and to stay with him and serve him in his need (2:25, 30). Hawthorne contends that Paul uses this term to signify that Epaphroditus is both "being commissioned and sent out with full authority to perform specific tasks of service,"[19] but this is not convincing. Earlier, writing to the Corinthian believers (2 Cor 8:23), Paul uses "apostles" in a non-technical sense. But there is an important difference between Paul and Epaphroditus, for Paul says that he has been appointed by God to be an apostle (Gal 1:1), whereas Epaphroditus has been sent on the mission by humans. The act of being sent by someone is not sufficient to defend Hawthorne's contention.

The latter term, *leitourgos* ("minister" in 2:25), is also used in a religious context in the LXX (Joel 1:9, 13; 2:17; Neh 10:37; Num 4:41; 16:9). In the NT, it is used with religious connotation in Luke 1:23 and Hebrews 10:11 and to refer to the resurrected Christ in Hebrews 8:2. Paul uses the term in relation to his own divine appointment to preach the gospel among the gentiles in Romans 15:16, further qualifying his ministry as a "priestly duty." Nevertheless, *leitourgos* is also used in the LXX (2 Sam 13:18; 1 Kgs 10:5; Sir 10:2) to describe a person functioning in public office. Within Paul's letters, the term is used for the secular rulers (Rom 13:6). Paul's use of this term for Epaphroditus is important, since he was not sent by the church to perform, in technical sense, a priestly religious duty or to function in a public office. Rather, he was sent "to take care of my [Paul's] needs" (2:25) and to bear the gifts from the Philippians to the apostle (4:18). However, because Epaphroditus is risking his life through his service, he is ministering like a priest in the Jewish temple. Dunn's observation is vital here, for he maintains that, by using the word for the secular rulers in Romans 13:6, Paul is making an effort to break

---

19. Hawthorne, *Philippians*, 117.

the barrier between sacred and secular services.[20] Duties that are performed in God's name and in fear of God as a servant are performed as a *leitourgos*. After all, the ideal in executing responsibilities, even within a household, is to do them as if unto the Lord (Col 3:17, 23). When we carry out any duty in a God-oriented manner, we are ministers of God.

In 2:26, Paul mentions the reason for sending Epaphroditus back. Though Epaphroditus is in distress and longs to see his people in Philippi, who are facing opposition, his strong emotional distress does not reflect negatively on his maturity to face difficulty away from his native city. However, both the terms together imply "a persistent continuation" in "homesickness and in mental distress."[21] While Paul uses the word *epipothōnēn* (*epipothein* means "long for, desire") previously in 1:8 to describe his longing to see his loved ones in Philippi, the term *adēmonōn* (*adēmonein* means "be in anxiety, be distressed") explains the gravity of Epaphroditus's mental tension which is as similar as to the experience of Jesus in Gethsemane (Matt 26:37; Mark 14:33). According to Paul, the reason for Epaphroditus's emotional distress is because the believers in Philippi have come to know about his illness. We do not know how the Philippian believers have come to know about it or whether their distress is caused, on the one hand, by their concern about Epaphroditus's physical condition, or, on the other, by their complaint against him for failing to fulfill their mission.[22] The former feeling is natural if his illness was serious and prolonged, and it explains why Paul is sending him back with great regard for his sacrificial service. However, if the latter condition is assumed, there is an apologetic motive for Paul's commendation of Epaphroditus. The former appears to be closer to the actual condition, because Paul does not express dissatisfaction about the service rendered by Epaphroditus. In 2:29, Paul says that he believes Epaphroditus's safe return will make his sending community glad.

Paul reiterates the extreme physical condition that Epaphroditus suffered and recognizes God's mercy in saving his life (2:27) without mentioning the manner in which he was healed. Hansen is insightful in emphasizing the God-centered miracle of experiencing divine mercy in healing. Earnest prayers offered by the apostle and others for the restoration of his health are immaterial compared with God's mercy.[23] The apostle's double-mention of Epaphroditus's

---

20. J. D. G. Dunn, *Romans 9–16*, WBC 38B (Dallas: Word Books, 1988), 764.
21. Hawthorne, *Philippians*, 117.
22. For various interpretations about the prevailing condition at that time, see Hansen, *Philippians*, 204, fn. 443.
23. Hansen, 205.

closeness to death (2:27, 30) highlights the severity of his illness. His earnest longing to rejoin his people in Philippi is the result of his physical condition and not *vice versa*. The striking feature of Epaphroditus's life, which he shares with Jesus and Paul, is his willingness to risk his life to serve the interests of others. Paul continuously teaches the believers in Philippi to aim for such a lifestyle within the community (2:1–18). Earlier, Paul mentions Jesus, who took on human likeness and became obedient unto death on the cross in order to save sinful humanity. Even Epaphroditus's own willingness to die for the benefit of the believers is visible in his self-sacrificial, missional lifestyle. Paul's hope that the believers in Philippi will seek to have the mind of Christ and live in unity is expressed in the life of Epaphroditus. This makes him an authentic model for imitation, along with Jesus and Paul, so that the Philippian believers will become more like Jesus (notice "us" in 3:17b).

For Paul, the outpouring of God's mercy is experienced not only by Epaphroditus but also by himself, for he says, "[b]ut God had mercy on him, and not on him only but also on me, to spare me sorrow upon sorrow" (2:27). Paul's insistence within the letter to rejoice in every circumstance in life (2:18; 3:1; 4:4) is counterbalanced here. The exhortation to rejoice in the Lord does not mean to be immune to the pain and suffering of others. Christian living is not blind towards other members in the body of Christ. Instead, when one lives a Christlike life, prioritizing others' interests above one's own, then it is praiseworthy to experience sorrow on behalf of others. Paul's confession that God's mercy has spared him from "sorrow upon sorrow" suggests successive waves of sorrow beating against his life. Although he does not view his imprisonment as a sorrowful experience, Epaphroditus's near-death experience of illness caused much heartache in the apostle, for Epaphroditus risked his life to serve him. For Paul, Epaphroditus's death would have shaken his inner tranquility, something which his own suffering in the jail for Christ has not caused.

In 2:28, Paul begins with "Therefore" (*ouv*), implying that the experience of God's mercy in healing Epaphroditus spared Paul from more sorrow, which now necessitates Epaphroditus's return to Philippi. As Hawthorne observes, this may be a sudden reversal of the original plan to send Epaphroditus to join the apostle's team permanently, but in Paul's evaluation, his return is now inevitable. He must return to Philippi as early as possible, which implies urgency. The past tense verb in Greek, *epempsa* ("I sent," aorist), can be taken as an epistolary tense (assuming that Epaphroditus was the bearer of the letter), which means that the aorist (past tense) is being used from the readers' perspective (as the present action the author describes will be passed by the time they receive and read it).[24] For Paul, sending Epaphroditus back has two benefits (in 2:28).

First, it will make the believers in Philippi glad (*palin charēte*) to see their emissary return safely after his illness. They will be able to rejoice again in the mercy of God for restoring Epaphroditus to life. According to Hansen, this joy "is God-centered; rejoicing in Paul's theology is praise for God's mercy and delight in God's presence."[25] In fact, the manifestation of God's mercy in each other's lives is the true reason for us to be glad and to praise God. In addition, Paul's character as a Christlike leader is revealed here, for he seeks the gladness of his beloved people in Philippi above his own need to have Epaphroditus serve him in jail. For that, Timothy can be retained in Rome, but not Epaphroditus, since his illness has made the Philippian believers anxious.

Second, Paul himself will be "less anxious" about Epaphroditus, because his family members and fellow believers in Philippi will be able to give him the necessary care. In fact, the word *alupos*, meaning "free from anxiety," refers to doing away with anxiety one has in the present.[26] Paul's anxiety is connected with his concerns for the believers in Philippi and Epaphroditus's well-being. Their suffering and sorrow aggravated his anxiety, but it can now be relieved, since he is able to give them a reason to rejoice in the mercy of God because of the miraculous healing of Epaphroditus from his near-death experience.

Having given the Philippians ample reasons and explanations for the circumstances for Epaphroditus's return to Philippi, Paul commands them to receive Epaphroditus with great joy in 2:29. With apostolic authority, he uses an imperative verb, meaning "welcome" (*prosdechesthe*), in order to restrict any complaints about Epaphroditus's unplanned return as a failure of the original mission. Thereby, this command also secures the peaceful return of his brother and fellow-worker (2:25) to Philippi. The manner of welcome that Epaphroditus deserves, having "almost died for the work of Christ" (2:30), is not to be measured according to the standards of the world. He must be received and honored "in the Lord" (2:29). Though "in the Lord" could have various interpretations, the most relevant understanding in this context would be to receive him as a Christian brother in the community of God, as they all share in the same spiritual locale (i.e., "*in* the Lord," emphasis added). Their preparation, attitude, and joy in welcoming Epaphroditus ought to be congruent with their existence in the Lord.

---

24. Hawthorne, *Philippians*, 118–119.
25. Hansen, *Philippians*, 207.
26. BDAG, 48.

In 2:30, Paul says that Epaphroditus must receive a warm welcome because he has risked his life for "the work of Christ" to help Paul on behalf of the Philippian believers in ways that they could not do in person. If Epaphroditus was originally intended to be a permanent member of Paul's team, representing the Philippian church by serving him while in jail, then the unexpected sudden return could be interpreted as a partial failure of the mission. However, Paul does not quantify Epaphroditus's service by measuring it according to the length of his duration or the variety of services he has rendered. Rather, the apostle is more interested in the quality of his service, which is visible in his self-sacrificial devotion to the entrusted task of carrying their gift to him at any cost. Hence, Paul ends his commendation by repeating the word *leitourgia*, a term used earlier (2:17) to describe the faithful service of the Philippian believers. In 2:30, he uses this same term to describe their help to Paul through the sacrificial service of Epaphroditus.

PHILIPPIANS 3:1–4:1
EXHORTATION TO BE CHRIST-FOCUSED

A pluralistic religious context presents many challenges to Christian believers on a daily basis, whether in Roman Philippi or India. In countries such as India, it can become difficult for Christians to resist religious ideas, values, and assumptions that have been imported from their pre-Christian religion and culture, even if they are contrary to the standards of the gospel. For example, in spite of the teaching about the sufficiency of Christ for our salvation, we don't consider all earthly pedigrees appropriated by birth completely irrelevant in our daily Christian living. Our general tendency is to seek ways to accommodate the two together. Paul launches a strong attack against such accommodations among the Philippians (i.e., adherence to Jewish law combined with faith in Christ Jesus).

Unlike the rest of the letter, Paul allows his emotion to dominate his rhetoric in 3:1–4:1. Through a variety of literary tools, he cautions the believers in Philippi about the danger lying close to them while verbally abusing his opponents ("the dogs," "evil doers," and "those mutilators of the flesh," 3:2). Adding strength to his persuasion, according to Hawthorne, Paul uses a number of figures of speech, including: (1) anaphora, adding emphasis through repetition (e.g., the use of *blepete*, meaning "look out for" or "watch for," in three consecutive clauses), (2) paronomasia, juxtaposing similar sounding words with opposite meanings to evoke stark contrast (e.g., *peritomē/katatomēn* or circumcised/mutilator), (3) polysyndeton, making quick successive use of the same conjunction (e.g., *kai,* meaning "and"), (4) alliteration, starting words with same consonants in Greek, and (5) chiasmus, presenting ideas or concepts in reverse order for a rhetorical purpose.[1] These figures of speech flow naturally out of Paul and do not break his flow of thought, but strengthen the rhetorical effect of his words in persuading his audience.

Further, the connection between Philippians 3:1–4:1 and the preceding section remains in the eye of contentious debate because some scholars in the past have argued that 3:1–21 is a remnant of a later letter that was interpolated here at an editorial stage.[2] Initially, the reason for this argument was the use of

---

1. Hawthorne, *Philippians*, 123.
2. Beare, *Philippians*, 100–141, maintains that 3:2–21 is a later interpolation (Letter B). The original letter continues after 3:1 at 4:2–9 (Letter A). He generally maintains a three-letter

to loipon, translated as "further" (NIV), in 3:1a. Yet it is not clear whether 3:1 should be treated as a concluding remark for 1:27–2:30 or an introductory remark for 3:2–4:1. If taken as a concluding remark for 1:27–2:30, then *to loipon* in 3:1a, translated as "finally," would be introducing the command to "rejoice in the Lord!" (3:1b). "[R]ejoice in the Lord" is a recurrent theme of exhortation to a persecuted community struggling to survive at multiple levels (i.e., against internal strife, division, and external violent opposition). For those who contend against the literary integrity of the letter, this position is natural and logical. However, recent discussions consider *to loipon* in 3:1a as an introduction to a new theme or section (compare 1 Thess 4:1).[3] In this case, 3:1–4:1 is seen as a further elaboration of the earlier themes.

Philippians 3:1–4:1 connects with Paul's assertion in 1:28 (that they should be fearless while facing those who oppose them) by asking the believers to conduct themselves according to the gospel, as he has demonstrated in his own preaching and life.[4] They ought to pay attention to what they believe (the message of the mutilators vs. the gospel preached by Paul), to who teaches them the gospel (false teachers vs. Paul who is modeling Jesus Christ, 3:2–3, 15–19), and to their identity as citizens of heaven (3:20). Moreover, several vital words are used in 3:1–4:1 that are also found in 1:27–2:30. For example, as Thompson lists, the terms and ideas that link chapters 2 and 3 include: "glory" (2:11; compare 3:19, 21); "earthly" (2:10; compare 3:19), "heavenly" (2:10; compare 3:20), "be found" (2:7; compare 3:9), "regard" (2:3, 6, 25; compare 3:7, 8), "death" (2:8; compare 3:10), "Lord Jesus Christ" (2:11; compare 3:8), and "take" (2:7; compare 3:12, 13).[5]

Further, concerning the literary structure of 3:1–4:1, Thompson maintains that 3:2–3 and 18–21 form an *inclusio* for 3:4–17, cautioning the audience concerning the false teachers. While 3:2 and 18–19 speak about the false

---

hypothesis (with Letter Cat 4:10–20). Beare, *Philippians*, 1–5. In contrast, others uphold the literary integrity of the letter, including: Loveday Alexander, "Hellenistic Letter-Forms and the Structure of Philippians," *JSNT* 37 (1989): 87–101; David E. Garland, "The Composition and Unity of Philippians: Some Neglected Literary Factors," *NovT* 27 (1985): 141–173; Robert Jewett, "The Epistolary Thanksgiving and the Integrity of Philippians," *NovT* 12 (1970): 43–53; William J. Dalton, "The Integrity of Philippians," *Biblica* 60 (1979): 97–102. A similar conclusion upholding the literary integrity of Philippians through rhetorical analysis is maintained by Watson, "A Rhetorical Analysis of Philippians," 57–88. Some argue for a two-letter hypothesis (Letter A: 1:1–3:1a; [4:2–7]; 4:10–23; Letter B: 3:1b–4:1, 8–9); see John T. Fitzgerald, "Philippians, Epistle of the," *ABD* 5:321.
3. Fowl, *Philippians*, 143–144; Thompson, *Philippians*, 90–92. Thompson states that the word "finally" "can either be a closing formula or a transitional particle (92).
4. Watson, "A Rhetorical Analysis of Philippians," 76.
5. Thompson, *Philippians*, 92.

teachers (i.e., their anti-cross lifestyles and selfish goals), Paul uses "we" in 3:3, including himself with his audience and identifying them as citizens of heaven (3:20–21).[6] By this *inclusio*, Paul contrasts the two.[7] If so, Paul's autobiographical statements in 3:4–17 must be read in the light of the *inclusio*. These autobiographical statements play an important role in dissuading his audience from following false teachers. He presents himself (and others who "live as we do," 3:17) as the right model for following Christ.

Thus, the literary structure of Philippians 3:1–4:1 may be identified as follows. First, intentionally repeating himself, Paul cautions the Philippian believers concerning the false teachers who contradict the true identity of the Christians in Philippi (3:1–3). Second, Paul counts his every fleshly credential as loss in order to gain Christ. Paul confesses his tireless persistence in pressing on to know Christ (3:4–14). Third, with the goal of winning the prize on the last day, every mature Christian ought to join Paul in following the example of Jesus Christ (3:15–17). Fourth, Paul contrasts the bad models destined to doom with those who join him in imitating Christ's example as the citizens of heaven (3:18–4:1).

3:1–3 BEWARE OF FALSE MODELS AND THEIR TEACHING

The new section in 3:1 begins abruptly. Although the larger literary integrity of the letter seems undeniable, the sudden shift here in tone, topic, and theme is puzzling to some. Paul begins the section with *to loipon*, which is often translated as "finally," suggesting that it is the end of a section (see 2 Cor 13:11; Phil 4:8). However, Paul also uses *to loipon* elsewhere to indicate a shift to a new topic (see 1 Thess 4:1, 2; 2 Thess 3:1). In this context, the phrase must be rendered as "beyond that, in addition," indicating a transition to a new topic.[8] However, in 3:1c, Paul says: "It is not trouble for me to write the same thing to you again and it is a safeguard for you." Reed, reading this in its Hellenistic context, argues that this is merely an "epistolary hesitation formula." For him, it functions as a transitional device with a specific function and form within a literary piece.[9] This transitional phrase suggests that the apostle considered the topic very important to him, and so he does not hesitate to repeat himself. But

---

6. Thompson, 90.
7. Thompson, 90.
8. BDAG, 602–603.
9. Jeffery T. Reed, "Philippians 3:1 and the Epistolary Hesitation Formulas: The Literary Integrity of Philippians, Again," *JBL* 115 (1996): 63–90.

what does he not hesitate to repeat? According to Fowl, in the light of earlier references to "rejoice" (1:18; 2:17–18, 28, 29) and its repetition in 3:1b, Paul is referring to his command to "rejoice."[10] They ought to rejoice like Paul, who rejoices in the jail (1:4, 18; 2:18), but they must also pay careful attention to his earlier instructions (3:18), which are repeated now in 3:2–21, regarding the false teachers.[11] Thus, the content that he repeats is his command to rejoice in the Lord, just as he does in jail, without being intimidated by the hostile environment, while also beware of false teachers and their ill-intentions. After all, Paul is convinced that his exhortation will "safeguard" the Philippians.

Throughout the letter, Paul repeatedly exhorts the believers to "rejoice" (2:18; 3:1; 4:4), as it is the best response amidst persecution and suffering. As O'Brien maintains, this is not a superficial cheerfulness out of blindness to the prevailing environment, but rather a positive calculation of the future with a complete trust that God is at work to bring about his absolute purpose, including the advancement of the gospel despite persecution and suffering.[12] Interestingly, this is the only specific location where Paul commands the believers to rejoice "in the Lord" (3:1; compare 4:10). While the command to rejoice might be a culturally colored, friendly refrain[13] rather than a farewell expression,[14] it does remind the believers that their existence is in the sovereign Lord (2:11; 4:1), the sole basis of their hope (2:19), confidence (1:14; 2:24), and salvation (3:20–21). In 4:1, Paul commands them to "stand firm in the Lord." For Paul, the risen Lord is the mystical space for the believers' spiritual existence and the ground for their corporate union.[15]

In 3:2, Paul is deeply troubled about his opponents, and his writing is full of invective and sarcasm. We can discern elsewhere in his letters (compare Gal 5:12; 2 Cor 11:13–15) that these opponents have consistently followed Paul in his mission, teaching the gentile converts things that were contradictory to the gospel of Christ, influencing it coercively with their Jewish cultural elements and their cultural imperialistic agenda. Thus for Paul, they "masquerade as servants of righteousness" (2 Cor 11:15).

---

10. Fowl, *Philippians*, 144.
11. Thompson, *Philippians*, 105; Fee, *Philippians*, NICNT, 293.
12. O'Brien, *Philippians*, 349.
13. Hansen, *Philippians*, 213.
14. Beare translates 3:1a as "Finally, my brethren, I bid you farewell in the Lord" (*Philippians*, 142). Contra. Reed, "Philippians 3:1 and the Epistolary Hesitation Formulas," 63–90.
15. O'Brien, *Philippians*, 350.

Hence, as part of his rhetoric in 3:2, Paul repeats *blepete*, a Greek imperative meaning "consider, note,"[16] thrice in quick succession. Literally, in Greek, Paul says, "Consider those dogs, consider those evildoers, consider those mutilators," repetition that emphasizes the need to be careful. The imperative must be understood as bringing something to someone's attention,[17] whereas the traditional translation of the word, "watch, look to, beware of," requires it to be "followed by an objective clause introduced by *mē* . . . or by the preposition *apo*."[18] Paul intends to make them aware of the danger lying close to them in false teachers so that they can identify them properly.

Paul employs three oppositional though somewhat ambiguous terms to define the opponents: *tous kynas* ("dogs"), *tous kakous ergatas* ("evildoers"), and *tēn katatomēn* (literally, "the mutilation"). The first two don't reveal anything specific about the opponents' identity, but the last surely points towards their Jewishness. Among Jews, it was common to call the gentiles *kynas* ("dogs," compare Mark 7:27) with contempt, because they were considered impure and defiled.[19] Paul's opponents, by enforcing circumcision (i.e., their Jewishness) upon these gentiles, were seeking to assimilate them into Jewish culture. Thereby, they strictly differentiated themselves from the gentiles. Such actions would speak louder than words to pronounce the gentile believers within the church as "dogs."[20] But Paul returns his opponents' words to them defining who they are really.

Similarly, he calls them *tous kakous ergatas* ("evildoers") because he sees them as cultural imperialists whose primary mission is to assimilate the gentile Christians into Jewish culture rather than Christ. Paul considers their reliance upon their cultural deeds as self-righteous, which is evil, because they are holding people back from the righteousness that comes by faith (3:9), leading them to boast "in the flesh" rather than "in Christ" (3:3). Hence, for Paul, they are "evildoers" of whom the believers in Philippi need to be cautious.

Their identity as "evildoers" is closely related to their practice of circumcision, for Paul calls them "mutilators of the flesh" (3:2). *Katatomē*, which can be translated as "mutilators," a term that Paul coins,[21] "is a sarcastic twist on the significance of circumcision: circumcision, the sign of the Jewish covenant,

---

16. BDAG, 179.
17. BDAG, 179.
18. Hawthorne, *Philippians*, 124–125 (Greek transliterated).
19. Otto Michel, "κυών," *TDNT* 3:1101–1104; Ryan, "The Reversal of Rhetoric," 68–70.
20. Hansen, *Philippians*, 219; Ryan, "The Reversal of Rhetoric," 70.
21. Thompson, *Philippians*, 105.

has not more value than mutilation if it replaces faith in Christ as the basis of belonging to the people of God."²² In the first century, circumcision formed part of the Jewish cultural identity,²³ but unlike its spiritual meaning in the OT (Deut 10:16; Jer 4:4), Paul valued it, not as the physical mark borne in one's body, but as the reality of inner-transformation experienced in a repentant human heart (Rom 2:28–29). In other words, Paul's objection to the emphasis on circumcision in the teachings of his opponents is primarily due to its lack of spiritual dimension and its self-righteousness based on Jewish law. This self-righteousness led Paul's opponents to claim ethnocentric superiority as possessors of the law and encouraged a Jew versus gentile hierarchy within the body of Christ. For Paul, such a divisive, ethnocentric, and law-based gospel of righteousness is incompatible with the all-inclusive, universal, and faith-based gospel of righteousness in Christ.

Thus in 3:3, Paul gives reasons for his caution to the believers against the false teachers. Paul finds their mistaken claims contradictory to the true Christian identity. Thus 3:3 is Paul's most important assertion, and his words of caution in 3:2 only provide a dark background against which Paul wants to reconstruct Christian identity. He says, "*we* who are the circumcision" (3:3, emphasis added), making "we" (*hēmeis*) intentionally emphatic. Later in 3:20, there is an emphasis on "*our* citizenship is in heaven" (emphasis added), and together these verses form a parenthesis around 3:4–19, which state Paul's autobiographical background, personal ambition, and the call to imitate his model in following Christ. This teaching constructs the true identity of the Philippian believers "in Christ." Paul's purpose is to open their spiritual eyes so that they, gentile Christians in Philippi, along with Paul, a Jewish Christian, can together create the true community of Christ.

The flip side of the assertion, "we are the circumcision," is that the gentile Christians are not required to undergo the circumcision rite, something that was insistently taught by Paul's opponents in Philippi. The believers in Philippi already share in the grace of God just like Paul, a Jew (1:7), in becoming children of God (2:14). God is at work among them constantly (1:6; 2:13). In

---

22. Hansen, *Philippians*, 219.
23. J. D. G. Dunn, "The New Perspective on Paul," in *Jesus, Paul and the Law: Studies in Mark and Galatians* (London: SPCK/Louisville: Westminster John Knox, 1990), 192, 196. Elsewhere, Dunn states that "[t]he basic point is that *circumcision was inextricably bound up with Jewish identity*, that is, with the identity of the Jews as the people of Israel, the people chosen by God from among all the other nations to be his own." J. D. G. Dunn, "'Neither Circumcision nor Uncircumcision, but . . . ,'" in *The New Perspective on Paul*, rev. ed. (Grand Rapids: Eerdmans, 2005), 315 (emphasis added).

contrast, the physical mark of circumcision among the Jews symbolized their covenantal status,[24] the basis of their claim to religious superiority, and their articulation of ethnocentric cultural identity in the first-century context. But for Paul, believers founded "in Christ" (3:1) do not need to fulfill this ritualistic requirement in the flesh because they are inwardly circumcised (i.e., in their heart, Rom 2:27–28) and already practice this "circumcision" (morally) by shining amidst a warped and crooked generation "like stars in the sky" (2:15). This inward circumcision contrasts with Israel, which failed both ethically and missionally to shine like stars among the gentiles and therefore did not fulfill the original schema of divine will. Thus circumcision is actualized in its true spirit by those who, united in Christ, live a life worthy of the gospel of Christ (compare 1:27).

In three subsequent participle phrases in 3:3, Paul precisely states how the believers in Philippi are the circumcised: (1) "we who *serve* God by his Spirit," (2) "who *boast* in Christ Jesus," and (3) "who *put no confidence* in the flesh" (emphasis added).

First, by saying, "we who serve God by his Spirit," Paul is referring to the spiritual function of those who are internally circumcised. The participle word "serve" (*latreuontas*) is specifically employed within the LXX and Christian writings for "the carrying out of religious duties, especially of a cultic nature, by human beings" (Exod 23:25; Josh 22:27).[25] According to Fee, the word is being used here ironically to contrast with 3:2, where the "mutilators" are engaged in something that was prohibited to those functioning within the temple system. Thereby, their engagement in the illegitimate function disqualifies them. He says, "[t]he verb, therefore, . . . represents the 'service' of God's people in terms of their devotion to him as evidenced in the way they live before him . . . [meaning] the true circumcision live (= 'serve') in Christ by the power of the Spirit."[26] This is coherent with Paul's repeated appeal to the believers in Philippi to have the mind of Christ, prioritizing the interests of others before their own (2:3–4).

However, a broader application of the term is much more relevant here, which includes the role of the Spirit in both formal worship and daily living. Jesus told the Samaritan woman at the well that the one who worships God,

---

24. Dunn, "'Neither Circumcision nor Uncircumcision, but . . . ,'" 316.
25. BDAG, 587.
26. Fee, *Philippians*, NICNT, 300 (brackets added). Contra. Thompson, *Philippians*, 106. Thompson understands the term *latreuontas* to mean "worshipping." Thus, for him, it refers to a worshipping response of believers to God in the Spirit.

who is Spirit, must worship him in Spirit and truth (John 4:19–24). In Romans 12:1, Paul employs the same term to speak about a spiritual form of worship that includes ethical living.

Further, the Philippians' life of service is energized by the Spirit of God. Paul's dative rendering of the Spirit, *pneumati*, followed by the genitive "of God" is vital for understanding both the nature and sphere of our living. *Pneumati* is used here in an instrumental sense ("by the Spirit"). The Spirit enables believers in Christ to fulfill God's will (Gal 5:16–25; Rom 8:1–11). Hansen observes that, in contrast to the teaching of his opponents, Paul's usage can be better understood in his own theology. For example, in Galatians, the presence of the Spirit not only characterizes the community of Galatian believers, but the Spirit is the energizing and guiding agent that helps believers break free from the bondage of the law (Gal 5:16–18).[27] Thus Paul contrasts the mission-mutilation of his opponents with the spiritual function of the Philippian believers as the community of God.

Second, for Paul, those "who are the circumcision" also "*boast* in Christ Jesus" (3:3 emphasis added). The term "boasting" (*kauchōmenoi*) refers to the very *act* of boasting in something that is the *source* of pride.[28] Paul perceives that the Philippian believers' present life is being energized by the Spirit in order to fulfill the divine will – not as any human accomplishment, but as a result of divine grace. This grace is available and operational "in Christ," which is the mystical space of a believer's existence (Gal 2:15–16, 20–21; 3:27–28). Another reason for boasting in Christ Jesus is that he is the sovereign Lord, who emptied himself and, taking human form, died upon the cross (2:5–11). The present hope of future glory (3:20–21) and the foretaste of eschatological salvation through the forgiveness of sins, here and now in Christ's death, is the actual ground and content of boasting. For Paul, while his opponents have "the law" as their source and substance of boasting before the people, the Philippian believers simply boast in the crucified messiah. Thus in 3:7–8, Paul boldly declares that all his earthly trophies are nothing but "garbage."

Third, the claim that we "*put no confidence* in the flesh" is a negative corollary of the preceding claim. He who boasts "in Christ Jesus" does not put "confidence in the flesh." A believer cannot exist simultaneously in these mutually exclusive spheres of existence. The term *sarx*, translated as "flesh," refers to a wide range of human existence: from the physical flesh (Gal 4:13–14) to

---

27. Hansen, *Philippians*, 221.
28. BDAG, 537.

sinful human nature that is oppositional to God and works out evil desires (Gal 5:16, 19; Rom 7:5; 8:9). According to Fowl, "the flesh" is a "shorthand for a standard of judging God's desires for oneself and the world that is, ultimately, contrary to God's desire and purposes."[29] In this context, as is generally accepted, putting "confidence in the flesh" means Jewish reliance upon their fleshly descent, nationalistic identity, and ritualistic Judaism founded upon the law. Paul's characterization of the opponents as "mutilators of the flesh" in 3:2 and his repudiation of his own Jewish credentials in 3:5–7 point to this meaning of "confidence in the flesh."[30] Hawthorne maintains that it is "striving to achieve an adequate status before God, but without dependence upon God."[31] This describes someone who counts upon one's own righteousness through the Law and seeks to stand in God's presence without accepting the absolute impossibility of being made righteous before God without grace. In other words, when we put no confidence in the flesh, we place our absolute trust in God.

Paul calls his believers' attention to the danger of false teachers among them and instructs them about their need to define their identity "in Christ" in order to sharpen his rhetoric while unleashing a verbal arsenal against his opponents. His use of the first person plural pronoun, "we," not only allows him to identify with his believers in Philippi, but also helps him present himself (using "I" or by saying "my example") as a model of the true (inner) "circumcision" that he describes later. In section 3:4–14, Paul provides readers with a specific example in everyday practical life of the absolute rejection of earthly credentials in order to know Christ, participate in Christ by sharing in his suffering, and intentionally press on to win the prize on the last day.

3:4–14 ALL THAT IS NEEDED IS CHRIST JESUS

Within the caste-ridden Hindu society of India and Nepal, claims of superiority based on class and social position are not rare to hear. Even within a Christian context, one's confidence in the flesh often results in hierarchical relationships between Christians based on socio-cultural factors. We often hear boastful claims based on someone's family heritage (such as Syrian Christian, Brahmin caste), dominant tribal/clan identity, or financial background. Such details are often highlighted while introducing someone in public or in testimonials,

---

29. Fowl, *Philippians*, 149.
30. Hansen, *Philippians*, 222.
31. Hawthorne, *Philippians*, 128.

and specific caste backgrounds are often mentioned in matrimonial advertisements. Converts from higher castes, such as Brahmin, often receive greater preference within the church than those who come into the church from lower castes. Ever since the beginning of the modern missionary movement, caste- or identity-specific churches and mission organizations have emerged in India.

With Paul's sudden shift from the collective "we" in 3:3 to the personal "I" in 3:4–14, he explains the implications of the true Christian identity. In these verses, Paul presents himself as an ideal Jew of the first century who has every valued social credential to claim superiority and pride in the society at the time. The string of personal statements recounting his heritage and achievements not only counter the tall claims of his opponents and their vanity, but they also present a concrete example of taking pride "in Christ" and putting no "confidence in the flesh" (3:5–7). Within a culture of constant social competition because of the desire to earn and display credentials for a higher social position, Paul claims to have impeccable righteousness based on the law, his family heritage gained by birth, and his own overwhelming zeal for the Jewish law. However, Paul does not count these credentials as gain in order to know Christ (3:7–11) and states his personal ambition to attain that "for which God has called me heavenward in Christ Jesus" (3:14).

Paul disavows all his earthly credentials in favor of being one of the true "circumcision," who *serves* "God by his Spirit," *boasts* "in Christ Jesus," and *puts* "no confidence in the flesh" (3:3). His intention in listing his heritage, personal achievements, and impeccable religious standing before others is not to compete with those who take pride in earthly things, but to tell his audience how little he values these things compared with knowing Christ. Moreover, just as Jesus emptied himself of all his divine prerogatives in order to become incarnate in human likeness (2:6–8), Paul also rejects his credentials in the flesh in order to know Jesus more in his life (3:7–11).

3:4–6 Paul's Life in Judaism

In 3:4, Paul puts himself on an equal footing with his opponents as far as religious pedigree is concerned. Hence, continuing his thought from 3:3, Paul says, "though I myself have reasons for such confidence." In other words, Paul considers his identity as a member of the "circumcision" at least as impressive, arguably even more impressive, than anyone else who thinks (*ei tis dokeiallos*, 3:4b) he has a good religious pedigree. At this time, Paul must have had the Judaizers in mind, though he speaks in more general terms. Further, the term *pepoithēsin*, an accusative, identifies the actual ground of Paul's confidence.

His reason for refuting reliance upon earthly credentials is not because he lacks them, for his conscience is robust[32] rather than crushed by the Mosaic Law, and this gives him the basis to claim, "I have more" (3:4). The expression is elliptic, which requires a greater affirmation of confidence in the flesh. This makes him an ideal Jew with every important pedigree "in the flesh" to claim superiority over others with similar claims – and yet he refuses to do so "for the sake of Christ" (3:7).

In 3:5–6, Paul lists his social, religious, and ethnic credentials that together form the possible ground of his reliance "in the flesh." He lists seven important credentials that define his superior position compared to the Judaizers, who proudly uphold their particular credentials to coerce the gentile converts in Philippi to submit to the requirements of the law. The list includes both acquired and earned social credentials, which substantiates his claim that "I myself have reasons for such confidence" (3:4). First, Paul's acquired social status is by virtue of his birth into a particular family, religious community, sect, and social group. The listed credentials marking Paul's higher social status are: "circumcised on the eighth day, of the people of Israel, of the tribe of Benjamin, Hebrew of Hebrews" (3:5). Second, he has earned his social status within society by his own efforts, arguing as follows: "in regard of the law, a Pharisee; as for zeal, persecuting the church; as for righteousness based on the law, faultless" (3:6).

Paul's claim that he was "circumcised on the eighth day" proves two things about his family. First, it proves that his parents were law-observant Jews who followed the legal stipulation of the OT (Lev 12:3). The tradition of being circumcised on the eighth day goes back to God's command to Abraham: "For the generations to come every male among you who is eight days old must be circumcised" (Gen 17:12). Second, it also implies that he was born into a devoted Jewish family and was not a proselyte. In other words, he was a Jew by birth.

He continues with three more ethnic details that make him firmly rooted in the Abrahamic lineage. Writing to the Roman and the Corinthian church, Paul repeatedly claims his membership of the nation of Israel (Rom 9:3–4; 11:1; 2 Cor 11:22), which he simply reasserts here, saying he is "of the people of Israel" (3:5). While his claim to belong to the "people of Israel" implies his ethnic identity (*genos*) stretching back to Abraham, the patriarch, it also

---

32. Kirster Stendhal, "The Apostle Paul and the Introspective Conscience of the West," in *The Writings of St. Paul*, ed. Wayne A. Meeks (New York: W. W. Norton, 1972), 422–434.

signifies his religious privilege as one of "God's chosen people."[33] In his diatribe in Romans, where he contends against his Jewish opponents, Paul recounts the religious privileges attached to the Israelite identity, saying: "[t]heirs is the adoption of sonship; theirs the divine glory, the covenant, the receiving of the law, the temple worship and the promises. Theirs are the patriarchs, and from them is traced the human ancestry of the Messiah" (Rom 9:4–5). Ethnically speaking, Paul possesses every credential that places him at the highest social layer of the first-century Jewish society.

"Israel" is a wider ethnic term compared to his claim that he is "a Hebrew of Hebrews." This latter phrase is not merely a reference to his fluency in the Hebrew language (Acts 21:40; 22:2), but as Silva observes, it "appears to have a climactic intent and thus could be understood in the sense of 'pure-blooded'; certainly a denial that he had any mixed ancestry would fit in well with the previous items, which focus on qualities related to his birth."[34] Within the first-century Palestinian nationalistic context, Hebrew identity signified ethnic purity.[35] Unlike Hellenized Jews, who compromised Jewish cultural purity to thrive in the Hellenistic world, those contending for Jewish cultural essentialism (as during the Maccabean revolt) resisted cultural mixture for political reasons (1 Macc 2). In other words, the claim is not merely for the purity of blood, a "blue-blooded" Jew, but is also a certification for his faithful adherence to cultural purity despite being born and brought up outside of Palestine (Acts 21:39). In other words, his diasporic upbringing has not diluted his pure Jewishness.

Regarding his acquired social status, Paul also claims that he is "of the tribe of Benjamin" (Rom 11:1). While a longer list of reasons for pride related to the tribe of Benjamin could be listed (as Hawthorne mentions),[36] the outstanding feature is that the first king of Israel came from this tribe (1 Sam 9:1–2). Even when political crisis embroiled Jerusalem, leading to the rebellion of Israel against the Davidic monarchy, the tribe of Benjamin remained loyal to Judah (1 Kgs 12:21).

The next set of credentials is those that Paul has earned from his hard labor and meticulous lifestyle. As Hansen rightly states, they "display Paul's personal achievements: his membership in an elite group of spiritual leaders within Judaism, his participation in the nationalistic effort to defend Judaism, and his

---

33. Hansen, *Philippians*, 223.
34. Silva, *Philippians*, WEC, 176.
35. George, *Paul's Identity in Galatians*, 236.
36. Hawthorne, *Philippians*, 132–133.

perfection in his obedience to the law."[37] Using *kata*, a preposition translated as "according to," Paul claims that, with regard to his strict adherence to the law, he belongs to the sect of the Pharisees. Generally, the name Pharisee is accepted to be related to the Hebrew word *Pᵉrûšîm*, meaning "separatist," who are believed to be the "spiritual descendants of the Hasidim, a group of pious Jews who attached themselves to the Maccabean opposition to the Seleucid King."[38] In first-century Palestinian society, Pharisees were religious leaders who adopted a strong fundamentalist position in obeying the law. Apart from the law of Moses, in order to fulfill every bit of the law perfectly, they also valued hundreds of other oral traditions.[39] In fact, during his defense before the Sanhedrin, Paul shrewdly used his Pharisaic sectarian identity and faith in the resurrection of the dead to split the jury (Acts 23:6–7). He also made proud claims for his Pharisaic upbringing and his education at the feet of the foremost Pharisee, Gamaliel (Acts 22:3; 5:34).

In 3:6, Paul refers to two important credentials that have political significance based on the Jewish religion. The *zēlos*, commonly translated as "zeal," which is preceded by the preposition *kata* ("according to"), refers to his strong enthusiasm, similar to the militant Zealots in first-century Palestine. In the post-Maccabean context, the Zealots took inspiration from Mattathias (1 Macc 2:26–27), Elijah (1 Kgs 19:14), and Phinehas (Num 25:7–13) in practicing their zeal for the law.[40] They abhorred Roman domination and constantly rebelled to overthrow their rule, culminating in the great Jewish War of AD 66–70. They opposed Rome in order to establish a Jewish theocratic kingdom.[41] According to the Zealot standard, by wanting to overthrow everyone – be it the powerful Romans or the emerging Christians who were threatening to abolish or corrupt the Mosaic law – Paul did not hesitate to rise up in arms. Hence, he confesses that he was violently zealous, like the Zealots, in "persecuting the church." In Galatians 1:13–14, Paul recounts his violent, Zealot-like zeal for the law, saying: "For you have heard of my previous way of life in Judaism, how intensely I persecuted the church of God and tried to destroy it. I was advancing in Judaism beyond many of my own among my people and was extremely zealous for the traditions of my fathers." Paul's use of the noun form *zēlōtēs* (Gal 1:14) to represent his fervency for the Jewish tradition attests to

---

37. Hansen, *Philippians*, 225.
38. Stephen Westerholm, "Pharisees," *DJG* 610.
39. Westerholm, 610–612.
40. George, *Paul's Identity in Galatians*, 164.
41. George, 101–103.

its similarity to the violent zeal of the Zealots.⁴² If so, Paul has a very strong religio-political pedigree to boast about, particularly in the light of the strong Jewish nationalism that would peak very shortly in Palestine (AD 66).

Finally, beyond his earlier claim of belonging to the sect of Pharisees, Paul now claims that his righteousness based on the law is "faultless." Lightfoot is right in observing that Paul's claim should be viewed against the backdrop of his Jewish religious heritage, in which he cannot be accused of any "sins of omission."⁴³ Such a claim to blamelessness in fulfilling the requirements of the law brings to mind the rich young ruler, who replied to Jesus: "All these I have kept since I was a boy" (Luke 18:21). This is a strong piece of evidence for the modern, anti-Lutheran critical conclusion that Paul never actually suffered a heavy, guilty conscience, crushed by the demands of the law.⁴⁴ Instead, at conversion, he had a robust conscience, and on that basis, he could later look back at his past life in Judaism with satisfaction. However, the shift that took place in Paul after his encounter with Christ on the way to Damascus is evident in his later Christo-centric theology.

3:7–11 Knowing Christ Jesus

Having enlisted all the credentials about which he could take pride in the flesh (like the Judaizers), Paul makes a sudden volte-face from the expected line of argument by repudiating his social status, privileges, and earthly gains in the world in order to know Christ Jesus. This goal for his life reflects more of a *Yesu bhakta* (devotee of Jesus), sold out to gain experiential knowledge of his *ishtadevata* (beloved deity), rather than a conquering apostle (as the modern, Western scholarship of the colonial era wanted us to believe). Within the Hindu *Bhakti* tradition, after experiencing one's personal inadequacies in order to fathom the greatness of the deity, a devotee recognizes his/her dependence upon absolute divine grace to attain salvation. At this level, the taste of the deity's grace leads the devotee to relinquish worldly entanglements in order to grow deeper in the love of God; thereby, one desires greater (experiential) knowledge of the *ishtadevata*. Paul, in his post-converted life, is a devotee of Jesus Christ (*Yesu Khristu*), who – like any *bhakti* saint of Hinduism – falls in

---

42. Compare George, *Paul's Identity in Galatians*, 101–103; Mark R. Fairchild, "Paul's Pre-Christian Zealot Associations: A Re-Examination of Gal 1.14 and Acts 22:3," *NTS* 45 (1999): 514–532.
43. Lightfoot, *Philippians*, 148.
44. For a broad survey on old and new perspectives about Paul, his conversion, and theology, see Stephen Westerholm, *Perspectives Old and New on Paul: The 'Lutheran' Paul and His Critics* (Grand Rapids: Eerdmans, 2004).

awe of the love, grace, and mercy displayed in God's Son, Jesus Christ, and so Paul wants to love and experience more and more of Christ Jesus at any cost. This requires him to renounce completely any confidence in the flesh through the law. The chief end of a *bhakta* is ultimately to experience union with the beloved deity. But Paul, a Jew, does not understand this union with Christ Jesus as one that leads to oneness with or merger into God. Instead, it is a mystical union with Christ – to be "found in him" (3:9) – without implying a divine-human merger. In 3:8, Paul says that his goal is to know "Christ Jesus my Lord," for which he counts every reason for his confidence in the flesh as rubbish.[45]

Speaking in the language of profit and loss, Paul presents himself before the believers in Philippi as a positive model, who has every vital reason for confidence in the flesh (more than the Judaizers), but values knowing Christ Jesus as more profitable. Interestingly, the central point elaborated in 3:8–11 is stated concisely in 3:7: "But whatever were gains to me I now consider loss for the sake of Christ." The word *hēgēmai* ("I have considered") in first person perfect form implies that Paul arrived at this logical deduction in the past. Hence his conclusion is the net result of a process of radical re-evaluation about his own life after his encounter with Jesus on the way to Damascus (Acts 9:1–9). Paul's new Christo-centric vision of life reverses his past judgments about the goal and purpose of his life (2 Cor 5:16). As a devotee of Christ Jesus, Paul is captured by a sudden new spiritual reality (3:8, "the surpassing worth of knowing Christ Jesus my Lord"), and so he prioritizes Christ, for whose sake he now counts as loss all his pride in his fleshly credentials.

In 3:8–11, Paul further explains the meaning and significance of the profit and loss he incurs as an exemplary Christian. This passage echoes Christ's cruciform path (2:6–8) in Paul's life, where he presents himself as one who imitates Christ and willingly relinquishes all for the sake of Christ. Like Christ, Paul's relinquishment is voluntary, and it is grounded in his attitudinal shift (3:7). In the light of Paul's emphasis on the transformed mind controlled by the Spirit (2:1–5; 4:2), Paul underlines the unique twofold relation that he, as a devotee of Christ, shares with Jesus. In 3:8, he addresses Jesus as "Christ" (*Christos*) and "Lord" (*ho kurios*), coloring this high title for Jesus with a sense of his personal relationship by using the pronoun "*my*."

The two important christological titles, Christ and Lord also have political meaning in Philippi. Paul, who is a prisoner in Rome and has been captured

---

45. George, "Divine Grace in the Making of Paul, the *Yesu Bhakta*," 74–96.

by Jesus Christ, declares the Lordship of Jesus upon his personal life. The title *Christos*, meaning Messiah, evoked political connotations among Jews. In first-century Jewish thought, the Messiah could be a human figure or a pre-existent figure, as in the apocalyptic tradition (1 En.; 4 Ezra; Sib. Or. 5; 11 QMelch).[46] According to N. T. Wright, the use of "Christ" with the personal name "Jesus" could be translated as "King Jesus."[47] Interestingly, within the Roman colonial context, the title referred to the king of another kingdom who subverted the *Pax Romana* and was hostile to the Roman claim for universal domination. Even in Thessalonica, Paul's Jewish audience heard him speaking of another king, not Caesar, as he preached about Christ Jesus (Acts 17:3; John 19:15).

Further, the title "lord" (*kurios*) is also an imperial title. In the LXX, the term *kurios* was used for translating the Hebrew *tetragrammaton*, YHWH. Hence Zealots, who recognized the God of the OT alone as YHWH, refused to confess Caesar as the *kurios* (Josephus, *War* 2.8.1; 7.10.1). In the Hellenistic world, *kurios* was used as a high title for the Hellenistic rulers.[48] Since the first-century BC, *kurios basileus* became a widely used royal title among the Romans in the east.[49] *Kurios* was used in titular form for Julius Caesar, Augustus, Tiberius, Caligula, and Nero.[50] In Philippians 2:9–11, Paul acknowledges that Jesus Christ is the sovereign "Lord" before whom every knee will bow, and he became his personal Lord after his conversion (3:8, "my Lord"). Although Paul views his own life as modeled after the life of Jesus, he relates with Jesus only as his Lord, to whom he submits his entire being. This absolute devotion to Jesus is essential, for no other power shares authority over Paul.

In the light of the surpassing worth of "Christ," Paul's sovereign "Lord," everything else becomes "garbage" (3:8). Notice the change from the perfect form, *hēgēmai* ("I have considered"), in 3:7 to the present form, *hēgoumai* ("I consider"), in 3:8, which intensifies Paul's negative attitude towards his socio-religious pedigrees from mere "loss" to "garbage." The Greek term *skubala* (3:8) refers to "useless or undesirable material that is subject to disposal,

---

46. J. H. Charlesworth, "From Jewish Messianology to Christian Christology: Some Caveats and Perspectives," in *Judaism and their Messiahs at the Turn of the Christian Era*, ed. Jacob Neusner, William Scott Green, and Ernest S. Frerichs (Cambridge: Cambridge University Press, 1987), 229–247.
47. Wright, *What Saint Paul Really Said*, 52.
48. W. Foerster, "Κυριος," *TDNT* 3:1049.
49. Bietenhard, "Κυριος," *NIDNTT* 2:511.
50. Fantin, "Paul's Use of Κυριος as a Polemic Against Caesar," 1–18.

refuse, or garbage,"[51] and Paul uses it here to convey the radical shift in his attitude. He no longer desires the things that he earlier thought was very important. Note the passive aorist form of the verb *edzēmiōthēn* (3:8, translated as "I suffered loss"), which refers to his intentional choice of knowing Christ and his self-inflicted decision to count all confidence in the flesh as "garbage."

In 3:8–11, Paul mentions a threefold goal for losing confidence in fleshly credentials: (1) to "gain Christ," (2) to "be found in him," and (3) "to know Christ." First, Paul's goal "that I may gain Christ" (3:8), as Hawthorne observes, uses a *hina* clause (a purpose clause with the subjunctive mood), suggesting not only absolute submission in the past to "gain" Christ, but also an incomplete action that is continuous in the present and will also continue in future.[52] This gain is of greater worth in comparison with Paul's nationalistic pride or his ability to boast in the purity of his blood or his impeccable performance of the law with extreme zeal. In fact, Paul's attitude towards his past religious pedigree as "garbage" emboldens his yearning to "gain Christ."

Second, Paul's yearning to "be found in him" (3:9) is characteristic of a devotee (*bhakta*) who is submerged in the desire for intimacy with his beloved God (*ishtadevatha*). The expression "in him" is parallel to "in Christ," which in Pauline theology is synonymous with a believer's mystical location (Gal 1:22; 5:10; 1 Cor 1:2; 1 Thess 1:1). This expression is a "short-hand for the sphere of influence (or energy-field) that is the community . . . It is impossible to avoid the conclusion that Paul's understanding of the church involves a deep and mystical identity between this community and the risen Jesus mediated by the Holy Spirit."[53] Thus Paul considers that being "found in him" is a gain, because in this mystical space of existence ("in Christ"), Paul's own righteousness (3:6) based on the law is replaced by a righteousness that comes from God through faith (3:9). The righteousness that Paul receives based on faith is sourced from the ground of his being, which is Christ Jesus. Paul makes a clear distinction between the two forms of righteousness from two different sources, which are mutually exclusive and irreconcilable because they are available in two different spheres of existence: one in the sphere of one's own achievement based on the law and the other "in Christ" based on faith.

There are two important issues related to 3:9. First, what does Paul mean by saying "righteousness . . . that comes from the law"? In the latter half of

---

51. BDAG, 932.
52. Hawthorne, *Philippians*, 140.
53. Luke Timothy Johnson, "Paul's Ecclesiology," in *The Cambridge Companion to St. Paul*, ed. J. D. G. Dunn (Cambridge: Cambridge University Press, 2003), 206–207.

the twentieth century, scholars have disputed the Lutheran understanding of righteousness based on the law as the merit earned by the legalistic obedience of the law.[54] Dunn argues that "the need to attain one's own righteousness was not part of the traditional Jewish teaching; righteousness was rather the practice of the devout within the covenant."[55] Hence, to Dunn, "they indicate the same conviction that righteousness was Israel's, to be practiced by covenant-loyal Jews and defended as Israel's by its practitioners." Thereby, it is evident that Paul was not contending against "self-achieved righteousness."[56] Arguing against Dunn, Kim maintains that Philippians 3:5–6 lists credentials that are not merely self-chosen, as Dunn argues, but rather self-achieved. Pointing out a contradiction in Dunn's argument, Kim observes that the prevalence of competition in outdoing contemporaries to fulfill the requirements of the law among Jews proves their sense of personal achievement. Hence, Kim asks, "[i]f Paul was not conscious of his personally achieved righteousness but only the 'national righteousness' of Israel on Phil 3:2–10, should he not have referred to it as 'our own righteousness,' including his Jewish opponents in his claim . . . ?"[57]

However, the truth appears to lie in between the two positions, as Westerholm maintains. The Sinaitic law provided the broad framework for how the people of God (Israel as a nation) were to live among the nations. However, as an individual Jew, Paul judged his performance (3:9, "my own") of the law, with his militant zeal and perfect obedience, to be "blameless," as was his righteousness.[58] "The righteousness of the law for Paul included both his Jewish heritage (the Israelite family into which he was born, his circumcision as an infant) and the conformity of his own behavior with the requirements of the law." While for Gentiles conformity to the law alone was applicable, Paul regarded "native Jewishness as preferable."[59] So in 3:9, Paul's disavowal of the righteousness that "comes from the law" is a double-loss to him, for both his native Jewishness and his personal achievements in zealously performing the law surpassed all his Jewish contemporaries.

---

54. For a broad survey on the topic, see Westerholm, *Perspectives Old and New on Paul*, 3–97, esp. 22–41.
55. Dunn, *Theology of Paul the Apostle*, 369.
56. Dunn, 370.
57. Seyoon Kim, *Paul and the New Perspective: Second Thoughts on the Origin of Paul's Gospel* (Grand Rapids: Eerdmans, 1998), 75–81, cited from 77.
58. Westerholm, *Perspectives Old and New on Paul*, 312.
59. Westerholm, 401–404, cited from 403.

Philippians 3:1–4:1

The second important consideration regarding 3:9 is whether to understand the expression *pisteōs Christou* as an objective or a subjective genitive. Although, it is generally translated as "faith *in* Christ," can it also be translated as "faith (fullness) *of* Christ"? While the traditional position ("faith *in* Christ") understands "Christ" in the genitive form as the object of an individual's faith (the objective genitive),[60] the recent interpretive proposal arguing for the subjective genitive maintains that "Christ" in the genitive form must be viewed as the subject of *pisteōs* ("faithfulness").[61] The traditional position provides an entirely credible meaning, because Paul uses the noun form "faith" three times (1:25, 27; 2:17) and the verb "believe" once (1:29) when referring to the Philippian believers' faith in Christ. For Hansen, this warrants our understanding of "faith" in 3:9 as "faith in Christ."[62] However, as Witherington argues, Paul is not obliged to use the verbal and noun form in the same fashion in the same text.[63] In recent years, an increasing number of scholars have espoused the subjective genitive here, treating the expression as "a shorthand reference to Christ's action," which is both God's fidelity towards humanity and humanity's fidelity towards God at the same time.[64] If the subjective genitive is acceptable, then, as Gorman states, "it means that for Paul the faith (fullness) or obedience of Christ expressed in his death (2:8), rather than circumcision or Law keeping, is the basis of membership in God's covenant people."[65] This position, although it lays emphasis on the role of Christ, does not reject the role of human response. It is "a *concentric* expression, which begins, always, from the faith of Christ himself, but which includes, necessarily, the answering faith of believers, who claim that faith as their own."[66] In other words, the mutuality of faithfulness (divine-human and human-divine) symbolized in the faith of

---

60. J. D. G. Dunn, "Once More, ΠΙΣΤΙΣΧΡΙΣΤΟΥ," in *Looking Back, Pressing On*, ed. E. Elizabeth Johnson and David M. Hay, vol. 4 of *Pauline Theology*, SBL Symposium Series 4 (Atlanta: Scholars Press, 1997), 61–81.
61. Richard B. Hays, "ΠΙΣΤΙΣ and Pauline Christology," in *Looking Back, Pressing On*, ed. E. Elizabeth Johnson and David M. Hay, vol. 4 of *Pauline Theology*, 57–60; Richard B. Hays, *The Faith of Jesus Christ: The Narrative Substructure of Galatians 3:1–4:11*, 2nd ed., The Biblical Resource Series (Grand Rapids/Cambridge: Eerdmans/Dearborn: Dove Booksellers, 2002).
62. Hansen, *Philippians*, 241.
63. Ben Witherington III, *Grace in Galatia: A Commentary on St. Paul's Letter to the Galatians* (Grand Rapids: Eerdmans, 1998), 180–182.
64. Hays, *Faith of Jesus Christ*, xxix, xxxi.
65. Gorman, *Apostle of the Crucified Lord*, 443.
66. M. D. Hooker, "ΠΙΣΤΙΣΧΡΙΣΤΟΥ," *NTS* 35 (1989): 341; Hays, *Faith of Jesus Christ*, xxxii. Such an expression of our faith/faithfulness in the obedience of Christ is, for Hays, one being "taken up into his life, including his faithfulness, and that faithfulness therefore imparts to us the shape of our own existence."

Jesus becomes the "pattern for the new life that he has inaugurated."[67] Thus, this model of faithfulness until death becomes dominant in Paul's escalated desire to "know Christ" by "becoming like him in his death" (3:10).

Finally, Paul's goal to be found in Christ elevates his desire to "know" Christ (3:10). Although the term *gnōnai* could be superficially understood as cerebral knowledge, the desire here to "know Christ" is experiential and based on shared intimacy. In 3:10b, Paul explains this desire "to know Christ" as a knowing of both "the power of his resurrection" and "participation [*koinonia*] in his suffering." These two aspects of knowing Christ are not separate from each other. Without participation in Christ, there is no knowledge of the power of his resurrection, which emphasizes an experience-based, personal knowledge of Christ. In 3:8, knowing Christ through "personal acquaintance" with Jesus can be compared with the experience of a devotee who becomes filled with mystical knowledge.[68] Hansen states that "[s]ince the desire *to know him* is the goal of one who is *found in him*, this knowledge is relational and experiential. The purpose of life *in Christ* is personal, intimate knowledge of Christ."[69]

The actual content of the "power of resurrection," according to Hansen, is to know God's power that raised Jesus from the dead. Paul himself, preaching the divine offer of salvation to all, bears testimony to the act of God (1 Cor 15:15; Eph 1:19–20). In the present, "[t]he power of God is demonstrated in the life of the believer by the power of the Holy Spirit (Rom 15:13; 1 Cor 2:4–5)."[70] Paul experiences this surpassing power of the resurrection in the Roman jail. In fact, his suffering in the jail is the occasion of his participation in Christ's suffering as well as the divine revelation of the power of the resurrection. The apostle's dilemma, to depart or to remain in the body (1:23), resurfaces here. Paul is clear that it is important for him to live for the well-being of the believers in Philippi, and yet his words "to die is gain" (1:21) imply his yearning to experience the power of the resurrection. Thus his knowledge of the power of the resurrection comes through his *koinonia* in Christ's suffering. For Paul, *koinonia* is a not an abstract idea, but a concrete act of sharing in mission. Paul also uses *koinonia* to refer to the partnership of the believers in his mission through their sacrificial gifts and sharing in his troubles (1:5, 7; 4:14). So even his death opens up the possibility for him to participate in the actual death of Christ, whereby he becomes like Christ Jesus (2:8).

---

67. Hays, *Faith of Jesus Christ*, xxxi.
68. BDAG, 203.
69. Hansen, *Philippians*, 243.
70. Hansen, 244.

This partnership in death with Christ is a prelude to sure glorification at the resurrection from the dead in the eschatological time, without which there is no resurrection from the dead (3:11). Viewing his life through a christological lens (2:6–11), Paul recognizes that his identification with Christ in death will surely lead to his glorification through his resurrection with the exalted Christ in "the highest place" (2:9). In short, Paul's desire to "know Christ" is of "surpassing worth" (3:8) because it fills him with the hope of the resurrection on the last day, emboldening him to suffer loss in this world in order to receive eternal life beyond death through the same divine power by which Christ Jesus was raised from the dead (2:8–9).

3:12–14 Persistence in the Race to Win the Prize

After recounting his reasons for being able to have confidence in the flesh and then saying that he considers that confidence as a loss in 3:4–11, Paul hastens to clarify some possible misunderstanding that his words might create. As a pastor, he wants to make it clear that his transformation, which was initiated at his conversion on the way to Damascus (Acts 9), was a process and not simply a one-time event. In 3:12–16, Paul seeks to tell his audience, both by negation and affirmation, that he is still persistent in his efforts to achieve his long-cherished goal. Philippians 3:12–14 is crafted very skillfully, as O'Brien maintains, by "a series of clauses in contrasting parallelism. The first set consists of negative statements (vv. 12a, 13a) in which Paul's disclaimers are mentioned, while the second set (vv. 12b, 13b–14) focuses on his ongoing determination to fulfil his ultimate aim."[71] In his post-conversion Christian life, Paul has a new set of priorities. Central to this section is Paul's single-minded devotion, amidst all hardships, to accomplish what God has appointed him to do. Unlike his life in Judaism, when he engaged in competition, outdoing his contemporaries to achieve a place among the elite religious performers (or group) by obeying the law, Paul has no human agenda as a Christian. Rather, he only pursues the goal that God has fixed for him.

Paul begins 3:12 with a firm disclaimer: "not that . . . or already" (*ouch hoti . . . ē ēdē*). In fact, this disclaimer introduces the present state of his incomplete journey. Paul's renunciation of all his pedigrees under Judaism is not an end in itself, but a continuing pursuit of attaining the ultimate goal (i.e., I have not "already arrived at my goal," 3:12). However, what is this goal that Paul has not yet attained? The answer lies in how we understand the object

---

71. O'Brien, *Philippians*, 418.

of the Greek verb *elabon*, meaning "I have obtained," which does not have a direct object and so opens up room for multiple proposals among scholars. First, Thompson and Beare maintain that the referent is resurrection or eternal life, as mentioned in 3:11.[72] Second, Hawthorne treats the verb *elabon* as a constative aorist tense that encapsulates Paul's entire experience, past to present, with its meaning, "to comprehend," where the object of the verb refers to the fuller significance of Christ. Hawthorne states: "Paul means to say that he does not lay claim to having fully grasped the meaning of Christ at this point in time."[73] Arguing in favor of this position, Hansen points out that "[t]wo times at the end of this sentence Paul uses an intensified form of the same verb" to mention how Christ apprehended him and how intensely he himself desires to know Christ.[74] Although the former proposal could be a possibility in the light of 3:11, it is unnecessary to assume that the apostle considers that his readers might be thinking of him as already resurrected from the dead (i.e., an eschatological experience). Similarly, the latter suggestion is not without merit, but it limits the scope of knowing Christ in Paul's life.

But for Paul, rather than having a mental or spiritual comprehension of Christ, the way to attain the righteousness that "comes from God on the basis of faith" is to know and be found in Christ (3:9). Thus according to Müller, Paul "has in mind the full knowledge of Christ, and the full-grown communion with Him and conformity to Him to which he has not yet come, the entire sanctification, spiritual and moral maturity and perfection which he has not yet attained."[75] By renouncing his past life under Judaism and his search of righteousness based on the law, Paul, as a *Yesu bhakta*, is taking up the single-minded goal of becoming like Christ through self-emptying and by continuing his journey of becoming like Christ in death. Paul wants the believers in Philippi to learn through his example that Christian maturity and perfection is a continuing process of becoming like Christ. This understanding fits well with the larger imitation motif in Philippians. Later in 3:17, the apostle appeals to the believers to join with him in imitating his example by seeking to become Christlike. Earlier in Philippians 2, Paul says that he, Timothy, and Epaphroditus exhibit Christlike virtues that are worthy of imitation by the believers in Philippi (2:5–11; 17–30; 4:9).

---

72. Thompson, *Philippians*, 111; Beare, *Philippians*, 128.
73. Hawthorne, *Philippians*, 151.
74. Hansen, *Philippians*, 250. See O'Brian, *Philippians*, 421–422.
75. Müller, *Philippians*, 121.

In 3:12b, the verb *diōkō*, "I pursue," explains the intense rigor and energy that Paul expends to "take hold of that for which Christ Jesus took hold of" him. The verb denotes, "to move rapidly and decisively towards an objective."[76] The effort Paul used to persecute (*diōkō*) the church in the past (3:6) is now directed toward obtaining the new goal of his life in Christ. The act of Christ gripping him firmly (*katalambanō*) echoes the event of his conversion on the way to Damascus, when the revelation of Christ permanently changed the course of Paul's life (Acts 9). Paul understands the purpose of this divine act as knowing Christ, being found in him, and being transformed into his likeness. For Paul, the divine revelatory act set the goal of his post-conversion life. To obtain this, Paul is determined to make every effort, even counting all his earthly credentials as loss.

In 3:13a, Paul bases his persuasion on his sibling relationship in Christ with the Philippian believers, and reiterates his disclaimer, saying, "I do not consider myself yet to have taken hold of it." Notice the emphatic position of *egō*, meaning "I," followed by *emauton* ("myself"), which differentiates his personal assessment of his own present state in the heavenward pilgrimage (3:14, compare 3:20) from that of others. The verb "I consider" (*logidzomai*) means "to hold a view about something" or "be of the opinion."[77] It is not a random judgment by Paul, but a conclusion reached after careful deliberation. He wants the believers in Philippi to know that his journey of knowing Christ, being sanctified and made righteous, and being found participating in his suffering is unfinished.

In 3:13b–14, Paul visualizes himself as an athlete (1 Cor 9:24–27), who is conscious, determined, and persistent to complete the race. The image in Paul's mind is of a runner, who fixes his eyes on the goal in front and not on what lies behind, bending his body forward with his arms pumping briskly to enable him to move faster towards the finish line. This powerful image richly communicates his single-mindedness, his willingness to undergo tireless exertion for the Christian race, and his focus on the finish line.

Paul wants his readers to know that he does one thing (*hen de*) almost simultaneously with another in his race: "Forgetting what is behind and straining towards what is ahead" (3:13b). In Greek, the *men . . . de . . .* construct literally translates as "on the one hand . . . on the other hand . . . ," which is further balanced by two participle phrases in 3:13b. On the one hand, he

---

76. BDAG, 254.
77. BDAG, 598.

continues forgetting (*epilanthanomenos*) that which lies behind. The act of forgetting refers to those things that he now counts as garbage (3:5–8). He does not want to be encumbered by the past. On the other hand, he continues stretching out (*epekteinomenos*) to obtain the goal that lies ahead. Paul explains "straining towards what is ahead" (3:13b) by saying, "I press on towards the goal" (3:14). Paul repeats *diōkō* (3:14, "I press on") from 3:12, underlining the intense effort he is expending in the pursuit of winning the prize. The use of *diōkō* in the present tense again tells readers that Paul is still continuing his race in the present "towards the goal" (*kata skopon*). The term *skopos,* meaning "goal," uniquely found only here in the entire NT, "is an image commonly used for the target in archery. In combination with *diōkō*, it suggests the runner looking at the finish line."[78] So Paul intends to say that he is constantly struggling to obtain "the prize" (*to brabeion*). Paul qualifies "the prize" with a genitive expression (*tēs anō klēseōs touTheou*) in 3:14, which literally means "of the above calling of God." Repeatedly, the term *brabeion*, meaning "prize, award,"[79] is understood in the context of the ancient Greek Olympic games, in which an athlete received the prize from the *Agonothete*, a high-ranking official.

However, different positions have been argued to explain the relationship between the prize and the genitive expression, *tēs anō klēseōs tou Theou*, in this context. First, treating the genitive as a genitive of apposition, Thompson argues that "the prize is the upward calling," which is the Christian life leading to the resurrection (3:11) of those who are conformed to the death of Jesus Christ.[80] Similarly, Hendriksen maintains that the prize is given at the end of the race to those who, like Paul and all the saints, are "called upward to meet the Lord in the air and to remain forever with him in the new heaven and earth (1 Thess 4:17)."[81] Hansen rejects such deductions because they imply waiting for the call in the future rather than the one Paul is already running.[82] Coenen also rejects these deductions because they contradict the technical sense of the term. According to Coenen, the call refers to the divine act that brings the one who is called-out into fellowship with Christ and other members of the church.[83]

---

78. Thompson, *Philippians*, 112. See also, BDAG, 931; Hawthorne, *Philippians*, 154.
79. BDAG, 183.
80. Thompson, *Philippians*, 112.
81. Hendriksen, *Philippians*, 175.
82. Hansen, *Philippians*, 256.
83. L. Coenen, "καλέω," *NIDNTT* 1:275.

Second, Beare suggests that grammatically, "prize" could mean "the high vocation to which God has called" Paul and others, "but the better sense seems to be that he is thinking of Christ, whom he longs to know or to gain (vv. 8, 10)."[84] For Beare, "it is high in the sense that it is a call from the earthly to the heavenly," given to all who are called into God's service.[85] Beare's position appears to be a better proposal, for it does not overstretch the imagery of the Hellenistic games and retains its theological emphasis. Hansen argues that, in this sense, the genitive "of the call" is subjective, implying God's call for all to remain united in Christ. So the term "heavenward" refers to the direction and origin of the call.[86]

Thus Paul says, "for which God has called me heavenward in Christ Jesus" (3:14), in order to assure his readers that his encounter with Christ at the gate of Damascus gave him a goal to pursue without ceasing, which is to win the prize of knowing Christ and experiencing the perfection that is available to him (and others) in Christ Jesus. Now, his entire race to obtain "the prize" is through living, walking, and breathing in Christ. He rejects the past burden of personal achievement through the law in order to run a winning race in Christ.

3:15–17 IMITATING THE GOOD MODEL

Whether in ancient Greece or in India, the imitation of an enlightened master (*guru*) has been the model for discipleship. A true disciple was always exhorted to imitate the *guru* carefully in order to attain greater spiritual enlightenment and deeper experiences of god. Similarly, Paul exhorts believers to join him in carefully replicating a Christlike life. The direct language of imitation is not employed until 3:17, but the command (using an infinite verb in 3:15) to fall in line with a good model of conduct as mature members of the community contributes to the same motif. Paul adopts this strategy in nurturing Christlike community among believers in Philippi (2:5–11, 17, 19–30; 3:4–14; 4:9). The imitation theme also appears in Paul's earlier letters (1 Thess 1:5–6; 2 Thess 3:7; Gal 4:12; 1 Cor 4:14; 11:1). In 3:15–17, Paul recognizes the significance of imitating the example of Paul and others in knowing and becoming like Christ so that believers might win the prize at the end of the race. Among Stoics, imitation was a tool to train a disciple, and among Jews it was a part of the religious demand itself ("You are to be holy to me because I, the LORD,

---

84. Beare, *Philippians*, 130.
85. Beare, 130.
86. Hansen, *Philippians*, 256–257.

am holy," Lev 20:26).[87] In 3:15, Paul says, "[a]ll of us, then, who are mature should take such a view of things," offering his conversion, attitudinal transformation, and new purpose in life as worthy models for other mature Christians. Paul's process of perfection in Christ is both corrective in nature to what the Judaizers were teaching in Philippi and descriptive in scope for believers to live by as citizens of the heavenly commonwealth. Paul exhorts all (*hosoi*, literally, "as many as") to recognize their Christian walk as an unfinished journey, beginning at their conversion and continuing till their participation in the death and resurrection of Christ. To run like a winner in the Christian race, they ought to shed their socio-cultural and religious pedigrees and run with single-minded focus on Christ to reach the goal of knowing Christ perfectly. "[T]herefore" (*oun*, 3:15), the Christian runners, including himself (notice the use of *phronōmen*, meaning, "let us think"), whom Paul calls "mature" (*teleioi*, 3:15), must adopt the viewpoint he exemplifies in 3:2–14. More specifically, Keener observes that the verb *phroneō* means "believers should think with their intention focused on pursuing the 'upward' goal (3:14), that is, towards heaven (compare 3:10–11, 20–21)."[88]

The referent of the term *hosoi*, translated as "all of us," is qualified by the subsequent term *teleioi*, meaning "perfect" or "mature." This exclusive meaning restricts the group whom Paul imagines to those who are willing to live by the gospel and the standards he is preaching. It does not include those who preach and teach a different gospel with wrong motives. Again, the meaning of the term "mature" must be understood in the light of Paul's disavowal that he is already perfect (3:12). Although some have understood it differently, Müller's proposal appears to be relevant in the context. He states that, whenever Paul calls himself and others perfect in Christ after 3:12, he is not speaking "in the sense of ethical perfection, but of perfection in principle."[89] They are in no way

---

87. For a brief discussion on various backgrounds proposed by scholars for the idea of imitation in the Hellenistic and Jewish world and the various debates surrounding it, see Yung Suk Kim, "'Imitators' (*Mimetai*) in 1 Cor 4:16 and 11:1: A New Reading of Threefold Embodiment," *HBT* 33 (2011): 147–163. Andrew D. Clarke, "'Be imitator of me': Paul's Model of Leadership," *TynBul* 49 (1998): 329–360; Kathy Ehrensperger, "'Be Imitators of Me as I Am of Christ:' A Hidden Discourse of Power and Domination in Paul?" *LTQ* 38 (2003): 241–261; Robert G. Hamerton-Kelly, "A Girardian Interpretation of Paul: Rivalry, Mimesis and Victimage in the Corinthian Correspondence," *Semeia* 33 (1985): 65–81; Dustin W. Ellington, "Imitating Paul's Relationship to the Gospel: I Corinthians 8.1–11.1," *JSNT* 33 (2011): 303–315; Elizabeth A. Castelli, *Imitating Paul: A Discourse of Power*, LCBI (Louisville: Westminster/John Knox Press, 1991).
88. Keener, *Mind of the Spirit*, 232.
89. Müller, *Philippians*, 125.

ethically perfect in its absolute sense, but by virtue of God's grace upon them in Christ, they are perfect in principle. By analogy, Müller explains, "[j]ust as a little child is a perfect human being, but still is far from perfect in his development as man, so the true child of God is also perfect in all parts, although not yet perfect in all the stages of his development in faith."[90] So while Paul acknowledges his imperfection in the sense of knowing and experiencing the power of Christ in its completeness (3:12), he also acknowledges the potential perfection of a child of God, who must realize his or her perfection in a progressive sense in Christ (3:15). Hence, those who consider themselves as runners in the race, making progress to win the prize, are "mature." They are exhorted to think of their perfection in Christ unlike the Judaizers, who are pursuing righteousness by the law.

However, Paul knows that some Philippians may think otherwise (notice *kai,* which as an adversative could mean "But"[91]), perhaps due to the influence of the Judaizers. According to Fowl, "[i]n epistolary literature the notion of 'thinking otherwise or in a contrary manner' indicates discord in a friendship."[92] It not only contradicts Paul's emphatic exhortation to be united in one mind (2:2) but also explains the concrete social context of disunity in Philippi. In Greek, "if" followed by the indicative mood verb (*phroneite*) refers to an actual situation.[93] Paul believes that any further solution to the problem of disunity in Philippi beyond his profound ethical exhortations in 1:27–3:14, both by firm directives and exemplifying ideal models, is purely dependent upon God's direct intervention by revelation. In 3:15, he says, "God will make clear to you." Paul has always expressed his faith in God's active role in the faith pilgrimage of the believers in Philippi. On at least two earlier occasions, Paul declares his confidence that God, as the initiator of the good work among the Philippians, will surely keep directing that work to fulfill his purpose (1:6; 2:13).

For this success, the believers in Philippi have "to live up to what we have already attained" (3:16). Interestingly, Paul uses here the infinitive verb, *stoichein,* which is a military term[94] that means to "be in line with a person or thing considered as standard for one's conduct,"[95] almost in an imperative sense. The believers in Philippi, a miniature Rome, would have often seen

---

90. Müller, 126.
91. Hawthorne, *Philippians*, 156.
92. Fowl, *Philippians*, 164.
93. Hawthorne, *Philippians*, 156.
94. Fee, *Philippians*, NICNT, 360.
95. BDAG, 946.

instances of Roman soldiers falling in line at the command of their commanding officer. Paul evokes this familiar image in their minds by using a military term to command the sort of response he expects from the believers amidst persecution from the outside, internal conflict and division, and attacks from the Judaizers, who are disturbing the peace of the community.

However, the model that the believers are supposed to be in line with depends upon the meaning one ascribes to the following clause: *eis ho ephthasamen* (literally, "to what we have attained") and the dative pronoun *to auto* (literally, "by the same"). Evidently, Paul is referring to something that is already commonly held by the believers (notice the shift from the third person to the first person plural verb, *ephthasamen*, in 3:16). Within the context of the letter, the former phrase, "what we have attained," refers to the gospel Paul has preached and taught, both through his words and actions. The latter expression, "by the same," refers to the preceding phrase. Earlier in 3:1, in warning the Philippians about their need for caution about the teaching of the Judaizers, Paul says that he is not hesitant to repeat what he has told them earlier. Rightly, Hawthorne summarizes this, saying, "[t]ogether these words constitute Paul's appeal to the Philippians to fall in step with him and together with him begin to live up to whatever level of knowledge they have already acquired by revelation."[96] In fact, they are to sustain the standard they have already attained and are not to lower it for any reason. Paul repeats the idea of being in line with a good model of conduct by employing imitation language in 3:17. So until God clarifies the points of dissent among them (3:15), they need to keep up with the received standard, like soldiers falling in step with the gospel that has been taught in words and demonstrated in Christlike lifestyle by Paul, Timothy, Epaphroditus, and others.

In 3:17a, Paul exhorts the entire community of believers to join with him in imitating his example of living a Christ-oriented life. He says, "Join together [with me] in following *my* example" (3:17a, emphasis added). Paul employs the self-coined term *symmimētai*, meaning "co-imitators," to command them to join with him in imitating Christ. Unlike other imitation passages, he calls others to imitate Christ by following his example (3:17). Thus the exhortation is non-hierarchical and non-coercive, without a will to exercise power or dominate others. In 3:17, Paul does not present himself as the sole authentic model of imitation. The prefix *sym* implies that he is only

---

96. Hawthorne, *Philippians*, 157.

one among many good models whom the Philippian believers can join in the process of imitating Christ.

This insight into Paul's appeal from 3:17 challenges Castelli's contention, based on Galatians 4:12, that Paul indulged in forced sameness at the cost of destroying other possible models of imitating Christ by presenting himself as the sole coercive model of imitation. According to Castelli, "Paul and the Galatians do not function as mutual or reciprocal models; Paul remains the privileged model for the community he addresses."[97] For her, the imagery of fatherhood in Galatians 4:1–3 establishes a hierarchical relationship between Paul and the Galatians, and the call to become like him in 4:12 shapes a power relation that erases differences as "a pragmatic and conceptual part of Paul's consolidation of his apostolic authority."[98] However, Castelli's claim cannot be accepted because Paul addresses the Galatians using sibling language, as he does in Philippians 3:17. Moreover, in Philippians 3:17, Paul is one among other good models of imitation, and in Galatians 4:12, Paul claims to have already become like them in some sense. In other words, Paul is speaking about mutual cultural dislocation, becoming like each other without ceasing to be oneself.[99]

The non-hierarchical, non-coercive, and pastoral nature of Paul's imitation language become even more convincing in Philippians 3:17b. Apart from the invitation to be a co-imitator in following his example of becoming Christlike, he changes the pronoun from "my" to "us" in 3:17b, thereby including his companions – and possibly others (compare 4:3) – as authentic models for imitation. Notice the exhortation "to pay careful attention"[100] (*skopein*, 3:17) to those among the Philippians who walk like Paul and his companions among them. By seeking to put the interests of others first, Paul and his companions (2:5–8, 17, 20, 30) are good models of the cruciform life of Christ and deserve the careful attention of the Philippians. In the OT, obedience to God that emerges from a personal relationship is often described as a "walk," as with Enoch (Gen 6:9) and Abraham (Gen 17:1).[101] Similarly, all who live out the gospel of Christ, as preached by Paul and his companions, are authentic models of Christlikeness. In other words, the call to follow the example of Paul is not founded upon his inherent authority but depends upon Paul's (and others') single-minded imitation of the cruciform life of the incarnate Christ.

---

97. Castelli, *Imitating Paul*, 115–116.
98. Castelli, 119.
99. George, *Paul's Identity in Galatians*, 204–205.
100. BDAG, 931.
101. G. Bertram, "πατέω," *TDNT* 5:942–943.

In this light, Paul constructs a corporate model of becoming like Christ in 3:17, which is not limited to any individual. Rather, "the ultimate model of Christ, visible in the world, is made up of more than one individual stitched together into one larger body."[102] To give a modern example, the giant sculpture "The Monolith" in Oslo, Norway, has 121 figures engraved in a single large block of granite, and while every engraved image is significant, the overall block communicates one single message in unison.[103] No single figure is capable of communicating the final message completely, but "by being stitched together into one they not only overcome each other's incompleteness, they also together communicated one message, one story, and one idea to the whole world."[104] In other words, by paying careful attention to those who walk among them and practice Christlikeness, the Philippian believers are learning to be united into the larger body of Christlike disciples.

However, Paul further elucidates his appeal to imitate good models of Christlikeness by describing his inner anguish about those who live as bad models. Speaking about these bad models in 3:18–19, Paul is in tears before the Philippians. In 3:18–21, Paul contrasts the bad and good models in terms of their character, origin, and eschatological end.

---

102. George, "'Join Together with Me in Imitating My Example'," 105.
103. "The Monolith," http://www.vigeland.museum.no/en/vigeland-park/monolith.
104. George, "'Join Together with Me in Imitating My Example'," 105.

CHRISTIAN DISCIPLESHIP BY IMITATION IN THE CONTEXT OF THE *GURUKULA PATHASHALA* SYSTEM IN INDIA

Unlike Jesus's call to his followers in the gospels "to follow" him (*akolutheō* in Greek), which is the epitome of Christian discipleship, Paul's call to imitate (*mimētai* in Greek) authentic models in order to become Christlike is central to Pauline Christian discipleship. In the Greek world, as Abraham J. Malherbe states, philosophers such as Seneca valued the concrete exemplification of their teachings above words before their pupils, because it had greater influence, authority, and effectiveness in shaping them.[1] In this sense, Paul is culturally at home as a pastor and leader among his readers when he invites his new converts to imitate him and others who personally concretize the gospel before their eyes in fashioning the community.

Even in the ancient Asian education system, especially in the *Gurukula Pathashala* of India, disciples (*Shishya*) lived with their master (*guru*), who taught them the way to liberation from worldly entanglements. This learning was never merely cognitive but promoted a holistic transformation of a disciple's lifestyle through careful observation and imitation of the *guru*'s daily routine, behavioral pattern, and ethical and spiritual practices. To a great extent, the importance of imitation as a tool in discipling is common among Greek, biblical, and Indian (or Asian) contexts.

However, Paul's idea of imitation is different from the practice of imitation in the *Guru-Shishya* relationship in India. In the latter pattern of relationship, the *guru* is viewed as a "god" who leads a soul to liberation from *maya* (illusion) through mystical or spiritual practices, whereas Paul's call to imitate him in becoming Christlike is not a means to liberation but a consequence of being united "in Christ." In other words, a believer ought to aspire to be like Christ – hence imitate Paul and others – because of one's own spiritual existence in him. Further, unlike Indian religious *guru* traditions, the scope, aim, and arena of imitation for Paul is not limited to the private sphere of one's life but extends to ethical living based on the cruciform life of Jesus Christ and the gospel within an ever-broadening communal context.

In other letters, Paul presents himself as the sole authentic model for imitation in becoming like Christ (1 Cor 4:16; 11:1; 1 Thess 1:6; 2 Thess 3:9; 1 Tim 1:16; 2 Tim 1:13). However, in Philippians, the model of imitation is not monolithic but rather composite in nature (3:17). Paul, his fellow companions, and unknown Christians in Philippi who are living according to the gospel he preached all together exemplify a composite model of authentic Christlike life in Philippi. (See exegetical discussion on 3:17; 4:9.) For Paul, these models possess the mind of Christ because they do not seek their own interests but the interests of others (2:17, 19–30; compare 2:6–9). In short, their humble, cruciform lifestyles make them authentic models to fashion the community of believers in Philippi. Paul reinforces the importance of imitating the right models towards Christian discipleship by earnestly appealing to the believers to watch out for those living contrary to the truth of the gospel, whose end is destruction (3:1–2, 18–19).

---

1. Abraham J. Malherbe, *Paul and the Thessalonians: The Philosophical Tradition of Pastoral Care* (Philadelphia: Fortress Press), 52–53.

3:18–4:1 DISTINGUISH BAD AND GOOD MODELS

In India, we often underline the importance of imitating a good model in life by repeating a saying negatively. One such saying in the Hindi language, "*Jaisa guru, vaisa chela, dono narak me thelamthela,*" means, "As the master so the disciple will be, finally both will blame each other in hell."[105] If the model of imitation is bad, the end for both master and disciple will be in hell. Nothing can be done there except to curse each other while suffering eternal destruction. Hence, one must select a role model for life with great caution.

In this section, Paul returns to the topic of those who are dangerous to the faith and to healthy ethical living among the Philippian Christians. Earlier in 3:2, Paul exhorts them to be cautious of some whom he calls "dogs," while in 3:18 he describes them as "enemies of the cross of Christ" who live a life that is contrary to the model that Paul and his companions have displayed before the Philippians. Drawing a contrast between those who live as "enemies" and those who belong to his pattern of living (compare 3:20, noting the use of "our"), Paul becomes emotional: "For, as I have told you before and now tell you again even *with tears*" (3:18, emphasis added). Hawthorne observes the literary features of 3:18–19, saying, "[i]ts features are short, verbless sentences; constructions that are broken off without proper completion; clipped phrases

---

105. Another variant of the saying is, "*Andha guru, behera chela, dono narak me thelamthela*" meaning "Blind master, deaf disciple, finally both will blame each other in hell."

whose meaning defies proper explanation; strong words, whose force lies not in lexical definitions, but in the sound and suddenness with which they come."[106]

This section can be divided into two parts. In the first part (3:18–19), Paul mentions in ambivalent terms those who are living contrary to the model he demonstrated before the Philippians, identifying the motives and destiny of these bad models. In the second part (3:20–21), Paul identifies himself as part of a contrasting group of good models who are waiting in anticipation for the return of the Messiah and whose eschatological hope is to inherit a glorious body (3:20–21). This section concludes with an appeal to "stand firm in the Lord" (4:1).

3:18–19 Character and Destiny of Bad Models

Paul begins 3:18 with "for many" ("*polloi gar*"), explaining the reason for his emphasis in 3:15–17 on the need for the Philippian believers to fall in line with the gospel standards by carefully imitating good models of Christian living. Moreover, his tearful reminder to take careful note of "the enemies of the cross of Christ" underlines the necessity and urgency of their response. On the one hand, Paul is sad about the willfully rebellious lifestyle of some Christians in Philippi. On the other hand, he is equally concerned about the threat that their lifestyle poses to the believers. The fact that he has told them about his concern earlier (3:18, "I have often told you before"), probably during his earlier missionary visit, and repeats it now indicates the serious and persistent problem of having such bad models among them.

A key issue associated with 3:18 is the actual identity of "the enemies of the cross of Christ." In the light of the internal literary evidence (3:2–4; 1:15–17), they seem to be some Christian Judaizers in Philippi who are relying upon the law to become perfect. The circumstantial evidence in favor of this is that their lifestyle could be deceptively dangerous to Philippians as a confusing model for imitation. In 3:2, Paul calls them "dogs," which implies their unbecoming lifestyle. According to I. H. Marshall, the term "enemy" does not refer to those who openly declare antagonism to the gospel, but to those who live a life that implies antagonism to the cross.[107] Hence, these are not outsiders, such as those who violently react to the believers in Philippi (1:28), because the apostle's concern is with the manner in which they live. Notice, Paul's use of the word *peripatousin* (3:18 literally meaning "they are walking") refers to

---

106. Hawthorne, *Philippians*, 163.
107. I. Howard Marshall, *The Epistle to the Philippians*, ECS (London: Epworth Press, 1993), 100.

the way these Christians lived.[108] Further, the fact that Paul is weeping for them implies that they are from within the community, because his behavioral pattern is to be tearful for fellow Christians (compare Acts 20:31). We can therefore deduce that these "enemies" believe in Christ, and yet they desire to be perfected by their obedience to the law. This nullifies the grace available in knowing Christ and maturing in Christ. Thereby, the "enemies" do not run their Christian race with a singular focus but are in conflict with others due to their self-centered living.

Hence in 3:19, the apostle lists four negative facts about their lifestyle: (1) "their destiny is destruction"; (2) "their god is their stomach"; (3) "their glory is in their shame"; (4) "their mind is set on earthly things." O'Brien identifies sharp contrasts within the first three statements between "destiny," "god," and "glory" and "destruction," "stomach," and "shame," respectively. Further, the fourth statement contrasts "mind," which hitherto has had a positive meaning, with the negative object, "earthly things."[109]

Regarding the first statement, Paul's claim that the destiny of "the enemies of the cross" will be destruction is connected to his Christology, which is that Jesus is the incarnate Savior, appointed by the Father, who established a way for human salvation by his obedience to death on the cross and will be exalted by God (2:6–9). Furthermore, Christ is the returning Savior who will transform the mortal bodies of the citizens of his kingdom into glorious bodies (3:20–21). Anyone who has not submitted their lifestyle to the standards of the gospel of Christ will inevitably suffer destruction at the end. By searching for perfection beyond Christ Jesus through the law of Judaism, these "enemies" forfeit eternal life ("resurrection from the dead," 3:11).

The second statement, their "god is their stomach (*hee-koilia*)" (3:19), is similar. The primary meaning of *koilia* ("stomach") refers to "the organ of nourishment," but elsewhere in the NT, the term is used for the "seat of inward life, of feelings and desires," denoting "the hidden innermost recesses of the human body."[110] Hence Hansen rightly argues that "Paul uses the term stomach to represent 'unbridled sensuality, whether gluttony or sexual licentiousness'" (based on Rom 16:18 and 1 Cor 6:13).[111] If so, Paul is saying that these enemies serve selfish desires of all kinds, and this contradicts the Christlike model visible in Paul, Timothy, and Epaphroditus (2:17, 21, 30).

---

108. O'Brien, *Philippians*, 452.
109. O'Brien, 454.
110. BDAG, 550–551.
111. Hansen, *Philippians*, 266.

Unlike Paul (3:13–14), these enemies do not press forward to know Christ and be sanctified in him, because they are not preaching Christ with single-minded devotion. Their idol is physical desire, "the stomach."

The third statement, "their glory is in their shame" (3:19), reflects their unethical, unchristian, and unspiritual lifestyle. As Hansen suggests, Romans 1:27 and Revelation 3:18 use the term "shame" to describe a degraded moral state or "shameful nakedness."[112] In simple words, the "enemies" take pride in things that reveal their shame. In the north Indian Hindi language, a peacock's proud display of its beautiful feathered tail is used metaphorically to describe people who foolishly and arrogantly display their obnoxious, shameful selves in public. Yet while they arrogantly display or brag about their particular credentials of glory before others, they often fail to realize that – like a peacock lifting its beautiful tail – they are at the same time uncovering their shameful nakedness before people.

In the final statement, Paul says that "their mind is set on earthly things" (3:19). As discussed earlier, in 2:2 Paul exhorts the believers in Philippi to be "of one mind," and in 2:5 he asks them to "have the same mindset of Christ Jesus." As mature Christians, he says they should focus on their upward calling (3:13–16). Yet those who do not think and act in accordance with the gospel of salvation in Christ set their minds on "earthly things" (3:19), and they are dangerous to the community of believers because they do not seek the interest of others before their own. They become blind to the heavenly and eternal realities and engrossed in amassing "garbage" of the earth, just as Paul did in his past life. In other words, they have not yet realized the surpassing worth of knowing Christ our Lord (3:7–8).

The gravity of the plight of "the enemies of the cross of Christ" becomes glaring when Paul goes on to describe the identity, destiny, and eternal hope of those who are joining with him in imitating his example of Christ (3:20–21). The Philippian believers must take serious note of the two contrasting models of imitating Christ, for their failure to choose the right role model will determine their eternal destiny.

---

112. Hansen, 266.

"DUAL CITIZENSHIP" OF CHRISTIANS IN A HOSTILE AND PLURALISTIC RELIGIOUS CONTEXT

In the context of the rise of religio-cultural nationalism, Indian Christians often hear voices emanating from certain corners of society that question their patriotism and, mingled with this threat, a demand that they flee from the country to the "Christian" West. Their religious (Christian) identity is often the reason to doubt their loyalty towards the nation, despite all their acts of charity in the name of Christ and their sacrificial support in nation building. Their religious (Christian) identity is viewed as irreconcilable to their Indianness. Within the pluralistic religious context of India, where Christianity is a minority religion, some from the dominant community practice hatred, hostility, and the politics of violence to intimidate Christians and to demand a Christian response to the artificial dichotomy between religious and national identities. Is it possible for Christians in India to reconcile these two by being faithful disciples of Christ and also loyal towards the nation of India?

Writing to the Philippian believers who were living in a similarly hostile religio-political first-century context, Paul implicitly refers to the dual citizenship of Christians at least twice (i.e., their citizenship in the kingdom of Jesus Christ and in Philippi, the Roman city, 1:27; 3:20). Talking about the kingdom of Jesus Christ is similar to the Gandhian idea of *Ramrajya* ("divine rule") in performing *rajdharma* ("the rule of justice"), though they are not identical. First, M. K. Gandhi used *Ramrajya* in his political imagination during the national struggle for freedom from the British rule to establish a nation, *Rashtra*, for socio-economic prosperity, justice, and peace. The ethics governing Christian existence as citizens of Christ's kingdom are similar, though they are not a political concept of governance: to live a cruciform life while maintaining unity in the Spirit and self-sacrificially seeking the interests of others (2:1–5). Ultimately, Paul's idea of the kingdom of heaven seeks to actualize the trans-cosmic kingdom values in a historical context by fostering social tranquility, economic security of the weak, and harmonious coexistence in unity.

For Paul, every true Christian operates in two overlapping realms simultaneously. His confession that "our citizenship is in heaven" (3:20) calls all disciples of Christ to fulfill their obligations as citizens of heaven by living on earth in a manner that is worthy of the gospel. Does this mean that the two will not be in conflict? Partially, no. Even when Paul sends the letter, he is not only languishing in prison for Christ's sake (1:13), but the believers in Philippi are also suffering hostility for the sake

> of their faith (1:28). Moreover, to confess Christ as "the Lord" denies Caesar his sovereignty in the Empire.
>
> However, are these two realms irreconcilably polarized? Surely, no. To resolve the dichotomy, Paul views historical reality through a theological lens, placing Jesus Christ above every power that will ultimately submit to his universal authority, which transcends every geopolitical boundary. Christ is the true Lord enthroned by God, the Father (2:9–11). Hence, Christians must carefully balance a simultaneous coexistence in these conflicting kingdom realms without rejecting either.

3:20–4:1 Our Hope as Citizens of Heaven

Paul's emphatic use of *hēmōn* ("our"), a first person plural pronoun, at the beginning of 3:20 underlines his distinct identity, along with those who join him in imitating his example of Christ. He contrasts this identity with those who are behaving as "enemies of the cross of Christ" (3:17–19). While Paul portrays a dark portrait of the latter group in 3:18–19, he paints a positive portrait of those whose "citizenship [*to politeuma*] is in heaven" in 3:20–21. His purpose in these verses is to encourage a particular pattern of behavior through imitation.

Earlier in 1:27, Paul employs the imperative form, *poleteuesthe*, to command ethical behavior among the Philippians without strong political meaning.[113] In 3:20, Paul explicitly states that the heavenly citizenship of the Christians in Philippi is already a reality. Strathmann observes that the consequence of this reconstructed identity highlights detachment from earthly things from those who are far from their motherland and living in the world as a foreign colony of the heavenly city. He observes that "[w]hat we have here is rather a figurative use of the term in the sense of state or commonwealth and with a view to describing the fact that Christians are inwardly foreigners, not specifically in relation to the earthly state . . . but very generally in relation to the earthly sphere."[114] The term states "their membership of the heavenly kingdom of Christ, to which they belong as it were by constitutional right."[115] At present, the kingdom (or empire) of heaven is the home city of Christians.[116]

---

113. Hermann Strathmann, "πολιτευομαι, κτλ," *TDNT* 6:534.
114. Strathmann, 535.
115. Strathmann, 535.
116. Strathmann, 535.

Paul's reconstruction of political identity is important since Philippi was a strongly Roman city, and Paul emphatically and regularly uses high imperial titles, such as "Lord" and "Savior," for Jesus Christ (3:20). The politically subversive implication of Paul's identity reconstruction is explicit here. Marchal maintains that "[b]y his redeployment of terms like *sōtēr* and *kyrios*, both commonly used titles for Caesar, Paul exposes how the Roman Empire is the parody of the 'real thing,' God's empire."[117] Paul believed that "at the name of Jesus every knee should bow, in heaven and on earth and under the earth and every tongue acknowledge that Jesus Christ is Lord, to the glory of God the father" (2:10–11). For him, Christ Jesus is the sovereign Lord, who has "the power that enables him to bring everything under his control" (3:21). In addition, in the OT, the title "Lord" is used for Yahweh, which Paul now applies to Jesus Christ.

If so, Christians in Roman Philippi are primarily citizens of a different empire, and their primary allegiance is to the "Lord" and "Savior" of that empire, though they do not cease to be citizens of the Roman Empire. Although many in the Christian community at Philippi might be Roman citizens, their first priority is to behave as citizens of the kingdom of Christ Jesus. The fact that their "citizenship is in heaven" indicates that the Christians are already in the kingdom, but the heavenly origin of the awaited "Savior" implies that the kingdom is "not yet" consummated.[118] Now, they bear dual citizenship, both a spiritual citizenship (heavenly) and a physical citizenship of the human empire (the earthly Roman Empire). The two kingdoms are not mutually exclusive spheres, but the spiritual citizenship of heaven is vital for Christians.

For Paul, this sovereign Lord of the heavenly kingdom is the "Savior" (3:20), the eschatological figure who will establish his kingdom in the end. In the Pauline corpus, apart from this instance, the title "Savior" for Jesus Christ is only used in Ephesians 5:23.[119] In this absolute sense, the title was used only for Caesar in the Roman world. Paul's claim that the Savior by his power will "bring everything under his control" (3:21) is a theologically grounded political statement of subversion. A persecuted minority community at loggerheads with the majority culture (both ethically and because of their higher allegiance to the Sovereign Lord) would undoubtedly be encouraged by Paul's reminder that our all-powerful Savior will come in the future

---

117. Joseph A. Marchal, *The Politics of Heaven: Women, Gender, and Empire in the Study of Paul* (Minneapolis: Fortress Press, 2008), 40.
118. Fee, *Philippians*, NICNT, 379.
119. Fee, 381.

not only to control everything that hurts and threatens us at present, but also to transform (*metaschēmatisei*) our lowly bodies into like his glorious body. Thompson says that Paul's assurance "corresponds to the declaration in Romans 8:29 that believers who share the destiny of Christ in their present suffering (Rom 5:2–5; 8:18) will be conformed (*symmorphon*) to the image of the Son." In 1 Corinthians 15:50–55, Paul assures believers that they will be transformed and receive an incorruptible body at the coming of the messiah.[120] This transformation will be done by "power" (*energeia*, 3:21). In the NT, the term *energeia*, meaning "a state or quality of being active," is always used for the divine being.[121] For Paul, the "power" that works in Christ to bring everything under his control is God, who is at work in the believers (compare 2:13). In fact, God has already exalted Christ to the highest position and put everything under his lordship (2:9–11). By this power and authority, Christ controls all (*ta panta*, meaning "everything," 3:21) principalities – visible and invisible, high and low, spiritual and physical. As Lord, Paul claims that Jesus Christ, upon his return, will be the supreme authority, even over the Roman Empire. Hence, from the eschatological perspective, those who set their minds "on earthly things" will suffer destruction, along with all the powers and principalities, when the Savior returns. Thus the citizens of heaven not only hope for the final consummation of the messianic kingdom at the return of the Lord Jesus Christ, but also for their conformation to his glorious body as the final mark of their salvation, having known Christ and his power of resurrection (3:10–11).

Disagreement over 4:1 continues among scholars regarding its relation both to the preceding and subsequent passages. While Hawthorne argues that 4:1 is an introductory verse for 4:2–9,[122] others such as Thompson consider it a concluding verse for the rhetorical unit, *probation* (chs 2 and 3).[123] These particular positions are based on how one understands the referent of "in this way" (4:1), because the introductory word *hōste*, meaning "therefore," followed by an imperative, *stēkete* ("stand firm"), can function in either way. However, Paul's command to "stand firm" in 1:27 and 4:1 forms an *inclusio* around this body of argumentation in the letter and explains the purpose of his persuasive theological statements. Amidst external hostility as well as internal

---

120. Thompson, *Philippians*, 116.
121. BDAG, 335.
122. Hawthorne, *Philippians*, 177.
123. Thompson, *Philippians*, 117; Müller, *Philippians*, 136, fn. 1. See Silva, *Philippians*, WEC, 216–217. Silva, however, does not deny the transitional function of the sentence.

conflict threatening the survival of the community, this literary insight (the *inclusio* form) points to Paul's primary concern for the Philippians. The latter position taken by Thompson appears to be more profitable than Hawthorne's in understanding Paul's mind, though this does not negate the transitional significance of 4:1 for 4:2–9.

However, Hansen keeps an open-ended view, arguing that 4:1 has significance for both the preceding and subsequent passages.[124] If 4:1 is treated as the concluding statement for the preceding section, then the expression "stand firm . . . in this way (*outōs*)" refers to righteousness by faith in Christ that is not based on the law (3:4–9), the single-minded pursuit of knowing Christ and winning the prize (3:9–14), and imitating Paul's example of following Christ as citizens of heaven awaiting for the coming of the Savior (3:15–21). Yet if 4:1 is treated as the introductory statement for 4:2–9, then the expression "stand firm . . . in this way" refers to being of "the same mind in the Lord" (4:2–3), rejoicing in the Lord and making it known before others (4:4–5), being free from anxiety and letting our hearts be guarded by the peace of Christ (4:6–7), and noticing and practicing excellence from what is learned, heard, received, or seen (4:8–9).

Another significance for 4:1 in this context is Paul's abundant use of the language of affection and love: *adelphoi* ("brethren"), *agapētoi* ("beloved"), *epipothētoi* ("longed for"), *chara* ("joy"), and *stephanos* ("crown"). The first three terms may be considered as words expressing Paul's affection, while the latter two are words of celebration and honor. The term "brethren" (*adelphoi*) is frequently used in Philippians (1:2; 3:1, 13, 17; 4:8, 21), which suggests a non-hierarchical relationship between Paul and the believers. In fact, earlier in 3:17, Paul already considers himself as a co-imitator of Christ with the Philippian believers. They are siblings in God's family ("children of God" 2:15). Further, the twin use of the term "beloved" (*agapētoi*) underlines his fond affection and deep love for the Philippian believers. The third word of affection, "longed for" (*epipothētoi*), is a cognate of *epipotheō*, used in 1:8 and 2:26 for himself and Epaphroditus, respectively. Paul's longing for the believers is full of the affection of Christ (1:8), which reveals the depth and intensity of his desire for those who are not only far from him now but are also threatened both internally and externally. He desires to be with them in this moment of crisis to ensure an amicable solution to the problems that persist among them.

---

124. Hansen, *Philippians*, 281–282. See O'Brien, *Philippians*, 474. They accept it as both an inferential and transitional sentence.

Similarly, an intense longing for the Philippian believers is expressed in the case of Epaphroditus (2:26).

The first term of celebration and honor, "joy" (*chara*), is "a fundamental Christian emotion," and the Philippian believers are the cause of Paul's joy.[125] The second term of celebration and honor, "crown" (*stephanos*), describes the Philippians not as a diadem worn on the head of kings, but rather a wreath placed on a victor's head in the Hellenistic games. In this sense, "the Philippians are a cause for Paul's festal-like joy, on the one hand, and informing them that they are also a source of great honor for him, on the other hand."[126]

These strong expressions of love and pride create a strong sense of bonding between Paul and his readers, where the expression "beloved" is perhaps best translated as "dear friends." This bond underlines the rhetorical effect of Paul's letter as he celebrates the believers' partnership in his mission amidst suffering and expresses his deep concern for and correction of those who are deviating from the right path.

---

125. Hawthorne, *Philippians*, 178.
126. Hawthorne, 178.

PHILIPPIANS 4:2–23
CONCLUDING REMARKS

In many personal letters sent today, the author first addresses any primary concerns and then makes some quick comments and exhortations at the end. Though these exhortations are important, they do not reflect the main purpose of the letter. Similarly, having completed the main arguments, which began in 1:27, Paul begins to conclude his letter with polite requests in 4:2–3. Following his regular practice (Gal 5:1; 1 Thess 3:8), Paul offers some apparently random exhortations and words of gratitude (4:2–23). As Hawthorne observes, Paul repeats several important terms and ideas in an unstructured string of exhortations, such as "joy," "stand firm," "to be of the same mind," "contended at my side in the cause of the gospel" (4:2–9), which underline the unity of the letter. The use of sibling language, along with a dense use of words in the first person singular ("I"), emphasize the personal nature of the letter.[1] As in other letters, such as Galatians 6:17 and 2 Corinthians 13:11, Paul makes an adverbial use of *loipon* ("finally," 4:8) and commands them to "be of the same mind" (e.g., Rom 12:16; 15:5; 2 Cor 13:11).[2] Silva maintains that this section is exceptional because 4:2–3 shows a close link with the preceding section of the letter, whereas 4:10–20 appears to be a detached unit that is independent from the letter. This detachment has caused some to consider 4:10–20 to be a part of some other letter.[3]

4:2–9 FINAL EXHORTATION

In this section Paul addresses the pertinent issue of a personality clash within the church between two important female figures, Euodia and Syntyche. We do not know much about them except that, as their names indicate, they were of gentile origin. This has led many scholars to conjecture extensively about who they were and the nature of the conflict between them. Paul's earlier exhortations to stay united in the same mind is invoked again in relation to them, but one must not limit the entire issue to these two women, because 2:1–4 envisions the community at large. Nevertheless, Paul feels that it is important

---
1. Hawthorne, 176.
2. Thompson, *Philippians*, 122.
3. Silva, *Philippians*, WEC, 219.

to address the conflict brewing between Euodia and Syntyche, perhaps because they toiled earlier with him as his faithful companions and the "true companion" (4:3) has not yet stepped in to help them resolve their differences.

Further, although 4:4–9 appears to be an unstructured string of repetitive and random exhortations adopted from Hellenistic sources, a "closer observation will show that these commands are integrally related to the major themes of the entire letter and the specific conditions of the church in Philippi."[4] Interestingly, for Fowl, "Paul is advocating something much more substantial, demanding, and even subversive for the Philippians" because he has already taught that the commonwealth of heaven in Philippi stands "as an alternative political body, ruled by a different Lord, to that body constituted by the citizens of Philippi under the dominion of Caesar."[5] If so, one needs to consider Paul's exhortations within this specific context in order to recognize their significance.

4:2–3 A Plea to Be United

Philippians 4:2–3 is a humble request based on the personal relationship that the apostle has shared with Euodia and Syntyche. The phrase, stand firm "in this way," in 4:1 is precisely what Paul envisages when he says "to be of the same mind" in 4:2. Paul's appeal to behave in a certain fashion and his request for mediation by the "true companion" (4:3) suggest that the two women were not living in mutual harmony and unity. Hence, Paul urges strongly, "I plead" (*parakalō*), to both Euodia and Syntyche without taking sides.[6] For some reason unknown to us, these two women have not been conducting themselves in line with Paul's earlier exhortation to the members of the commonwealth of heaven. He urges them specifically to "be of the same mind in the Lord," something he says earlier to the entire community (2:2–4). This means that the problem of disunity and conflict in the community is wider and not limited to these two women.

If so, why does Paul specifically mention them by name? Most likely, they were his former team members and extended significant support to him in the past. In 4:3, Paul identifies them as those who "have contended at my side in the cause of the gospel." In 1:27, Paul uses the same image to speak of the way the entire community in Philippi ought to behave. Contending for "the cause of the gospel" side by side implies their united stance in advancing the gospel. During Paul's mission work in Philippi, these two women probably

---

4. Hansen, *Philippians*, 286–287, cited from 287. See Fowl, *Philippians*, 180–181.
5. Fowl, *Philippians*, 181.
6. Hansen, *Philippians*, 282.

withstood opposition from outsiders to ensure that the gospel flourished in Philippi. Hence, they must have been influential personalities in the community. The image of these women as leaders in Philippi need not surprise us, because historical evidence proves that women in Philippi played a greater role in the city's social life compared with any other part of the empire.[7] For Paul, the falling out between them is harming the larger interest of the church in Philippi, and their reconciliation is necessary for the healthy spiritual life of the community.

The common space for being "of the same mind" is "*in* the Lord" (*enkuriō*, 4:2, emphasis added), which is synonymous with Paul's favorite expression, "in Christ." This is the mystical space of their coexistence beyond bipolarities, hierarchies, and differentiations (Gal 3:26–28), where selfish sociocultural claims cease to operate. Hence, the two women are exhorted to be of "the same mind." Otherwise, their conduct contradicts their existential space and causes disruption in the community.

Paul's agony is not limited to the conflict between the two women, for he is also concerned that his unnamed confidant, "my true companion" (literally, "true yoke-fellow"),[8] has not yet stepped in to bring reconciliation between them. In Paul's confinement, he needs the anonymous figure to act ("help") in the "same mind," seeking others' interests first (2:2–4) in order to limit the damage that the women's conflict could cause to the community. Although the identity of the "true companion" remains mysterious, Paul's indirect reference to the particular individual (*se*, "you," in singular form, 4:3) would have been enough for the church to know exactly whom Paul is addressing. In Philippi, there were some, such as Clement and his other "coworkers," who labored with him for the advancement of the gospel. Paul values them, though they are not specifically named here. Clement's Latin name indicates that he was a Roman and a respected member of the community.[9] Perhaps, for this reason, Paul names him, but it is equally possible that Paul remembers him contending in mission on a particular occasion alongside him, Euodia and Syntyche.

The idea of someone's name appearing "in the book of life" (4:3) was known among the Jews. In Exodus 32:32, as an intercessor pleading for forgiveness on behalf of Israel, Moses asks the Lord to blot out his name from the book. Similarly, the book of life is referred to in Jewish apocalyptic literature

---

7. Hawthorne, *Philippians*, 179; Fee, *Philippians*, NICNT, 390–391, fn. 31.
8. The identity of the unnamed figure has been debated and conjectured differently. For a list of proposals, see Hawthorne, *Philippians*, 179–180.
9. Hansen, *Philippians*, 285.

(Dan 12:1; 1 En 47.3; 1QM 12.3) and the NT (Luke 10:20; Heb 12:23; Rev 3:5; 13:8). Mentioning that their names appear in the book in heaven assures believers of their citizenship in heaven (3:20). Even in the Roman colony of Philippi, as Hansen observes, the citizens of the city who registered their names in the civic census register were bound by duty to live in harmony. Similarly, those who have their names written in the "book of life" are bound to live by its standard.[10]

4:4–7 Rejoice and Do Not Worry

In 4:4–7, we find a series of short commands and statements that do not seem to be connected to one another. The initial command, "Rejoice in the Lord always," is reinforced by the repetition, "I will say it again: Rejoice!" (4:4). The command to rejoice is a recurring theme in the letter (2:18; 3:1), which is addressed to a community that is a target of persecution from outside and strife within. Paul wants to teach his believers in Philippi that Christian joy is not determined by contextual or historical realities but should be a believer's continuous ("always," 4:4) and appropriate response of trust in God's activity. In other words, it is "the appropriate response when one rightly perceives the unfolding of God's drama of salvation even in the midst of suffering and opposition."[11] Hence, the sphere of a believer's activity or experience is "in the Lord." For a Christian, joy is not a spontaneous emotional outburst because of certain pleasant experiences, but an intentional response that is grounded in the Lord, recognizing what God is doing among his people and in the world at large.

The reasons given for *chara* ("joy") are different for Paul than for the believers in Philippi. While Paul rejoices in the progress of the believers (2:2) or the gospel (1:18), the believers experience joy in seeing their emissary, Epaphroditus, safely return back to them (2:28–30). Elsewhere in Paul's letters, "joy" is closely associated with the Holy Spirit. In Galatians 5:22, it is listed as a fruit of the Spirit. For Paul, it belongs to the Holy Spirit (1 Thess 1:6).

Paul's next command is: "Let your gentleness be evident to all" (4:5). The term *epieikēs*, translated as "gentleness," is difficult to translate adequately. In the Greco-Roman context, it was an admired quality. "Roman writers spoke of the *clementia* of Caesar . . . In the Septuagint the adjective *epieikēs* and the noun *epieikeia* are used for the gentleness and forbearance of God (1 Sam 12:22; . . . Wis 12:28; Bar 2:27 . . .), connoting judgment combined with

---

10. Hansen, 286.
11. Fowl, *Philippians*, 181.

mercy."[12] Apart from this context, it appears on only three other occasions within the NT. In 2 Corinthians 10:1, Paul appeals on the basis of the "gentleness of Christ," but in the pastoral letters, gentleness is one of the desirable qualities of a minister of God, as opposed to quarrelsome behavior (1 Tim 3:3; Titus 3:2). Hawthorne states that, for Aristotle, gentleness was a generous treatment of others, suggesting a just, but not literal, application of the law. In other words, to be gentle is to do justice without harm.[13] Paul commands the believers in Philippi to practice this virtue in the sight of others so that others may see it. Amidst hostility from others, the Christian response in Philippi ought to be in tune with the gentleness of Christ, which seeks justice without intending harm. Making "gentleness evident to all" (4:5) in effect overlaps with the exhortation to shine like stars among the warped and crooked generation (2:15–16). To some extent, the exhortation to be gentle is missional in essence, for it distinguishes the community of Christ from those who live outside of life in Christ.

The statement, "[t]he Lord is near" (indicative), is disconnected from the imperative, but it can be understood in connection with the preceding command as, "you must let others see your gentleness because the coming of the Lord is near." Reading 4:5 this way echoes the words of the psalmist in 145:18, which recognize the imminence of God in our day-to-day activities. However, in the light of Paul's words, the expression also means that the community of the faithful waits for the return of the Savior, who has power to control everything and to transform our lowly bodies to conform to his glorious body. The statement implies the imminent eschatological return (3:20–21) of the sovereign Lord, who will be exalted to the highest position, even above Caesar (2:9–11).

However, this statement at the end of 4:5, "[t]he Lord is near," can also be understood in relation to the command that follows: "Do not be anxious about anything" (4:6). If "[t]he Lord is near" introduces this command, it reminds us of the words of Jesus in Matthew 6:25–34. The believers in Philippi do not have to worry about anything, including the threats from outside, because the Lord controls everything. Their prayers, petitions, and thanksgivings are informed by the Lord's return, which does not leave room for anxiety.

Thus "[t]he Lord is near" can be interpreted in multiple ways, but it would be wise to conclude that it stands equally connected to both commands,[14] since

---

12. Thompson, *Philippians*, 136.
13. Hawthorne, *Philippians*, 182.
14. Fowl, *Philippians*, 183.

Paul may be intentionally communicating the imminence and immanence of the Lord by using an ambiguous expression.[15]

In 4:6, Paul encourages the Philippians to "present your requests to God," who is at work in you constantly (1:6; 2:13). In other words, the Philippians ought to open their hearts in God's presence as an expression of their trust in God's activity "in every situation" (4:6) and every aspect of life. No circumstance should make them anxious, because "[t]he Lord is near," and they are to "present their requests to God." According to Hansen, Paul uses a string of three synonyms for prayer – *prayer, petition, requests* – with additional emphasis on *thanksgiving*, which "encourages all types of prayer." The types of prayers include intercession (*proseuchē*), requests to meet certain needs (*deēsis*), and prayers for specific concerns (*aitēmata*).[16]

If so, Paul introduces the verse with "and" (*kai*), which "probably introduces the result of making requests to God."[17] The result of letting God know one's request is "the peace of God." The genitive form signifies God as the source of "the peace." In the Roman imperial context, the Peace of Rome (*Pax Romana*) was an important theme of imperial propaganda widely spread through Roman art and architecture.[18] The Roman *Pax* was understood as both the end of wars against external forces and the suppression of internal revolts. It was maintained high-handedly by the terrorizing will of the dominant power and by instilling fear and an acceptance of humiliation and enslavement among the defeated subjects.[19] In contrast, "the peace" that Paul is speaking about originates with and belongs to God. Psalm 29:11 says that "the LORD blesses his people with peace." The following expression, "transcends all understanding," qualifies God's peace. In the Roman imperial context of Philippi, Paul's claim for "the peace of God" is subversive, for it not only draws a direct comparison between God's peace and the *Pax Romana* aggressively propagated in Philippi, a Roman colony, but it also undermines Roman peace as inferior. For Paul, true peace comes from the reconciliatory act of God through his son upon the cross (2:6–11).

Unlike the Roman *Pax*, God's peace "will guard [*phrourēsei*] your hearts [*kardia*] and your minds [*noēmata*] in Christ Jesus." While the "heart and

---

15. Hawthorne, *Philippians*, 182.
16. Hansen, *Philippians*, 290.
17. Thompson, *Philippians*, 137.
18. Klaus Wengst, *PAX ROMANA and the Peace of Jesus Christ*, trans. John Bowden (Philadelphia: Fortress Press, 1987), 7–54.
19. Wengst, *PAX ROMANA*, 11.

mind" together refer to "the whole of Christian existence,"[20] the image for the verb "guard" comes from the Philippian context, where the Roman garrison was stationed to maintain peace by ensuring law and order within the city.[21] Paul intends to tell the believers in Philippi that God's peace will secure and protect a believer in Christ. "In Christ" is an important recurring expression in Philippians (1:1, 26; 2:5; 3:3, 14; 4:7, 19, 21) that identifies an alternate space of emancipation for the persecuted, minority Christian community in Philippi.

4:8–9 Obey and Live in Peace

The last command in a string of imperatives is introduced by *loipon* ("finally"). In 4:8, Paul uses six adjectives, each preceded by the relative pronoun "whatever" (*hosa*), and two nouns in separate conditional clauses that begin with "if . . ." Beare points out that all these terms signify "virtues of pagan morality" without exception and argues that "[i]t is almost as if he had taken a current list from a textbook of ethical instruction, and made it his own."[22] However, as Thompson argues, having defined the parameters of Christian moral conduct in Philippi based on the Christ's incarnational narrative, Paul does not end his letter with Hellenistic moral ideals. Instead, although he borrows vocabulary from the Hellenistic context, he redefines these ideas "in light of the cross, calling for a communal *phronēsis* determined by the Christ event."[23]

In 4:8–9, Paul exhorts the Philippians to do two important things: (1) "think about such things" (4:8) and (2) "put it into practice" (4:9). The twofold concluding imperative is quite natural for Paul, as thinking and doing are two important areas of discussion in the letter. The first command, "think about such things" (4:8), refers back to the preceding six adjectives and two nouns. The two nouns used in 4:8 are *aretē* ("excellent") and *epainos* ("praiseworthy"). According to the BDAG, the term "excellent" is used in 2 Peter 1:5b to refer to the highest form of virtue, an uprightness that is the opposite of lower standards of behavior. In 4:8, when it is used along with "praiseworthy," it refers to a "recognition of distinguished merit that was customary in Gr[eco]-Rom[an] society." In a social context, it evokes public recognition. Among Stoics, it was a favorite moral term.[24] Even Paul uses the term to refer to the moral excellence familiar from the Hellenistic cultural context. The Philippian

---

20. Thompson, *Philippians*, 137.
21. Hansen, *Philippians*, 294.
22. Beare, *Philippians*, 148.
23. Thompson, *Philippians*, 139.
24. BDAG, 130.

believers are commanded to think about "such things" of excellence, which are qualified by six adjectives: "true," "noble," "right," "pure," "lovely," and "admirable" (4:8). Together, they refer to the desired ethical qualities.

Within the Philippians' context, thinking about what is "true," the first word in this series of virtues, is to be unlike those who preach with false motives (1:18). The Philippians must discern the difference between the truth and falsehood by intentionally pursuing the truth. Even in Romans 1:18, 25, the truth is associated with God, which is a truth that human wickedness purposefully suppresses.

The second term, "noble," means "honorable, worthy . . . above reproach."[25] In the pastoral epistles, it is used with respect to the conduct of church leaders, whose lives must be above reproach, evoking admiration and respect from others (1 Tim 2:2, 11; 3:8; Titus 2:2, 7). Paul exhorts the Philippians to conduct themselves in ways that are above reproach, in full coherence with their heavenly citizenship, despite being victimized by some in the city (1:27; 3:20).

The third term, "right" (literally, "just"), is often used by Paul in the context of speaking about one's righteousness before God (Rom 3:10; 5:19; Gal 3:11). However, it is also used in a broad secular sense, meaning to do that which is just, based on cultural customs (Phil 1:7; Matt 20:4).[26] Hawthorne states that "[i]t concerns giving to God and men their due. It involves duty and responsibility. It entails satisfying all obligations."[27]

The fourth term, "pure," is a cultic term, which signifies the purity of an object dedicated in the temple. It must not be understood only in the sense of moral uprightness, though "it embraces the idea of purity in motives and actions including pure in every part to life (compare 2 Cor 11:2; 1 Tim 5:22; Jas 3:17; 1 John 3:3)."[28]

The fifth term, "lovely," as Fee points out, is taken from the Hellenistic background and is unused elsewhere in the NT. It includes every conduct that is "recognized as admirable by the world at large"[29] and means to cause "pleasure or delight."

Finally, the sixth term, "admirable," refers to the conduct that is generally praised by others. What Paul appears to be saying is that the Philippian believers must conduct themselves in a manner that will evoke praise from others.

---

25. BDAG, 919.
26. Hansen, *Philippians*, 298.
27. Hawthorne, *Philippians*, 188.
28. Hawthorne, 188.
29. Fee, *Philippians*, NICNT, 418.

In short, the Christians are exhorted to "think" about such things, which fall in the list of virtues Paul mentions. Their conduct ought to be such that it will evoke admiration from others rather than hatred or ill will.

In 4:9, Paul states the second aspect of the command, which is to put in practice those things that have been imparted by his teaching, preaching, and living before them. This exhortation is a call to imitate Paul and is an appropriate conclusion to his presentation of a series of true models (from Christ to Paul's companions). However, he narrows the scope of what needs to be put into practice in 4:9. The verse begins with *ha*, a definitive relative pronoun, which refers to a specific set of teachings imparted to the Philippians, which are referred to as "such things" in 4:8.[30] In other words, 4:8 is defined more narrowly in 4:9. Thereby, it limits all praiseworthy and excellent things to those virtues exemplified in Paul's teachings and personal living: namely, that Paul conducted himself self-sacrificially and put their interests above his own. This narrow scope of imitation in 4:9 does not contradict 3:17, because, as Hawthorne observes, "Paul may have deliberately placed the *enemoi* ("in me") at the end of the list, not only for rhetorical effect, but to say as forcefully as possible that everything he knew and believed and taught was embodied in himself."[31]

The four important terms used in 4:9, "learned," "received," "heard," and "seen," comprise a source of learning upon which they should model their lives. Hansen argues that the first two terms refer to Paul's teachings (i.e., the gospel) and the latter two terms refer to his actual life as he lived before them, preaching and practicing what he taught.[32] In a sense, Paul is a good model in whom the gap between speech and action merge into one. In contrast to those who preach Christ out of wrong motives (1:15), Paul commands his believers to follow the good model seen in him. Fee maintains that the call is to imitate the "kind of cruciform existence" that Paul has visibly demonstrated before their eyes.[33]

Paul concludes the command in 4:8–9 with a promise: "And the God of peace will be with you." Thompson maintains that Paul speaks of the "God of peace" elsewhere "in the context of real or potential conflict (1 Cor 14:33; Rom 16:20)."[34] For Paul, as Fee rightly maintains, the presence of God among

---

30. O'Brien, *Philippians*, 508.
31. Hawthorne, *Philippians*, 190 (Greek transliteration added).
32. Hansen, *Philippians*, 300.
33. Fee, *Philippians*, NICNT, 420.
34. Thompson, *Philippians*, 139.

his people is Jewish in nature, which in the context of the church is brought about through the presence of the Spirit.[35] If so, the promise to the Philippian believers is that if they conduct themselves according to the gospel preached to them in words and actions, then when there is internal and external discord among them, they will still enjoy the presence of God through the Spirit's presence among them. To a persecuted community, the promise of the personal presence of the "God of peace" is most encouraging.

4:10–20 THANKSGIVING FOR THEIR SUPPORT

Paul begins 4:10 with *de,* which (though not usually translated) is considered to indicate the beginning of a new section. According to Lightfoot, "[t]he *de* arrests a subject which is in danger of escaping," as in Galatians 4:20.[36] Paul makes a sudden and disconnected shift to a section about thanksgiving that otherwise might have been forgotten. Though some in the past have argued that 4:10–20 forms a part of another letter sent to the Philippians, this is unlikely because, as Fowl argues, the section repeats several important words and ideas from 1:3–11. For example, 1:3 and 4:10 both refer to rejoicing and thanking God; 1:5 and 4:15 both mention partnership; 1:6 and 4:13 both speak about God's care; 1:7 and 4:14 both mention the Philippians standing with Paul in his trials; 1:7 and 4:10 both identify the disposition that Paul shared with the Philippians (through the common use of *phronein*). In addition, the section connects with the rest of the letter, for this is not the only place where Paul expresses his gratitude to the Philippians. In 1:4–5, he thanks them for their partnership with him in advancing the gospel; in 2:16–18, he rejoices that he shares a relationship with them in Christ; in 2:25, he acknowledges their support by sending Epaphroditus to help him in his need. Thus, 4:10–20 is not the result of "an afterthought," but rather "a well-crafted frame within which the entire epistle fits quite nicely."[37]

In 4:10–20, Paul expresses his gratitude to the Philippians for their help in a countercultural manner. Based on G. W. Peterman's work, Fowl maintains that within the practices of Paul's culture, receiving and giving gifts had significant sociocultural ramifications. A clear acknowledgment of help in need established a hierarchical relationship based on a social convention between the giver and receiver of gifts. The receiver remained obligated to the giver in

---

35. Fee, *Philippians*, NICNT, 420.
36. Lightfoot, *Philippians*, 163 (Greek transliteration added).
37. Fowl, *Philippians*, 191–192, cited from 192.

a time of need unless the receiver could reciprocate by returning a gift in equal measure. If not, the receiver had to acknowledge the giver of gifts as socially superior.[38] However, in 4:10–20, Paul acknowledges the timely support of the Philippians in his need, but the ground of his gratefulness is "in the Lord" (4:10), which does not leave room for a hierarchical relationship.

If the term "I rejoice" (*echarēn*, aorist, literally, "I rejoiced") in 4:10 is an epistolary aorist verb, then Paul is speaking in the past tense when compared with the time that the Philippians actually read these words. Paul regularly uses the verb "rejoice" to mention a particular Christian disposition towards circumstances (1:4, 18; 2:2, 17–18; 3:1; 4:4). The reason for his joy is a revival of the Philippian believers' concern for the apostle after a gap of some time. The expression *ēdēpote*, translated as "at last" (4:10), implies that "the Philippians had let an inordinately long time elapse since last they sent Paul a gift."[39] This does not imply that Paul is passing a sly remark on their failure to send support at a regular interval, because "the following sentence gives the reason for the unavoidable delay in the arrival of the church's gift."[40] Paul says, "you were concerned, but you had no opportunity" (4:10). The reason for the delay is unknown, but Paul is sure that the lapse in time is merely due to a lack of opportunity to help.

Paul "greatly" rejoices that the Philippians are able to support him in his mission once again. His joy is not based on the materialistic support he is receiving from the Philippians, but rather because of their concern for him. In other words, the reason for his rejoicing is "not things, but people and how they behaved."[41] While the term *phronein* "describes an active interest in that person's affairs,"[42] the term *anethalete*, translated as "you renewed," is a botanical term, meaning "cause to grow/bloom again" exactly into the previous state.[43] In short, Paul rejoices that the Philippians have revived their concern for him to exactly the same state in which they partnered with him earlier (4:14–18). They have always been thoughtful of him and willing to help, but only now, after a gap of time, have they had the opportunity (*akaipeisthai*) to help him.

In 4:11–13, Paul expresses his strong contentment in all circumstances. He denies in explicit terms that he rejoices because he desires gifts from them:

---

38. Fowl, 190–191.
39. Bruce, *Philippians*, 123.
40. Martin, *Philippians*, TNTC, 174.
41. Hawthorne, *Philippians*, 196.
42. Hawthorne, 196.
43. BDAG, 63.

"I am not saying this because I am in need" (4:11a compare 4:17). Paul does not want the Philippian believers to misunderstand him or his positive disposition towards them. Paul's need here may refer to "lacking that which is essential,"[44] which does not mean that Paul has never been in want or unable to meet his basic needs. Paul's catalogue of sufferings in 2 Corinthians 6:3–10 specifically mentions hunger, while in 1 Corinthians 4:11, he says, "we go hungry and thirsty . . . we are homeless." The impression Paul gives is not that he has everything he needs in prison, but that he does not have a sense that he is lacking because he has learned to be content.

Further, Paul speaks about contentment and his confidence that he can do all things "through him" who gives him strength (4:11b–13). The term *autarkēs*, meaning "content,"[45] is unique to this verse in the NT. It is a moral term that was particularly important for Stoics, whose ultimate goal was to attain self-sufficiency or contentment by emotional detachment.[46] In Hindu and Buddhist philosophical thought, desire is the source of all pain. Hence, *nishkama karma* (literally, "work without expectation") is the highest virtue in human existence. Paul is not speaking about such a detachment from things; rather his contentment in all circumstances is due to his confidence in Christ, who is sufficient to provide all his needs (4:13). In the preceding verse, Paul rejoices "in the Lord" (4:10). In other words, Paul trusts God to meet all his needs. His behavior is not controlled by the circumstances he faces, nor is his contentment a result of self-discipline.

Using "I" in the emphatic position, Paul affirms that he has already learned (notice the aorist form of *emathon*) to be content. His struggles in mission (1 Cor 6:3–10; 12:8–9) and his eagerness to know Christ – and to consider everything he counted precious in the past as garbage (3:4–11) – has taught him the secret of contentment. He no longer desires to have more, but is able to rely on Christ, the source of his strength, to meet his needs. Paul's priority is to serve Christ throughout his life at any cost (1:21), whether he is in "need," "plenty," "well fed or hungry" (4:12). He can face all circumstances without complaints because he trusts in the one who strengthens him (4:13).

Interestingly, the reason for his contentment is embedded in the infinitive verb, *tapeinousthai*, which, as Hawthorne observes, signifies his knowledge of how "to humble himself" or "to be humbled." In other words, his ability to

---

44. BDAG, 1044.
45. BDAG, 152.
46. Hansen, *Philippians*, 310.

cope with every circumstance is key to his contentment.⁴⁷ But how does one attain such contentment in every circumstance? Seemingly, it is the result of a cognitive change. In 4:11b–12, Paul uses verbs of cognition, such as *emathon* ("I learned"), *oida* ("I know"), and *memyēmai* ("I have learned the secret"), which fit appropriately with his emphasis on cognitive transformation (2:2–3, 5; 3:10, 19–20; 4:2). To learn the secret of contentment, we must cultivate a mental disposition that enables us to cope with the circumstances of life. Similarly, to remain in unity, we must cultivate the unity of our minds in a Christlike manner. According to Fowl, Paul is referring to being initiated "into the secret of Christ-focused contentment" in 4:13.⁴⁸ For Paul, we can only derive strength from Christ if we are found in Christ (3:9), which he implies by his use of the preposition *en* ("in") in 4:13. In other words, Paul is not completely abandoning desire or teaching *nishkama karma* ("work without expectation") as it is taught in other religions, but he is living in total reliance upon God's provision while declaring his own inability to bring about the results that he expects God to accomplish.

In 4:14, Paul makes a sudden shift by using the adversative conjunction *plēn* ("yet"). He returns to "partnership," a key idea in the earlier part of the letter, with a word of appreciation: "it was good of you." Paul appreciates their loving gesture in extending personal care to him even though he could have been content without it. Instead of appreciating their gift in particular, Paul commends their act as "sharing in my [Paul's] trouble" (4:14). In other words, Paul appreciates them for becoming fellow partakers in the apostle's condition. The aorist participle *synkoinōnēsantes*, meaning "sharing in," suggests that Paul is thinking of a past event, perhaps his imprisonment itself, when Epaphroditus stayed with him on behalf of the Philippians to serve him in his need.

In a single long Greek sentence in 4:15–16, Paul recounts concrete instances from the past when the Philippian believers stood with him in mission. In 4:15, appealing to the common knowledge of the Philippians, Paul refers back to the first visit he made to the Macedonian region, particularly Philippi, during his second missionary journey (Acts 16:11–40). Paul acknowledges their partnership and expresses his gratitude for them. The Philippians are the only church that shared with Paul in *doseōs* ("giving") and *lēmpseōs* ("receiving"), terms that are commonly used in a business context. Paul uses them to refer to the material gifts he received from the church and the spiritual blessings

---

47. Hawthorne, *Philippians*, 199.
48. Fowl, *Philippians*, 196.

they received from him. This probably explains why Paul never suggests that he will repay the Philippians for the gifts he received from them. Their support of Paul is being repaid by the spiritual blessings they received in Christ. For Paul, their act of supporting him financially is grounded in Christ. Hence, he rejoices on their behalf in the Lord (4:10) and desires that more may be credited to their account (4:17). In other words, the participation of the Philippians in the advancement of the gospel by supporting Paul's needs is not a personal favor that requires an acknowledgment of their benevolence. Rather, it is done for God, who will "meet all your needs according to the riches of his glory in Christ Jesus" (4:19). To the credit of the Philippians, when no other church stepped in to share in Paul's afflictions by extending him material support, the Philippians alone supported him from the very early days of their acceptance of the gospel. Even when he went from Philippi to Thessalonica, the Philippian church sent him gifts more than once in his need (4:16). Though the Philippians helped Paul in the past, Paul feels content in all circumstances.

In 4:17, Paul makes a second disclaimer in order to avoid misunderstanding: "[n]ot that I desire your gifts." Although he makes this disclaimer earlier (4:11), he repeats himself, because he does not want his appreciation of them in 4:15–16 to be seen as a subtle attempt to ask for more gifts. Instead, Paul's "desire is that more be credited to your [Philippians'] account" (4:17). By adding the prefix *epi* to *zētein* ("to seek"), Paul intensifies his wish to increase *karpos* (literally, "fruit") to their account. Although 4:17 is overloaded with commercial language, *karpos* is an agricultural metaphor that can also be understood in a commercial sense.[49] However, as Thompson observes, Paul employs *karpos* as an agricultural metaphor in the NT for "ethical formation empowered by the Spirit (compare Gal 5:22; Rom 1:13)." In the letter to the Philippians, Paul prays for them to be filled with the "fruit of righteousness" (1:11). Further, he desires to reap "fruitful labor" among them (1:22) with a concern to see their progress in faith (1:25–26). Thus, what Paul intensely desires for the Philippians to have credited to their account is "the transformation of the community, their capacity for sacrifice."[50] The Philippians ought to imitate Paul in a self-sacrificial, missional model, willingly offering themselves for the advancement of the gospel and the progress of others (1:12–14; 2:17). Such a transformation in the Philippian community will increase "fruit" in their account.

---

49. Hawthorne understands the word "fruit" (*karpos*) in a commercial sense (*Philippians*, 206).
50. Thompson, *Philippians*, 143.

In 4:18, Paul continues to use commercial metaphors to speak about the gifts he has received, saying, "I have received full payment and have more than enough." While the first part of the sentence ("I have received full payment") is "used as a technical expression for the drawing up of a receipt in business," the latter part (I "have more than enough") underlines the generosity of the gift that has covered more than his needs. It was culturally acceptable in the first-century context for the recipient of a gift to acknowledge the generosity of the giver as a mark of his or her gratitude. Paul continues to affirm that the gift he received, which the believers sent through Epaphroditus, meets all his needs. Paul's words convey that he is hesitant to make too much of the participation of the Philippians in his mission by providing for his needs. Paul neither allows himself to be burdened with the sociocultural expectations associated with giving and receiving, nor refrains completely from acknowledging the generosity, sufficiency, and magnanimity of their gifts. In other words, Paul redefines their generosity theologically, which has two functions in this context. First, it functions as an expression of his gratitude towards them. Second, it explains why Paul never burdened himself with the responsibility of personally reciprocating for the gifts he received. Paul understood their magnanimity as a sacrifice offered to please God.

Drawing on language from the OT cultic system, Paul redefines the significance of their gift sent through Epaphroditus as "fragrant" and as an "acceptable sacrifice" that is pleasing to God (4:18). In the OT, on multiple occasions, the odor of the sacrificial offerings for God is described as pleasing to God (Gen 8:21; Lev 1:9, 13, 17), while the sacrifices themselves were merely acceptable to God (Ps 51:17). Such an understanding continued even in the NT. Paul speaks about his own ministry as spreading the fragrance of God to all (2 Cor 2:14) and offering our own "bodies as a living sacrifice, holy and pleasing to God" (Rom 12:1). In Ephesians 5:2, the self-sacrificial death of Christ is understood as "a fragrant offering and sacrifice to God." By infusing theological meaning from OT sacrificial language to the Philippians' support of Paul and his mission, he elevates their sacrificial missional partnership from a simple, contractual human act to a spiritually significant deed done unto God. In fact, Paul speaks of the Philippians' effort in sacrificial terms earlier in 2:17. Thus, if their sacrifice is pleasing to God, then it is undoubtedly important for Paul and his mission.

Hence, God (not Paul) will reciprocate for their sacrificial gifts in supporting Paul's mission to advance the gospel (4:19). Paul emphasizes his personal standing with God, saying, "*my* God *will meet all* your *needs*" (emphasis added). In 2 Corinthians 8:2–5, Paul mentions that the churches have shared in a collection project in spite of their own lack. Now, the Philippians are assured that God will never be their debtor. God is faithful to provide all their needs (*chreia*, 4:19), just as Paul's needs (*chreia*, 4:16) have been met in "full," and he has "more than enough" (4:18). According to Martin, "the preposition *according to*, *kata*, makes it clear that 'the rewarding will be not merely from His wealth, but also in a manner that befits His wealth – on a scale worthy of His wealth.'"[51] (emphasis in original). In fact, it is better for the Philippians to wait upon the Lord to be repaid for their sacrificial services than to expect the imprisoned apostle to reciprocate out of his scarcity. The expression *kata to ploutos autou en doxē* (literally, "according to his riches in glory"), as pointed out by Martin, may be understood either as "glorious riches," or "it may point forward to the glory reserved for believers in the future kingdom of God: 'in the glory'." He rightly concludes that a better understanding of the passage would be to read it as God supplying the Philippians' needs out of his glorious riches in Christ Jesus.[52] Hawthorne maintains that *endoxē* "should not be given any futuristic meaning but should be curtailed and limited here to a description of God's wealth."[53]

---

51. Martin, *Philippians*, TNTC, 183.
52. Martin, 183–184.
53. Hawthorne, *Philippians*, 208–209.

PARTNERSHIP IN MISSION: DEFINING THE DONOR-RECIPIENT RELATIONSHIP

The relationship between a sponsor and a missionary as partners in Christian mission is central to Paul's letter to the Philippians and also for our mission today. While in the past such relationships paved the way to reach unreached people with the gospel of God's love, they also compromised the essentials of mission in order to accommodate a donor's choice. A Christian leader once confessed to me that raising funds for infrastructure is easier than for a new grass-roots level Christian worker's salary. Though the latter is the priority in mission, the former often gets priority, depending upon the interests and availability of the donor.

Further, the status and power to dictate missional activities through funding has created a benefactor-client hierarchy between a donor at the top and a missionary/evangelist or a recipient church at the bottom. Flattering donors for funds is not uncommon in mission today, because the prevailing attitude is that the "donor is the boss." Hence, the power of money often determines the missional agenda in board rooms and mission reports. This not only leads to mission practices that do not reflect the gospel, but it legitimizes a donor's undue domination in God's mission. Such misguided hierarchical relations force aid recipients to become people pleasers rather than seeking to honor and please God. Moreover, the Asian cultural expectations and practices defining reciprocity in terms of subordination and submission have led to the servitude of the those who receive missional funds. These evils are not limited to missional partnerships between the East and West but are also common at the local level in countries such as India, where many rich native sponsors of a mission project attempt to dictate terms at all levels within a church.

In the letter to Philippians, Paul repeatedly expresses his appreciation and thankfulness for the encouraging support he has received from the believers in Philippi to organize, conduct, and culminate his call as an apostle to the gentiles (1:4–5, 7; 2:25–30; 4:3, 10–19). He thanks and prays to God for the Philippians due to their constant support while in jail (1:3–5), just as they supported him in the past when no other church in Macedonia stepped forward (4:15–16). Moreover, the present supply of gifts through Epaphroditus adds to their sacrificial support of Paul's mission.

However, Paul does not appear to be oblivious to the sociocultural obligations for receiving aid under the Greco-Roman benefactor system. In the first-century Greco-Roman context, this system established a social hierarchy that required intentional acts of gratitude from the receiver along with eulogies intended to increase the giver's status. Both parties were socially obliged to maintain the hierarchical relationship.[1] Although we cannot be sure about the Philippians' attitudes about extending financial and other forms of support to Paul, we do have interesting clues within the letter to understand how Paul responded. Reading these clues within the sociocultural benefactor system of the time, we can identify three important aspects to Paul's response to the Philippians in 4:18–19.

First, Paul's claim for self-sufficiency in 4:10–18 proves his hesitation to accept their gifts without qualification. Paul has, in fact, learned to live in plenty and scarcity of resources through God, who strengthens him in all situations (4:12–13). Paul does not desire to receive more but is content in all that he has received (4:17–18). Exemplifying the virtue of seeking others interest more than one's own (2:3–4), Paul desires "that more be credited to your (Philippians') account" (4:17).

Second, Paul's interpretation of the gifts as part of the cultic sacrificial system identifies them as something offered to God that pleases him. In other words, by ascribing a theological meaning to their benevolence, the apostle disappears into the shadow of the true receiver of all their gifts, which is God.

Third, in 4:19, Paul says that God will repay the Philippians for all their sacrificial gifts to Paul in the eschatological times. This statement is a logical progression from his assertion in 4:18 that God is the receiver of gifts and is pleased by them. Hence, the one who receives and takes pleasure in the sacrificial gifts will repay them "according to the riches of his glory to Christ Jesus" (4:19). It is beneficial for the Philippians to be repaid by God rather than Paul, for there is no comparison between Paul's resources and God's.

Thus Paul is ambivalent about the gifts he has received, oscillating between the opposite poles of gratitude and ingratitude. This attitude is countercultural and subverts the fundamental principle that defines every social relationship. Acting on behalf of God in the *missio Dei*, Paul neither gives nor receives anything personally. What the Philippians offer to him in his moments of need is first and foremost an offering to God. Hence, he is thankful to God, because through the believers in Philippi, God provides for his needs. Therefore, he is not under pressure to act according to the norms of the patronage system – in fact, he is absolutely free of them.

This discussion corrects our misconceptions about the partnership between donors and recipients in God's mission and restores God to the center of these relationships. From this, we can learn the following lessons.

> First, both donors and recipients are equal partners in God's mission. Second, the aid provided in mission does not oblige a recipient to reciprocate to any human donor because God is the ultimate giver and receiver of all things. By supporting a needy missionary or church, the donor is ultimately giving back to God what has already been received. Third, the recipient should overflow with thanksgiving to God for the donor and pray for greater rewards for the donor out of God's inexhaustible store. Fourth, a recipient of aid, whether in poverty or riches, ought to prioritize God's work as Paul does. One does not need to worry about funds too much because, as Hudson Taylor famously said, "God's work done in God's way will never lack God's supply." We can be assured of every necessary supply, for the God who repays from his riches of glory is capable to supply resources to continue his work in every situation.
>
> ---
>
> 1. Peterman, *Paul's Gift from Philippi*, 88–89.

Philippians 4:20 is a doxology, where *hēmōn* ("our"), a first person plural pronoun, upholds Paul and the Philippian believers' common belonging to "God and Father." While the definite article in front of "God" refers to the supreme divine being, the doxology confesses that the supreme being has become "our Father (*patrihēmōn*)," that is, the father of Paul and his believers in Philippi. In 1 Corinthians 8:6, God the father is the source and goal of all existence. He is the father of the Lord Jesus Christ (2 Cor 1:3; 11:31; Eph 1:2, 3), whom the believers in Christ can call "Abba! Father!" through the Spirit (Gal 4:6). The reference to God's fatherhood for these Philippians coheres with 4:19, which mentions how the divine providence will fulfill all their needs out of God's glorious riches in Christ Jesus. Further, all the "glory" (*doxa*) shall be to God "forever and ever." For Paul, ascribing glory to God means to acknowledge, affirm, and praise his divine honor, splendor, and power, which is and always has been and ever will be.[54] In the context of Philippians 2:10–11, every knee bowing before Jesus and confessing him as "Lord" will be "to the glory of God the Father."

---

54. G. Kittel, "δόξα," *TDNT* 2:247.

Philippians

4:21–23 FINAL GREETINGS

In India today, many personal letters end with loving regards from the author and his or her community to all the intended recipients. Similarly, in 4:21–22, Paul greets the Philippian believers and sends them greetings on behalf of the brothers and sisters in Rome. Then in 4:23, he concludes with a benediction of grace in the name of Jesus Christ. Such a conclusion is in line with the letter-writing convention of the ancient Hellenistic world. However, Paul avoids "the standard 'farewell' (*errōso*) or 'good luck' (*eutuchei*) that one is accustomed to find at the end of pagan or even Christian letters."[55]

In 4:21, Paul commands some select members, perhaps the leaders, of the Philippian church to "[g]reet" (notice the imperative form, *aspasasthe*) all the saints (*panta hagion*), even though he has already addressed them in his salutation at the beginning of the letter: "To all God's holy people in Christ Jesus at Philippi, together with the overseers and deacons" (1:1). Paul does not name any specific member of the community, but greets all, perhaps to avoid "an additional reason for envy and rivalry in an already divided church."[56] He addresses the members of the church as "God's people" (literally, "saints," 1:1), which is repeated in 4:22 for the believers in Rome (literally, "all the holy ones"). The term "saints" in the OT is used for Israel (Exod 19:4). By calling the gentile believers in Philippi "saints," Paul reminds them that they have a new status "in Christ Jesus," and the unique status of Israel in the OT is transferred to them by faith. Just as Israel was set apart by God to be his treasure (Exod 19:5; Deut 7:6), the "saints in Christ Jesus" are God's own people. Their current spiritual status is modified by the fact that they are "in Christ Jesus." This great truth also applies to the believers in Rome, who are "God's people" as well (4:22).

Paul's greetings (4:22) on behalf of his friends in Rome are general, and yet they include some particular details. Although "all" with him in Rome send greetings to the Philippians, "Caesar's household" is mentioned in particular. In the first-century imperial setting, every individual working for Caesar, from the highest (governor) to the lowest (slave) position, could be described as belonging to Caesar's household.[57] The identity of those who are being addressed as "Caesar's household" is unclear. Certain assumptions about particular names

---

55. Hawthorne, *Philippians*, 212.
56. Hansen, *Philippians*, 329.
57. Peter T. O'Brien, "Caesar's Household, Imperial Household," *DPL* 83–84.

could be made, but they would only be educated guesses.[58] However, despite this uncertainty, Paul's reference to some in Caesar's household conveys to the persecuted group of Christians in Philippi that the power of the gospel has begun to intrude into the higher echelons of the Roman social order. The power of the gospel is rapidly advancing into the corridors of the imperial power.

Finally, in 4:23, Paul pronounces a benediction: "The grace of the Lord Jesus Christ be with your spirit. Amen." In 1:2, *charis* ("grace") along with "peace" originates from "God our Father and the Lord Jesus Christ," but Paul concludes the letter in 4:23 by associating "grace" exclusively with "the Lord Jesus Christ." This wording is exceptional for Paul, but as Hawthorne maintains, "[o]bserving this fact one quickly comes to understand that for Paul Christ has the right to perform the divine role with full authority."[59]

---

58. Hansen, *Philippians*, 331; O'Brien, "Caesar's Household," 84.
59. Hawthorne, *Philippians*, 215.

SELECTED BIBLIOGRAPHY

Alexander, Loveday. "Hellenistic Letter-Forms and the Structure of Philippians." *JSNT* 37 (1989): 87–101.

Ali, S. A. "The Problem of Suffering in Islam." In *The Problem of Death and Suffering in Indian Religions*, edited by Clarence O. McMullen. New Delhi: "LITHOUSE" Publications, 1983.

Arnold, Clinton E. *Acts*. Zondervan Illustrated Bible Backgrounds Commentary, edited by Clinton E. Arnold. Grand Rapids: Zondervan, 2002.

Barrett, C. K. *The Epistle to the Romans*. BNTC. Rev. ed. London: Hendrickson, 1991.

Beare, F. W. *The Epistle to the Philippians*. BNTC. 2nd ed. London: Adam & Charles Black, 1959.

Bercovits, J. Peter. "Paul at Ephesus and the Composition of Philippians." *Proceedings* 8 (1988): 61–76. Accessed 28 March 2018. http://web.a.ebscohost.com/ehost/pdfviewer/pdfviewer?vid=4&sid=45634aac-71d7-4a8a-8d1f-5fe9b9beef3a%40sessionmgr4008.

Berry, Ken L. "The Function of Friendship Language in Philippians 4:10–20." In *Friendship, Flattery and Frankness of Speech: Studies on Friendship in the New Testament World*, edited by John T. Fitzgerald. NovTSup 82. Leiden: Brill, 1996.

Black, David Alan. "Paul and Christian Unity: A Formal Analysis of Philippians 2:1–4." *JETS* 28 (1985): 299–308.

———. "The Authorship of Philippians 2:6–11: Some Literary-Critical Observations." *CTR* 2 (1988): 269–289.

Brawley, Robert L. "An Alternative Community and an Oral Encomium: Traces of the People of Philippi." In *The People beside Paul: The Philippian Assembly and History from Below*, edited by Joseph A. Marchal. Early Christianity and Its Literature 17. Atlanta: SBL Press, 2015.

Brewer, Raymond R. "The Meaning of *Politeuesthe* in Philippians 1:27." *JBL* 73 (1954): 76–83.

Brown, Colin, ed. *New International Dictionary of New Testament Theology*. 3 vols. Grand Rapids: Zondervan, 1975–1978.

Bruce, F. F. *Philippians*. GNBC. Basingstoke, Hants: Pickering & Inglis, 1983.

Carson, D. A., Douglas J. Moo, and Leon Morris. *An Introduction to the New Testament*. Grand Rapids: Zondervan, 1992.

Castelli, Elizabeth A. *Imitating Paul: A Discourse of Power*. LCBI. Louisville: Westminster/John Knox Press, 1991.

Caulley, Thomas Scott. "The Title *Christianos* and Roman Imperial Cult." *ResQ* 53 (2011): 193–206.

Charlesworth, J. H. "From Jewish Messianology to Christian Christology: Some Caveats and Perspectives." In *Judaism and Their Messiahs at the Turn of the Christian Era*. Edited by Jacob Neusner, William Scott Green, and Ernest S. Frerichs. Cambridge: Cambridge University Press, 1987.

Clarke, Andrew D. "'Be Imitators of Me': Paul's Model of Leadership." *TynBul* 49 (1998): 329–360.

Craddock, Fred B. *Philippians*. IBC. Atlanta: John Knox Press, 1985.

Dalton, William J. "The Integrity of Philippians." *Biblica* 60 (1979): 97–102.

Dunn, J. D. G. "'Neither Circumcision nor Uncircumcision, but . . . '." In *The New Perspective on Paul*. Rev. ed. Grand Rapids: Eerdmans, 2005.

_____. "The New Perspective on Paul." In *Jesus, Paul and the Law: Studies in Mark and Galatians*. London/Louisville: SPCK/Westminster/John Knox, 1990.

_____. *The Theology of Paul the Apostle*. Grand Rapids: Eerdmans, 1998.

_____. "Once More, PISTIS CRISTOU." In *Looking Back, Pressing On*, edited by E. Elizabeth Johnson, and David M. Hay. Vol. 4 of Pauline Theology. SBL Symposium Series 4. Atlanta: Scholars Press, 1997.

Ehrensperger, Kathy. "'Be Imitators of Me as I Am of Christ:' A Hidden Discourse of Power and Domination in Paul?" *LTQ* 38 (2003): 241–261.

Ellington, Dustin W. "Imitating Paul's Relationship to the Gospel: I Corinthians 8.1–11.1." *JSNT* 33 (2011): 303–315.

Fairchild, Mark R. "Paul's Pre-Christian Zealot Associations: A Re-examination of Gal 1.14 and Acts 22:3." *NTS* 45 (1999): 514–532.

Fantin, Joseph D. "Paul's Use of κύριος as a Polemic against Caesar with Some Remarks towards the Contribution of the Study to the Exegesis of 1 Corinthians 8:5–6." Paper presented at the ECGRW Seminar, University of Sheffield, 29 April 2002.

Fee, Gordon D. *Paul's Letter to the Philippians*. NICNT. Grand Rapids: Eerdmans, 1995.

_____. *Philippians*. IVPNTC. Downers Grove: InterVarsity Press, 1999.

Fitzgerald, John T. "Philippians in the Light of Some Ancient Discussions of Friendship." In *Friendship, Flattery and Frankness of Speech: Studies on Friendship in the New Testament World*, edited by John T. Fitzgerald. NovTSup 82. Leiden: Brill, 1996.

Fitzmyer, Joseph A. *The Acts of the Apostles: A New Translation with Introduction and Commentary*. AB 31. New York: Doubleday, 1998.

Fowl, Stephen E. *Philippians*. THNTC. Grand Rapids: Eerdmans, 2005.

Freedman, David Noel, ed. *The Anchor Bible Dictionary*. 6 vols. New York: Doubleday, 1992.

Funk, Robert W. "The Apostolic Parousia: Form and Significance." In *Christian History and Interpretation*, edited by W. R. Farmer, C. F. D. Moule, and R. R. Niebuhr. Cambridge: Cambridge University Press, 1966.

Selected Bibliography

Garland, David E. "The Composition and Unity of Philippians: Some Neglected Literary Factors." *NovT* 27 (1985): 141–173.

George, Roji T. "'Join Together with Me in Imitating My Example': Reflection on Paul's Call to Imitate in the Letter to the Philippians." In *Bible, Mission, and Theology: A Festschrift in Honor of Rev. Dr. Simon Samuel*, edited by P. V. Joseph. Dehradun: Luther W. New Jr. Theological College/Delhi: ISPCK, 2018.

———. "'God Sent His Son, Born of a Woman' (Gal. 4:4): The Idea of Incarnation, Its Antecedents, and Significance in Paul's Theology." *DTJ* 5 (2008): 65–85.

———. "Divine Grace in the Making of Paul, the *Yesu Bhakta*: Reclaiming the Role of Grace in the Self-Consciousness of Paul as a *Bhatka* in the Light of St. Tukaram's Bhakti Thought." *BTF* 45 (2013): 74–96.

———. *Paul's Identity in Galatians: A Postcolonial Appraisal*. New Delhi: CWI, 2016.

Gill, David W. J. "Macedonia." In *Greco-Roman Setting*. Vol. 2 of *The Book of Acts in Its First Century Setting*, edited by David W. J. Gill and Conrad Gempf. Grand Rapids/Carlisle: Eerdmans/Paternoster, 1994.

Gorman, Michael J. *Apostle of the Crucified Lord: A Theological Introduction to Paul and His Letters*. Grand Rapids/Cambridge: Eerdmans, 2004.

Goyandaka, Jayadayal. *Srimadbhagavadgita Tattvavivecani: English Commentary*. Gorakhpur: Gita Press, 2014.

Hagner, Donald A. *The New Testament: A Historical and Theological Interpretation*. Grand Rapids: Baker Academic, 2012.

Hamerton-Kelly, Robert G. "A Girardian Interpretation of Paul: Rivalry, Mimesis and Victimage in the Corinthian Correspondence." *Semeia* 33 (1985): 65–81.

Hansen, G. Walter. *The Letter to the Philippians*. PNTC. Grand Rapids/Cambridge: Eerdmans/Nottingham: Apollos, 2009.

Hawthorne, G. F. "Philippians, Letter to the." *DPL*, 707–713.

———. *Philippians*. WBC 43. Waco, TX: Word Books, 1983.

Hays, Richard B. "PISTIS and Pauline Christology." In *Looking Back, Pressing On*, edited by E. Elizabeth Johnson and David M. Hay. Vol. 4 of *Pauline Theology*. SBL Symposium Series 4. Atlanta: Scholars Press, 1997.

———. *The Faith of Jesus Christ: The Narrative Substructure of Galatians 3:1–4:11*. 2nd ed. The Biblical Resource Series. Grand Rapids/Cambridge: Eerdmans/Dearborn: Dove Booksellers, 2002.

Hellerman, Joseph H. *Reconstructing Honor in Roman Philippi: Carmen Christi as Crusus Pudorum*. SNTSMS 132. Cambridge: Cambridge University Press, 2005.

Hendricksen, William. *Philippians*. NTC. Edinburgh: Banner of Truth Trust, 1962.

Hengel, Martin. *Crucifixion: In the Ancient World and the Folly of the Message of the Cross*. Philadelphia: Fortress Press, 1977.
Hooker, M. D. "PISTIS CRISTOU." *NTS* 35 (1989): 321–342.
Hoover, Roy W. "The *Harpagmos* Enigma: A Philological Solution." *HTR* 64 (1971): 95–119.
Horrell, David G. "The Label Χριστιανός: 1 Peter 4:16 and the Formation of Christian Identity." *JBL* 126 (2007): 361–381.
Jeffers, James S. *The Greco-Roman World of the New Testament Era: Exploring the Background of Early Christianity*. Downers Grove, IL: InterVarsity Press, 1999.
Jewett, Robert. "The Epistolary Thanksgiving and the Integrity of Philippians." *NovT* 12 (1970): 40–53.
Johnson, Luke Timothy. "Paul's Ecclesiology." In *The Cambridge Companion to St. Paul*, edited by J. D. G. Dunn. Cambridge: Cambridge University Press, 2003.
_____. *The Writings of the New Testament: An Interpretation*. Rev. ed. Minneapolis: Fortress Press, 1999.
Judge, Edward A. "Judaism and the Rise of Christianity: A Roman Perspective." *TynBul* 45 (1994): 355–368.
Keener, Craig S. "Between Asia and Europe: Postcolonial Mission in Acts 16:8–10." *AJPS* 11 (2008): 3–14.
_____. *The Mind of the Spirit: Paul's Approach to Transformed Thinking*. Grand Rapids: Baker Academic, 2016.
Kim, Seyoon. *Paul and the New Perspective: Second Thoughts on the Origin of Paul's Gospel*. Grand Rapids: Eerdmans, 1998.
Kim, Yung Suk. "'Imitators' (*Mimetai*) in 1 Cor 4:16 and 11:1: A New Reading of Threefold Embodiment." *HBT* 33 (2011): 147–170.
Kittel, Gerhard, and Gerhard Friedrich, eds. *Theological Dictionary of the New Testament*. Translated by Geoffrey W. Bromiley. 10 vols. Grand Rapids: Eerdmans, 1964–1976.
Lightfoot, J. B. *St. Paul's Epistle to the Philippians: A Revised Text with Introduction, Notes, and Dissertations*. Peabody, MA: Hendrickson, 1987.
Malherbe, Abraham J. *Paul and the Thessalonians: The Philosophical Tradition of Pastoral Care*. Philadelphia: Fortress Press, 1987.
Marchal, Joseph A. *The Politics of Heaven: Women, Gender, and Empire in the Study of Paul*. Minneapolis: Fortress Press, 2008.
Marshall, I. Howard. *The Epistle to the Philippians*. ECS. London: Epworth Press, 1993.
Martin, Ralph P. *Carmen Christi: Philippians II. 5–11 in Recent Interpretation and in the Setting of Early Christian Worship*. SNTSMS 4. Cambridge: CUP, 1967.
_____. *Philippians*. NCBC. Grand Rapids/London: Eerdmans/Marshall, Morgan & Scott, 1980.

Selected Bibliography

———. *Philippians: An Introduction and Commentary.* TNTC. London: InterVarsity Press, 1959.

Melherbe, Abraham J. "Paul's Self-Sufficiency (Philippians 4:11)." In *Friendship, Flattery and Frankness of Speech: Studies on Friendship in the New Testament World*, edited by John T. Fitzgerald. NovTSup 82. Leiden: Brill, 1996.

Melick Jr., Richard R. *An Exegetical and Theological Exposition of Holy Scripture: Philippians, Colossians, Philemon.* NAC 32. Nashville: Broadman Press, 1991.

Metzger, Bruce M. *A Textual Commentary on the Greek New Testament: A Companion Volume to the United Bible Societies' Greek New Testament (Fourth Revised Edition).* 2nd ed. Stuttgart: Deutsche Biblgesellschaft/United Bible Societies, 1994.

Moule, H. C. G. *The Epistle to the Philippians.* TC. Grand Rapids: Baker Book House, 1981.

Moxnes, Halvor. "Patron-Client Relations and the New Community in Luke-Acts." In *The Social World of Luke-Acts: Models for Interpretation*, edited by Jerome H. Neyrey. Peabody, MA: Hendrickson, 1999.

Müller, Jac J. *The Epistles of Paul to the Philippians and to Philemon.* NICNT. Grand Rapids: Eerdmans, 1955.

Mullins, T. Y. "A Visit Talk in New Testament Letters." *CBQ* 35 (1973): 350–358.

———. "Disclosure as a Literary Form in the New Testament." *NovT* 7 (1964): 44–50.

———. "Formulas in New Testament Epistles." *JBL* 91 (1972): 380–390.

Oakes, Peter. *Philippians: From People to Letter.* SNTSMS 110. Cambridge: Cambridge University Press, 2001.

O'Brien, Peter T. "Caesar's Household, Imperial Household." *DPL*, 83–84.

———. *Introductory Thanksgiving in the Letters of Paul.* NovTSup 49. Leiden: Brill, 1977.

———. *The Epistle to the Philippians.* NIGTC. Grand Rapids/Carlisle: Eerdmans/Paternoster Press, 1991.

Pandey, V. C. "Problems of Death and Individual Suffering in Hindu Religion." In *The Problem of Death and Suffering in Indian Religions*, edited by Clarence O. McMullen. New Delhi: "LITHOUSE" Publications, 1983.

Peterlin, Davorin. *Paul's Letter to the Philippians in the Light of Disunity in the Church.* NovTSup 79. Leiden/New York/Köln: E. J. Brill, 1995.

Peterman, G. W. *Paul's Gift from Philippi: Conventions of Gift-Exchange and Christian Giving.* Cambridge: CUP, 1997.

Rapske, Brian. *The Book of Acts and Paul in Roman Custody.* Vol. 3 of *The Book of Acts in Its First Century Setting*, edited by David W. J. Gill and Conrad Gempf. Grand Rapids: Eerdmans/Carlisle: Paternoster, 1994.

Reed, Jeffery T. "Philippians 3:1 and the Epistolary Hesitation Formulas: The Literary Integrity of Philippians, Again," *JBL* 115 (1996): 63–90.

Reumann, John. "Philippians, Especially Chapter 4, As a 'Letter of Friendship': Observations on a Checkered History of Scholarship." In *Friendship, Flattery and Frankness of Speech: Studies on Friendship in the New Testament World*, edited by John T. Fitzgerald. NovTSup 82. Leiden: Brill, 1996.

Roetzel, Calvin J. *The Letters of Paul: Conversations in Context*. 2nd ed. Atlanta: John Knox Press, 1982.

Ryan, Scott C. "The Reversal of Rhetoric in Philippians 3:1–11." *PRS* 39 (2012): 67–77.

Sambaugh, John E., and David L. Balch. *The New Testament in Its Social Environment*. Philadelphia: Westminster Press, 1986.

Sanders, J. T. "The Transition from Opening Epistolary Thanksgiving to Body in Letters of the Pauline Corpus." *JBL* 81 (1962): 348–362.

Schreiner, Thomas R. *Paul Apostle of God's Glory in Christ: A Pauline Theology*. 1st Indian ed. Secunderabad: OM Books, 2003.

Schubert, Paul. *Form and Function of the Pauline Thanksgiving*. ZNT 20. Berlin: Topelmann, 1939.

Sharma, J. M. "The Social Aspect of the Problem of Death and Suffering in Hinduism." In *The Problem of Death and Suffering in Indian Religions*, edited by Clarence O. McMullen. New Delhi: "LITHOUSE" Publications, 1983.

Silva, Moisés. *Philippians*. BECNT. 2nd ed. Grand Rapids: Baker Academic, 2005.

———. *Philippians*. WEC. Chicago: Moody Press, 1988.

Stendhal, Kirster. "The Apostle Paul and the Introspective Conscience of the West." In *The Writings of St. Paul*, edited by Wayne A. Meeks. New York: W. W. Norton, 1972.

Still, Todd D. "More Than Friends? The Literary Classification of Philippians Revisited." *PRS* 39 (2012): 53–66.

Stowers, Stanley K. "Friends and Enemies in the Politics of Heaven: Reading Theology in Philippians." In *Pauline Theology: Thessalonians, Philippians, Galatians, Philemon*, edited by Jouette M. Bassler. Vol. 1. Minneapolis: Fortress Press, 1991.

———. *Letter Writing in Greco-Roman Antiquity*. Philadelphia: Westminster Press, 1986.

"The Monolith." http://www.vigeland.museum.no/en/vigeland-park/monolith.

Thompson, James W. *Philippians*. PCNT. Grand Rapids: Baker Academic, 2016.

Vincent, Marvin R. *A Critical and Exegetical Commentary on the Epistle to the Philippians and Philemon*. ICC. Edinburgh: T & T Clark, 1985.

Wallace, Daniel B. *Greek Grammar beyond the Basics: An Exegetical Syntax of the New Testament*. Grand Rapids: Zondervan, 1996.

Watson, Duane F. "A Rhetorical Analysis of Philippians and Its Implications for the Unity Question." *NovT* 30 (1988): 57–88.

Selected Bibliography

Wengst, Klaus. *PAX ROMANA and the Peace of Jesus Christ*. Translated by John Bowden. Philadelphia: Fortress Press, 1987.

Westerholm, Stephen. "Pharisees." *DJG*, 609–614.

———. *Perspectives Old and New on Paul: The 'Lutheran' Paul and His Critics*. Grand Rapids/Cambridge: Eerdmans, 2004.

White, John L. "Ancient Greek Letters." In *Greco-Roman Literature and the New Testament*, edited by David E. Aune. Atlanta: Scholars Press, 1988.

White, L. Michael. "Morality between Two Worlds: A Paradigm of Friendship in Philippians." In *Greeks, Romans and Christians: Essays in Honor of Abraham J. Malherbe*, edited by David L. Balch, Everett Ferguson, and Wayne A. Meeks. Minneapolis: Fortress Press, 1990.

Wintle, Brian. "Philippians." In *South Asia Biblical Commentary: A One-Volume Commentary on the Whole Bible*, edited by Brian Wintle. Udaipur: Open Door Publications, 2015.

Witherington III, Ben. *Paul's Narrative Thought World: The Tapestry of Tragedy and Triumph*. Louisville: Westminster/John Knox, 1994.

———. *Friendship and Finances in Philippi: The Letter of Paul to the Philippians*. Valley Forge, PA: Trinity Press, 1994.

———. *Grace in Galatia: A Commentary on St. Paul's Letter to the Galatians*. Grand Rapids: Eerdmans, 1998.

Wright, N. T. *What Saint Paul Really Said: Was Paul of Tarsus the Real Founder of Christianity?* Grand Rapids/Cincinnati, Ohio: Eerdmans/Forward Movement Publications, 1997.

Asia Theological Association
54 Scout Madriñan St. Quezon City 1103, Philippines
Email: ataasia@gmail.com Telefax: (632) 410 0312

OUR MISSION

The Asia Theological Association (ATA) is a body of theological institutions, committed to evangelical faith and scholarship, networking together to serve the Church in equipping the people of God for the mission of the Lord Jesus Christ.

OUR COMMITMENT

The ATA is committed to serving its members in the development of evangelical, biblical theology by strengthening interaction, enhancing scholarship, promoting academic excellence, fostering spiritual and ministerial formation and mobilizing resources to fulfill God's global mission within diverse Asian cultures.

OUR TASK

Affirming our mission and commitment, ATA seeks to:

- **Strengthen** interaction through inter-institutional fellowship and programs, regional and continental activities, faculty and student exchange programs.
- **Enhance** scholarship through consultations, workshops, seminars, publications, and research fellowships.
- **Promote** academic excellence through accreditation standards, faculty and curriculum development.
- **Foster** spiritual and ministerial formation by providing mentor models, encouraging the development of ministerial skills and a Christian ethos.
- **Mobilize** resources through library development, information technology and infra-structural development.

To learn more about ATA, visit www.ataasia.com or facebook.com/AsiaTheologicalAssociation

Langham Literature, along with its publishing work, is a ministry of Langham Partnership.

Langham Partnership is a global fellowship working in pursuit of the vision God entrusted to its founder John Stott –

> *to facilitate the growth of the church in maturity and Christ-likeness through raising the standards of biblical preaching and teaching.*

Our vision is to see churches in the majority world equipped for mission and growing to maturity in Christ through the ministry of pastors and leaders who believe, teach and live by the Word of God.

Our mission is to strengthen the ministry of the Word of God through:
- nurturing national movements for biblical preaching
- fostering the creation and distribution of evangelical literature
- enhancing evangelical theological education

especially in countries where churches are under-resourced.

Our ministry

Langham Preaching partners with national leaders to nurture indigenous biblical preaching movements for pastors and lay preachers all around the world. With the support of a team of trainers from many countries, a multi-level programme of seminars provides practical training, and is followed by a programme for training local facilitators. Local preachers' groups and national and regional networks ensure continuity and ongoing development, seeking to build vigorous movements committed to Bible exposition.

Langham Literature provides majority world preachers, scholars and seminary libraries with evangelical books and electronic resources through publishing and distribution, grants and discounts. The programme also fosters the creation of indigenous evangelical books in many languages, through writer's grants, strengthening local evangelical publishing houses, and investment in major regional literature projects, such as one volume Bible commentaries like the *Africa Bible Commentary* and the *South Asia Bible Commentary*.

Langham Scholars provides financial support for evangelical doctoral students from the majority world so that, when they return home, they may train pastors and other Christian leaders with sound, biblical and theological teaching. This programme equips those who equip others. Langham Scholars also works in partnership with majority world seminaries in strengthening evangelical theological education. A growing number of Langham Scholars study in high quality doctoral programmes in the majority world itself. As well as teaching the next generation of pastors, graduated Langham Scholars exercise significant influence through their writing and leadership.

To learn more about Langham Partnership and the work we do visit **langham.org**

www.ingramcontent.com/pod-product-compliance
Lightning Source LLC
Chambersburg PA
CBHW051927160426
43198CB00012B/2071